# PERSONAL AND CULTURAL SHADOWS OF LATE MOTHERHOOD

*Personal and Cultural Shadows of Late Motherhood* explores the topic of delayed motherhood from a Jungian psychoanalytic perspective, using both quantitative and qualitative research methods, including interview transcripts, diaries, dreams, and the Jungian Word Association Experiment. It provides a unique contribution to our understanding of the pressures faced by women today on the topic of delayed motherhood.

We may consider an affect to be in place when a woman allows her relationship to her body and its procreative capacity to slip away from consciousness, only to awaken at a point when redeeming her past choices becomes a hunger. This book delves into personal, cultural and collective spheres of influence that have been split off waiting for the right moment to reintegrate. Working with Interpretive Phenomenological Analysis and Jung's Word Association Experiment, the author identifies aspects of the psyche arousing late procreative desire and considers the differing accounts of maternal and paternal parents, alongside the effect of growing up beside a male sibling. The book examines women's procreative identity in midlife, identifies complexes of a personal, cultural and collective nature and considers how the role of mother is psychosocially performed, taking in feminist psychoanalytical thinking as well as Queer theory to explore new meanings for late motherhood.

This book will be of great interest to clinicians, researchers, and post-graduate students of Jungian, gender and psychosocial studies. Anyone with desire for motherhood in midlife will find this book relevant.

**Maryann Barone-Chapman**, PhD, is a Jungian Analyst, Supervisor and Professional Member of the Association of Jungian Analysts in London. Her involvement in Jungian psychology spans almost thirty years and spawned interest in female development leading her to research personal, cultural and collective complexes on delayed motherhood at Cardiff University's School of Social Science. Her published works have appeared in the *Journal of Analytical Psychology*, *Behavioral Science*, *Feminism and Psychology*, *Quadrant*, and edited volumes on Jungian psychology published by Routledge.

'Through this innovative study, Dr. Barone-Chapman explores the unconscious processes that necessitate a shift in midlife for women to seek a procreative identity. Psychosocial aspects of delayed motherhood are thoroughly researched through related literature, particularly the evidence of a historical patriarchal bias towards women, in psychoanalysis. Transforming Jung's Word Association Experiment (WAE) into a key feminist research methodology for accessing personal, cultural, and collective intergenerational complexes within delayed motherhood, Dr. Barone-Chapman revitalizes and modernizes Jung's important research tool for examining unconscious complexes and their symptomology. This book makes an important contribution to feminist post-Jungian studies and will be an invaluable resource in furthering interdisciplinary studies into motherhood, psychoanalysis, and the WAE.'

—Elizabeth Brodersen, PhD, Accredited Training Analyst and Supervisor, CGJI Zürich, Author, *Taboo: Personal and Collective Representations, Origin and Positioning within Cultural Complexes* (2019)

'Maryann Barone-Chapman has written a fascinating book about delayed motherhood, including (as she says) its "idealization, denigration, avoidance, and ambivalence," in psychological significance. From the personal to the archetypal, and from the literal to the symbolic, the meanings associated with delayed reproduction in women are compelling. Barone-Chapman has covered them all. Postponing childbirth and being able to become pregnant through new bio-technical means have implications for women all over the planet, but especially for those who are educated, and determined to lead their own lives. If you are a woman considering your own reproductive possibilities, or a clinician treating women struggling with infertility, indecision, and/or fear of decision-making, this book will help you see the complexity of women's newfound "autonomy." I very much appreciated the depth of Barone-Chapman's inquiry and her desire to see motherhood in a new register.'

—Polly Young-Eisendrath, PhD, Author, *Love Between Equals: Relationship as a Spiritual Path*

'This important book demonstrates the unconscious complexities of late motherhood, moving beyond any blame game towards a far-reaching understanding of the situation facing an increasing number of women today. Highly recommended.'

—Valerie Walkderdine, Distinguished Research Professor, Cardiff University

'Barone-Chapman majestically invites us to rethink what a mother complex is. Her research into the layers of a woman's decision to wait until midlife to become a mother reveals how consciousness grows from frustration and conflicts suffered with a trickster's ability to turn double binds around. This ground-breaking work points to the happy surprise of a child who can recognize how much more there is in the mother when women dream their agency forward to generate lives that are genuinely chosen.'

—John Beebe, MD, past president, C. G. Jung Institute of San Francisco, Author, *Integrity in Depth*

# PERSONAL AND CULTURAL SHADOWS OF LATE MOTHERHOOD

Jungian Psychoanalytic Views

Maryann Barone-Chapman

LONDON AND NEW YORK

First published 2020
by Routledge
2 Park Square, Milton Park, Abingdon, Oxon OX14 4RN

and by Routledge
52 Vanderbilt Avenue, New York, NY 10017

*Routledge is an imprint of the Taylor & Francis Group, an informa business*

© 2020 Maryann Barone-Chapman

The right of Maryann Barone-Chapman to be identified as the author has been asserted in accordance with sections 77 and 78 of the Copyright, Designs and Patents Act 1988.

All rights reserved. No part of this book may be reprinted or reproduced or utilised in any form or by any electronic, mechanical, or other means, now known or hereafter invented, including photocopying and recording, or in any information storage or retrieval system, without permission in writing from the publishers.

*Trademark notice*: Product or corporate names may be trademarks or registered trademarks, and are used only for identification and explanation without intent to infringe.

*British Library Cataloguing-in-Publication Data*
A catalogue record for this book is available from the British Library

*Library of Congress Cataloging-in-Publication Data*
A catalog record has been requested for this book

ISBN: 978-1-138-34976-6 (hbk)
ISBN: 978-1-138-34978-0 (pbk)
ISBN: 978-0-429-43343-6 (ebk)

Typeset in Bembo
by Taylor & Francis Books

 Printed in the United Kingdom by Henry Ling Limited

For John Leonard Chapman

# CONTENTS

*List of illustrations* viii
*Acknowledgements* ix
*Foreword* x
*Prologue* xvi

1 Return to Mother 1
2 Forgetting, Then Remembering 11
3 A Method Out Of Madness: Ethics 24
4 Intersubjective Spaces 39
5 Living In The Shadow 48
6 Meetings With The Unconscious 67
7 Trauma and Transformation 87
8 Creation and Destruction 100
9 Through a Mother Monster 109
   Epilogue 115
   Definitions 119

*Index* *125*

# ILLUSTRATIONS

**Figures**

| | | |
|---|---|---|
| 6.1 | Ms A and Jung's Word Association Experiment | 72 |
| 6.2 | Early Perseveration Through Repetition | 72 |
| 6.3 | Waves of Fears and Tears | 74 |
| 6.4 | Circumambulation of a Complex | 76 |
| 6.5 | Ms B and Jung's Word Association Experiment | 77 |
| 6.6 | Narrative of Despair | 78 |
| 6.7 | Correctly Recalled Words Above 32 | 79 |
| 6.8 | Incorrectly Recalled Words Above 32 | 80 |
| 6.9 | Ms D and Jung's Word Association Experiment | 81 |
| 6.10 | Trilateral Affects | 82 |

**Tables**

| | | |
|---|---|---|
| 4.1 | Ms A Special Meeting | 43 |
| 4.2 | Ms B Eight Years Later | 44 |
| 4.3 | Ms D Eight Years Later | 45 |

# ACKNOWLEDGEMENTS

There is a lifetime of people who deserve some credit. My parents, who purchased a thesaurus for me and read my earliest short stories with delight. My friend Alan Lewis, who as a writer believed in me long before I did. My Jungian tutors at The British Foundation for Psychotherapy/British Jungian Analytic Association who encouraged my taking a chance on a chancy subject, especially Miranda Kenny. Dale Mathers, for his collegiality as one writer to another. Valerie Walkerdine, who inspired when the page went blank. Elizabeth Brodersen, a generous and supportive friend. Phil Goss, a prince among men, particularly on gender bias. Nancy Krieger, for giving me a platform at ISAP and Gottfried Heuer at his Leading Edges series. David Freeman, for Rabbinical wisdom throughout the journey. Fanny Brewster, for unbridled vision and tenacity. Polly Young-Eisendrath, for simply being a bright light. John Beebe, who gets it from the heart. John Chapman, who got me to the church on time.

Grateful thanks also go to all the research participants who brought everything they were conscious of, and so much more that was in process of being known. Also, to my present and former analysands who taught me more about being in a female body while learning to deconstruct and reconstruct what it could mean to be a woman.

Finally, the book pays homage to those who have done so much for Analytical Psychology and Psychoanalytical thought, present and past.

Thank you.

# FOREWORD

*Personal and Cultural Shadows of Late Motherhood* engages me because it renews me in that space where I am most familiar. The space of the feminine as woman, mother, daughter, wife and aunt. The rhythms of my feminine life allow me to claim these titles, the roles that culture, society, and personal identification invoke with a myriad of images to satisfy an ego that shamelessly requires such invocations. Dr Barone-Chapman's book continuously asks me if I can have more of something, or less of this essence of something, related to being feminine in the same way in which she asks it of the women whose researched lives she has shared in her book. In our societal time of feeling the pressures of women 'having it all'—both the successful career and birthing children, we now see more women delaying having children. The presence of reproductive technology is named by the author as an influential element in the lives of women, and their decisions regarding becoming birthing mothers. Barone-Chapman continuously brings the reader back to this question: *Is delayed motherhood a personal area of conflict with a connection to the cultural and collective unconscious?* Through the research that Barone-Chapman has completed and discusses in this book, we travel with her and her co-research analysands. The author seeks a clear path, walking through the complexities of feminism, psychological complexes and inherent problems of gender theories we have inherited as practitioners of Analytical Psychology.

Maryann Barone-Chapman's written movement into psyche skates the surface of the egoic, moving back and forth in between space at its centre and outside the margins of the above central question. It can be exhilarating to find the self in a place of such movement of the between. It can be both familiar and unknown. The former, because as women we understand the nowhere land of delayed motherhood of which Barone-Chapman speaks. We know this place even when we have never given birth to children. We know this place because it belongs to all women. Her questions ask us to think about a particular space—the space of delayed motherhood. In a way, we have all as women delayed being mothers. We are not born and directly become mothers from our own mother's wombs. We age, and if we are fortunate, grow into some understanding of what mothering means. Some of us develop a sense of our bodies as future containers for conceiving children. Some of us rebel against such conceptions. We can also live in ambivalence regarding childbirth, as Barone-Chapman notes. Her writing makes us think more on this space of knowing about being mothers from a significant time—one of delayed time. A gaze to the future without the assurances of youth or perhaps even the blessings of a society. What exactly is delayed motherhood? What does it really mean for individual women as well as our collective? Equally as important to Barone-Chapman is the very idea of feminism itself. In her book she adds to her discussion of the Feminine, the presence of LGBTQ and what this recent increase of consciousness of this community could mean for our consideration of the Feminine.

In bell hooks' *Outlaw Culture*, in a chapter entitled 'Moving Into and Beyond Feminism: Just for the joy of it', Barone-Chapman echoes the 'edgy' space of Feminism, questions finding a space within a deeper one that can take us someplace that we were barely considering in 1994 at the time of hooks' writing, with any degree of acceptance—to the margins.

This is not experienced as a space of discomfort, as a place defined by another, but as a conscious space of choosing. There is a rapport between hooks' voice and Barone-Chapman's idea of a woman who can decide to delay birthing children until she thinks/believes she wants them. However, there is a contradiction to be considered even in this idea of delayed mothering. Barone-Chapman states that the 'polarities of idealization and denigration are at the epicenter of delayed motherhood' (p. 113). The margin does not offer safety, rather only a fluid space from which one can inhabit what Barone-Chapman calls the *pregnant pause*—a space of re-birth and creativity. This reminds me of hooks' definition of her state of mind where she can 'transgress boundaries'. hooks writes the following before beginning her interview essay:

> Initially excited to be interviewed for a book that would highlight women and performance, I was pissed to learn that it would be called Angry Women. In our culture, women of all races and classes who step out on the edge, courageously resisting conventional norms for female behavior, are almost always portrayed as crazy, out of control, mad. This title was good for selling books. Representations of 'mad' women excite even as they comfort. Set apart, captured in a circus of raging representations, women's serious cultural rebellion is mocked, belittled, trivialized. It is frustrating, maddening even, to live in a culture where female creativity and genius are almost always portrayed as inherently flawed, dangerous, problematic.

Luckily, despite stereotyped packaging and the evocation of the image of 'angry women,' this portrayal is challenged and subverted by the resisting representations that appear in the book.

> In this interview, I do not speak out in rage. The passion in my voice emerges from the playful tension between the multiple, diverse, and sometimes

contradictory locations I inhabit. There is no unitary representation to be formed here, no fixed sense of what it is to be black, female, from a working-class Southern background. For years, I was afraid to engage in radical political thought or movement. I feared it would close down creativity, confine me in an unchanging standpoint. Moving past this fear and embracing struggles to end domination, I find myself constantly at odds with workers for freedom who invest in the notion of a unitary self—a fixed identity. I continually resist surrendering complexity to be accepted in groups where subjectivity is flattened out in the interest of harmony or a unitary political vision. Turned off by culture vultures who want me to talk 'race only,' 'gender only,' who want to confine and limit the scope of my voice, I am turned on by subjectivity that is formed in the embrace of all the quirky conflicting dimensions of our reality. I am turned on by identity that resists repression and closure. This interview was a site where I could transgress boundaries with no fear of policing—a space of radical openness on the margins, where identity that is fluid, multiple, always in process could speak and be heard.

*(hooks, 2008)*

In her discussion of her idea of a *pregnant pause*, Barone-Chapman says, 'What the pregnant pause brings into question are the unconscious processes necessitating the narrative shift in midlife to see procreative identity, as a reparative motif for a one-sided, "half-alive" development in non-essentialist terms.' Is it possible then that the decision to wait to have a child, even in a biotechnological way—without a husband or male partner, is *only* a remedy? Is it to be a 'fact' of repair because our society cannot help but cast its own shadow on the decision of an older woman—with 'old eggs', to wait beyond the 'normal' years for having children? Whose right is it to choose? According to the author, women do not have the 'ultimate choice' as to when they will have children. There always appear to be outside influencing factors. Barone-Chapman, in referencing a study published in the *International Journal of Nursing* in 2010, found that delaying childbirth was the result of a 'complex interplay of relationship, stability, health and fertility with an element of chance'. The study also noted that having children past thirty years of age was currently a 'global trend'. This does not appear to have changed except in the direction of young women who are not committing to having children at all.

What of the relationship between mother and daughter as major criteria for whether or not to have children? How does the intergenerational trauma of our mothers and their mothers before them, influence our decision to bear children—when to bear children? If ever to bear them? Barone-Chapman (2007) addresses an important connection between the women of her own study. They all appeared to have a negative mother complex.

> The common complex linking these women is the negative mother complex, which played Trickster games in their lives as a trauma most often seen through the death of a father through mortality, symbolically, or the rise of the male sibling for pride of place. What kept coming up as both privation and

deprivation across affective behavior and narratives within the life stories of eight participants was the difference in the way girls and boys were raised as siblings, through parental expectations and in education, reflecting culture on gender.
(Barone-Chapman, 2007, p. 134).

Naomi Lowinsky in *The Faust Woman Poems* expresses emotional ideas of the negative mother complex, the absent father and the 'hungry daughters'. This is a recurring theme in the words of the women in *Personal and Cultural Shadows of Late Motherhood*—they never want to be like their mothers. This speaks to not only the personal experience of the type of mothering that the research analysands had seen as children, but also the culture in which they were raised. In this the place where 'doubt is an ethical benchmark', it appears that the decision of certain women in our society to delay childbirth can be an aspect of resonation with the Self. It appears as almost a protection against further re-traumatization by becoming and reliving their mother's lives through childbirth.

Barone-Chapman identifies the women of her study as ones who did not claim 'enough sovereignty'. This is considered as possible shadow in the mother-daughter relationship. As the author writes about her experience of the research analysands with whom she worked, she provides details that show the care, intensity and emotional endurance of being the analyst. This we see through her description of the transference relationship and her countertransference reactions. Her invocation of the Wounded Healer is appropriate and valuable as she thinks how the women with whom she engages share the places in which they are hurt. This woundedness is present even after the birth of the first child. The suffering of the women that appears to endure is from their own relationship with their mothers. Having children, no matter how delayed, has not sufficiently softened the pain of their negative mother complexes. What happens to the children of these wounded mothers who have delayed having their own children, perhaps hoping to avoid mothering?

Barone-Chapman asks the question: 'Is delayed motherhood a revolt against domination of the biological imperative to reproduce sooner rather than later?' Following this, I ask if domination is a 'natural', normed aspect of our societal lives? The author uses the words 'de-gender equality'. These words seem powerful when considering bell hooks' insistence for personal subjectivity and complexity. However, we can see that the collective voice, oftentimes as it has been expressed in the form of media, is not favorable towards 'older' women having children. There appears to be an age of 'safety' and older women, over the age of thirty-five, are at a 'higher risk' when birthing children. Even if this were true, and in some cases it may very well be, the culture of pejorative judgment against delaying motherhood remains strong today. In returning to Barone-Chapman's question of delayed motherhood as a revolt, it seems this is quite possible given the strength of the collective unconscious and conscious push to keep women birthing children within a particular time period. In the same manner that women are able to claim a longer work life, if this is their choosing, why can they not choose Psyche's time for the delivery of their children into the world as opposed to that of Chronos? Barone-Chapman notes that Jungian analyst and author Polly Young-Eisendrath wants women to ask the question regarding what *they* need for their own development. Here we can see how this becomes almost impossible if a girl child grows up lacking a sense of power and equality in a home that favors the masculine, whether sibling or father.

*Personal and Cultural Shadows of Late Motherhood* creates an opening through which to walk—a path on which to journey leading to discovery. On this journey we must question the historical path we have always taken in favour of looking in a new direction in terms of the necessary task to 'de-gender equality'. How can we stand, dance, create, as well as move about the space that wants to keep us held in identities because it is what we were taught and what we cling to out of fear? How do we allow the margins to exist without becoming marginalized by those who proclaim that we *are* 'marginalized'? I think that Barone-Chapman invites us to journey with her as we investigate and enquire more into the ways, perhaps of a deeper feminine wisdom, of those who delay motherhood. Who determines the rules as to how soon or too late it is to bring children into life? In today's political climate, women continue to fight and struggle for control of their bodies. We are engaged not only with encountering the old narratives of who we must be as mother, daughter, wife, sister, but must be engaged enough within ourselves to write new inner scripts that also support bringing other women with us on the journey.

I appreciate the work of Barone-Chapman who reminds us throughout this important and insightful, creative exploration of the feminine, that our task is to reclaim our bodies in as many ways as are possible. Barone-Chapman gives us another way to view our lives and those of women, both personally and not personally, known to us. There are ways in which we can know ourselves and know those who bring us the important stories, songs, and narratives we need to better live our multi-dimensional lives. In *Personal and Cultural Shadows of Late Motherhood*, Maryann Barone-Chapman provides us with such a rich and embracing narrative.

Fanny Brewster, PhD, MFA., LP, Philadelphia Association of Jungian Analysts, Professor of Depth Psychology at Pacifica Graduate Institute

## References

Barone-Chapman, M. (2007). 'The hunger to fill an empty space. An investigation of primordial affects and meaning-making in the drive to conceive through repeated use of ART', *Journal of Analytical Psychology*, 52(4), pp. 389–541.

hooks, b. (2008). *Outlaw Culture: Resisting Representations*. London: Routledge.

Lowinsky, N. (2013). *The Faust Woman Poems*. New York: Fisher King Press.

## Further Reading

Brewster, F. (2018). *Archetypal Grief: Slavery's Legacy of Intergenerational Child Loss*. London: Routledge.

'The task now becomes to unify the ego with the unconscious which contains the person's unlived life and unrealized potential'.
Murray Stein (2010) *Jung's Map of The Soul: An Introduction,* p. 177

# PROLOGUE

This book is about the desire to find motherhood later in life. By design it seeks to make an intervention on a subject area that cuts across gender, feminism, the psychosocial, equality, and unseen forces, that is, the unconscious. To access this unknowable realm, it was necessary to include Henderson's concept of the cultural unconscious as 'an area of historical memory' (Henderson, 1988, p. 103) to serve as a bridge between the collective unconscious and personal spheres of influence (Kimbles, 2014, pp. 83–85). In keeping with how these three zones operate as the *psychosocial* (Andrews, Day Sclater, Rustin, Squire and Treacher, 2000), since the beginning of time, I have drawn from Analytical Psychology's methods. These include the model of Jung's (1904–1906, 1904–1909) Word Association Experiment (WAE), which brought Freud's aetiology of the libido as a repressed sexual drive into question, shortly before Jung demonstrated there was an unconscious replete with associative networks not linked to infantile sexuality. What both men agreed upon initially was that complexes are real and can be demonstrated.

The discovery of the unconscious emerged into modern clinical understanding with Charcot's (1882) observation that hysterical paralysis originated as a split-off fragment with autonomous capacity to form spontaneous ideas with a disturbance that was separate from the ego and organized over a long period of time (Ellenberger, 1970, p. 149). 'Later, when Jung defined what he termed a "complex," he equated it with what Janet had called the *idée fixe subconsciente*' (ibid.). Complexes, based on Jung's (1918) findings, are images and ideas, gathering emotional tone through the observation of affect. Initially, I began with a semi-discursive instrument, Interpretive Phenomenological Analysis (IPA) (Smith, 2003), by deviating in the interpretation of the data by including clinically informed inter-subjective dynamics of transference and countertransference phenomena. This method put on display the ways in which a psychoanalytical psychodynamic approach and Jung's WAE created a dialectic as if to finish the sentence of the other, to create a whole complex understanding of *mater material*.

In parallel, this book is also designed to explore women's relationship, responses and reactions to the biologically pre-emptive role of becoming a mother, at a particular time called *midlife*, and to illustrate how it differs in conception and attitude to motherhood arising at an earlier time of life. We will uncover how affects become acculturated with conditions that attempt to control women's conduct. Indigenous cultural assumptions about the female body, the feminine and femininity have been and will continue to be called into question. Suspicions have been aroused around the topic of resistance from both subject and object positions, through the lens of gender bias in culture. Since the early post World War II years, motherhood has evolved from a biological pre-emptive normative identity to a challenged concept. It has contained not only ambivalence in opposition to maternal pre-occupation; latterly it has been re-formed into maternal subjectivity. The idea of the 'perfect mother', let alone one that is good enough, has become a minefield of uncertainty between women seeking comfort in groups with other mothers and the isolated mother who has difficulty feeling she is the right age to be among such a group. The problems constellating around delayed motherhood can include health issues for mother and child, repeated use of IVF (Barone-Chapman, 2007), and other forms of biotechnology to overcome socially derived secondary problems of ageing. While these issues have been written about in many ways, my objective in this book is to build a picture of how delayed motherhood has spawned women's connections to the past in the present. Early disconnection to their own lives can leave them stranded as they come up to forty years of age, due to a recapitulation of their early family trauma. This trauma has cast a pall over what defines a woman, long before the #MeToo movement began.

Weber's depiction of modernity's de-mystification of objects in the world in favour of scientific ways of making life (Weber, 1947), applies to the subject of delayed motherhood as context to 'a transformation of the collective psyche' (Jung, 1958, para. 589). Biotechnology in the form of IVF treatment may have become midlife's animism for the woman who is attempting to create and connect to soul by making life in a new way. In short, delayed motherhood has gathered cultural popularity. I have defined my approach as drawn from clinical skills and techniques as a Jungian Analyst familiar with symbol formation and complexes on the premise that midlife longing for motherhood is connected to the idea of being under a spell of dissociation from the self. 'Jung's practice of psychotherapy posited a concept of possession by complexes and a principle of relatedness and intra-psychic equilibrium which answers to it' (Stephenson, 2009, p. 142). Whereas, 'Moreno's model emphasized and accounted for psychosocial phenomena such as scapegoating as mechanisms which groups unwittingly exercise in the interest of reinforcing cohesion ... locating the self externally ... psychosocially in roles' (ibid.).

I began tracking the trajectory of delayed motherhood while living in New York in the 1980s and saw countless women opt for IVF treatment while juggling busy careers. Observation of a phenomenology around late motherhood, replete with high-toned feeling affects, continued when I was conducting mind-body workshops in London in the early 2000s with women at a fertility clinic who were in despair of a future without a child. I neither wanted nor expected any participants to tell me why they had delayed procreation. What I wanted to understand all along was where and how a complex had formed that influenced their relationship with making a life for themselves before making a family. This is the new order of a woman's life, especially if her life has not been infused with value within her home life from the start. Yet beyond the family, I found a wide arena of relational inter-subjectivity with the capacity to re-stimulate associative networks, funnelling down to where there is only the dream ego to observe. In this way I was able to walk alongside their experience of life to appreciate what caused them to seek reproductive identity at the eleventh hour of their procreative life.

In seeking to learn the complex nature of delayed motherhood I reviewed literature in Jungian and psychoanalytical frames, explored the value of feminist writings in both camps and within psychosocial research where psychoanalytical thought has prevailed. In this exploration my attention has been drawn to the inter-subjective field, where projected unconscious contents form a relational dependency. This has aroused an interest in extending the dynamics of transference and countertransference phenomena from the consulting room into the research framework. Through the complexity of time, gender identity, and confusion, the aetiology of delayed motherhood becomes more three-dimensional – intra-psychically, relationally and culturally. If the delay of motherhood has become so acculturated that the idea 'becomes associated with the ego … felt as strange, uncanny, and at the same time fascinating … the conscious mind falls under its spell' (Jung, 1928b, para. 590) as affect dysregulation of a personal complex becomes hidden from the conscious mind.

What interested me all along was the meaning and purpose of motherhood in midlife to the individual psyche as revealed on an affective level. I wanted to value what the attending complexes might represent in the personal realm, and how these might be mirrored as cultural and collective unconscious complexes in parallel. Within this frame we are exploring a woman's unconscious use of her body during the period of a *pregnant pause* (see Definitions) to the biological pre-emptive idea of becoming a mother in the age of bio-technological advancement. The female body may be the single most important evidence we have of where a culture places value in a patriarchal society, and in parallel, how such value creates an affective field of inter-subjectivity in psychosocial life. The methodology I was seeking had to be one that would allow the unconscious to speak for itself and be able to differentiate between personal, cultural and collective dimensions. I wanted to be able to see the unconscious on display without having to find it buried within narrative memory and discursive text.

Affect is not limited to Wundt's (1902) understanding of affect plus ideation, nor to sensation and ideation linked via fantasy (Walkerdine, Lucey and Melody, 2001), but to an invasion of feeling states. Upon writing 'A Review of Complex Theory' (Jung, 1934a) Jung's ideas had developed further as he witnessed the sentinels of fear and resistance guarding the road leading to the unconscious, after years of clinical work which began at the Burgholzli. Jung repeatedly differentiated his idea of the unconscious from Freud, who first conceived the unconscious as filled with immoral contents that needed to be repressed ((Jung, 1934a, para. 212). Jung separated feeling from affect on the premise that we can have command of our feelings, whereas affect operated as an intruder upon our will. In such moments we may find character slipping at any point when our adaptation is at its weakest, vulnerable to exposure (Jung, 1934a). Affects can have an explosive quality as well as an imploding resonance, catching us off guard and taking over our understanding of our relationship to our inner and external worlds. For instance, Jung never believed, as did Freud, that all pathology could be reduced to a sex drive. From this he began to form a unique understanding of psyche's structures.

We may also wonder if the *drive to delay motherhood until mid-life* is a body of evidence of a female complex beyond the personal, belonging to the cultural and/or collective unconscious (Jung, 1928b, para. 590), an aspect of an a priori condition to resist the notion woman = mother, as a pre-emptive biological destiny in its own right, since the advent of technology.

While researching and writing this book, I kept in mind the women whose desire for a child around the age of forty (and later) could no longer be ignored, dissociated from, or quelled. The achievement of creating a child creates a universe around the child in relation to how the mother creates her place in community. Within this particular midlife complexity, a curious psychosocial phenomenon offers a forensic perspective relevant to inter-generational studies, longitudinal trauma, generative identity, gender confusion, researching the unconscious, but especially how not to grow a daughter.

Maryann Barone-Chapman
London, 2020

## References

Andrews, M., Day Sclater, S., Rustin, M., Squire, C. and Treacher, A. (2000). 'Introduction', in M. Andrews, S. Day Sclater, C. Squire, and A. Treacher (eds), *Narrative Lives: Psychosocial Perspectives*. London: Routledge, pp. 1–10.

Barone-Chapman, M. (2007). 'The hunger to fill an empty space. An investigation of primordial affects and meaning-making in the drive to conceive through repeated use of ART', *Journal of Analytical Psychology*, 52(4), pp. 389–541.

Charcot, J.M. (1882). 'Sur les divers etats nerveux determines par l'hynotisation chez les hysteriques', *Comptes rendus hebdomadaires des séances de l'Académie des sciences*, XCIV (I), pp. 403–405.

Ellenberger, H.F. (1970). *The Discovery of the Unconscious: The History and Evolution of Dynamic Psychiatry*. New York: Basic Books/Perseus Books Group.

Henderson, J.L. (1988) The cultural unconscious. *Quadrant: Journal of the C.G. Jung Foundation for Analytical Psychology* 21(2), pp. 7–16.

Jung, C.G. (1904–1906). 'The Associations of Normal Subjects', C.G. Jung and F. Riklin. In *Collected Works, Vol. 2. Experimental Researches* (2nd edn). London: Routledge & Kegan Paul, 1992.

Jung, C.G. (1904–1909). 'Studies in Word Association'. In *Collected Works, Vol. 2. Experimental Researches* (2nd edn). London: Routledge & Kegan Paul, 1992.
Jung, C.G. (1928b). 'The Psychological Foundations of Belief in Spirits'. In *Collected Works, Vol. 8. The Structure and Dynamics of the Psyche* (2nd edn). London: Routledge & Kegan Paul, 1991.
Jung, C.G. (1934a). 'A Review of the Complex Theory'. In *Collected Works, Vol. 8. The Structure and Dynamics of the Psyche* (2nd edn). London: Routledge & Kegan Paul, 1991.
Jung, C.G. (1958). 'Introduction to Flying Saucers: A Modern Myth'. In *Collected Works, Vol. 10. Civilization in Transition* (2nd edn). London: Routledge & Kegan Paul, 1991.
Kimbles, S. (2014). *Phantom Narratives: The Unseen Contributions of Culture to Psyche*. New York and London: Rowman & Littlefield.
Smith, J.A. (ed.) (2003). *Qualitative Psychology: A Practical Guide to Research Methods*. London: Routledge, pp. 51–80.
Stephenson, C.E. (2009). *Possession: Jung's Comparative Anatomy of the Psyche*. London and New York: Routledge.
Walkerdine, V., Lucey, H. and Melody, J. (2001). *Growing Up Girl: Psycho-social Expectations of Gender*. Basingstoke: Palgrave Macmillan.
Weber, M. (1947). *The Theory of Social and Economic Organization*, trans. A.M. Henderson and T. Parsons. New York: Oxford University Press.
Wundt, W. (1902). *Outlines of Psychology*, 2nd edn. Ann Arbor: University of Michigan Press.

## Further reading

Jacobi, J. (1974). *Complex/Archetype/Symbol in the Psychology of C.G. Jung*. New York: Bollingen Foundation, Inc./Princeton University Press.
Jung, C.G. (1937b). 'The Lapis-Christ Parallel'. In *Collected Works, Vol. 12. Psychology and Alchemy* (2nd edn). London: Routledge & Kegan Paul, 1968.
Jung, C.G. (1954c). 'The Conjunction'. In *Collected Works, Vol. 14. Mysterium Coniunctionis* (2nd edn). London: Routledge & Kegan Paul, 1981.
Jung, C.G. (1954d). 'Adam and Eve'. In *Collected Works, Vol. 14. Mysterium Coniunctionis* (2nd edn). London: Routledge & Kegan Paul, 1981.
Murray, H.M. (1943). *Thematic Apperception Test*. Cambridge, MA: Harvard University Press.
Zepf, S. (2007). 'The relationship between the unconscious and conscious – a comparison of psychoanalysis and historical materialism', *Psychoanalysis, Culture and Society, Vol. 12*, pp. 105–123.

# 1
# RETURN TO MOTHER

The interactive channel of messages given and received, consciously and unconsciously, we know from Bion (1962), Benjamin (2004) and others, only requires two-ness to stimulate a response akin to the mother-infant dyad, transmuting culture into a potent close relation.

For those who have had early experiences leading to annihilation of self, the delayed turn to motherhood can be fraught with a history of interruptions lasting years and decades of traumatic disappointment. This was brought home to me when I faced the challenge of doing credible feminist research outside of patriarchal interrogation. In those borderlands of consciousness, the truth of image, perhaps of God, enabled not only my participants, but also me as their witness, to find liberation through experiencing the reality of one's desire for the ultimate *otherhood* of mothering. At times I found the stories of women hungry to fill an empty space to be intoxicating, as though they were under a spell of an addiction, which emerged in me as both empathic and repulsive counter-identifications of mother-generated complexes at work. This duality is important for becoming a mother in order to be someone's other.

Clinicians and academics, psychologically and politically minded people, have become acutely aware of the many frameworks women have been subjected to as carriers of psychosocial formulations from generation to generation. We/they have been encapsulated as a subject, object, abject, Mother, other, caregiver, mirror, and summarily as animus ridden or an anima woman. Each of these has carried an additional cultural frame to her nature, including receptivity, castrated, empathic, relationship-oriented, envious of a penis, an uroboros for renewal and the ultimate image of the contra-sexual unconscious – a chaos of characterizations that exemplifies the problem facing Jungians, no less than any other subscribers to a depth psychology, in which the female body is conceived both as part-object and as symbol. Yet the status of a maternal object that is also able to stand as a symbol, suggests, in Benjamin's terms, a real mother who can act as '… another subject whose independent centre must be outside her child if she is to grant him (or her) the recognition he (or she) seeks' (Benjamin, 1988, p. 24).

I was inspired by Young-Eisendrath's (1984, p. 18) conclusion to 'The Story of Sir Gawain and Lady Ragnell' in *Hags and Heroes*, where she names what women really want as sovereignty over their own lives. For women who have been negatively framed in personhood, occupation or professional life, I would add the right to determine how long it may take them to reach procreative identity. Seligman conjures up 'a creativity born of resolution and reconciliation of opposing psychic forces *with* an individual' (Seligman 1985, p. 83). Here we must include a woman's right to determine how long her developmental processes may take to reach procreative identity, if ever. This observed phenomenon in participants' narratives became the ethical, methodological junction toward accessing intra-psychic associations and inter-subjectivity as a research model. The tension I was holding with my participants was when the body mattered and when it didn't. Starting with Merleau-Ponty's (1968, p. 263) 'non-dualist corporeality' which sees body as an environment where process takes place and Simonsen's (2012) feminist and post-colonial thinking on phenomenology as quintessentially embodiment and embodied experience, I sought to learn more about the subjective and affective spaces of the body containing *living meaning* (ibid., p. 17). In this space action/lack of action is an ever flowing both/and articulation of emotions 'simultaneously passive/and active' (Simonsen, 2012).

Yet [*late*] desire for procreation at midlife, which seeks 'identification and closeness [between mother and child] must *also* be traded for independence; it means that being a subject of desire required repudiation of the maternal role, of feminine identity itself' (Benjamin, 1988, p. 134). Most participants had lived their lives in two parts, first as if they were Adam focusing on hunting and gathering in the world of work, and later, in the second half of life, they wanted to become Eve, to create the same relational security they had sought from their own mother but had failed to receive. The '"gaping wound" had the mother patriarch at its core. The mother's perfectionist ideals not only created a split in her daughter's femininity but also undermined her self-esteem and creativity' (Woodman, 1990, p. 99). Here, I found the female ego's very duality in its capacity to at once identify with and take up the role of the other while at the very same time denying the uncontrollable nature of the turn to otherness by asserting a concomitant need for recognition, which in turn aroused the feeling of being negated along with a deep wish to do something about it. Or as Chodorow (1978) put it, motherhood reproduces itself. I recall one participant who was able to express her hunger for a child succinctly, "I just want someone to feel I'm special".

A 'second return to mother' (Powell, 1993) in Jungian terms is a return to an original identification with mother and comes after a long attachment period to father. That need not literally mean the biological father, for it can represent the favouring of masculine ways and means. This orientation to the masculine is an Oedipal phase, reinforced by patriarchal primacy in cultures (ibid., p. 159) that can linger over an extended period past adolescence and into midlife. 'The anima too is a product of the patriarchy, as is the puer father who married the devouring mother' (Woodman, 1990, p. 99). At root, a second return is the profound change of a girl's identity into a deeper appreciation of herself as an adult woman, drawing on previously learned qualities of animus gained through higher education and the workplace.

> For a generation, aging and female reproduction have been lodged within the gendered and gendering debates regarding women's involvement in the workforce and demographic shifts toward delayed parenting which culminate in discourses on the 'biological clock'… emerging in the 1970s to capture the interconnections and fissures between social and physiological domains regarding women's bodies and reproduction.
> 
> *(Friese, Becker and Nachtigall, 2006, p. 1551)*

Could it be that human beings, particularly women (Hollway, 2006), are born with an in-built ability to care for another? Through the works of first and second wave feminists, commencing with Simone de Beauvoir's assertion, 'mother's feeling of being a valuable human being "is only an illusion"' (de Beauvoir, 1972, p. 14) as and against Chodorow's ([1978]1999) position that inequality is engendered through caring. Hollway separates the trajectories of girls and boys, making a case for shared parenting in order for both genders to enjoy advantages of connection and autonomy in childhood (Hollway, 2006, p. 25). Female researchers at Harvard (Gilligan, Lyons and Hammer, 1989; Gilligan, 2013) found that girls lost their authentic voice, the very nature of how they communicated in relationships until adolescence, when they began to interact with boys as members of the opposite sex, preferring not to speak out, for fear they might hurt someone's feelings. These findings raised questions as to the measure of an authentic self when faced with social pressures seen to be compromising 'leaving a further lacuna in the understanding of psychological health in girls' (and boys') development and its relationship to their capacity to care' (Gilligan, 2013, p. 27). Such socially constructed gendered trajectories, it is argued, impact on whether there develops an experience of self-worth in a child, 'the basis of a capacity to care'. With self-worth, maternal subjectivity prepares the ground to see a child accurately such that s/he can move through omnipotent struggles to individuation and improved gender relations where women are subjects not objects (Hollway, 2006, p. 55). Hollway (2006, p. 105) has embraced object relations for an understanding of early development, including the move from self-centred infantile love into genuine love by means of the capacity to be concerned for another 'without intruding into their otherness as "love's knowledge"'.

It was not surprising to then learn how desire for a child can also turn in on itself within a spectrum of maternal preoccupation, ambivalence and subjectivity. The barrier for women in finding their feminine ground is rooted not only in how their own mother related, or cared for her female child, but what valuing messages father also gave her (Barone-Chapman, 2007, p. 494) about her body difference and potential place in the world. There was fear and later repulsion at discovering some might have a 'child like me', reflecting a stain left by how their own mother had felt about them, a perversity of shared experience that came alive while working through their complex material on delayed motherhood: 'Today 86 percent of women ages 40–44 – near to the end of their reproductive years – are mothers, up from 80 percent in 2006, reversing decades of decline [in the US], according to a new analysis of census data by Pew Research Center' (Cain Miller, 2018). The *New York Times* further reported the increase occurred among women with advanced education and those who did not marry. With this additional remark we are getting more than population news, we are receiving a pejorative message from the patriarchy implying women who pursue higher education over having babies, are being selfish, thus, the medical advice goes, mother and baby are also at risk. Marriage becomes the moral red herring if a woman chooses to conceive out of wedlock.

With Rozsika Parker's work we get a significant bridge from clinically oriented conceptions to more social orientations in considering women's affective responses toward motherhood. Artist, feminist and psychoanalytical psychotherapist, Parker contributed to art and the women's movement by taking needlework out of a domestic female world into art history and criticism (Parker, 2010) and gave us 'permission' to acknowledge *maternal ambivalence* (Parker, 2005) and its off shoots in hate (Parker, 1995) and shame (Parker, 1997). Parker translated a Kleinian outlook on the transition to motherhood from the need for a woman's own infantile issues to be reworked from infantile ambivalence toward her mother to having a developmental purpose to be worked out with the child. Holding what Jung would have referred to as a 'union of opposites' within the goal of individuation, Parker sought to demonstrate that a balance of love and hate pervades the effort to achieve maternal thought. She argued that tolerating her ambivalence as part of a desire to know what being a mother really is about, would lead not only to *thinking* but to creativity. Baraitser and Noack (2007, p. 174) went on to extend Parker's work by suggesting that mothers may need to use infants-as-objects in much the same way as Winnicott had suggested infants need to use mothers as objects (Winnicott, 1968). Baraitser and Noack (2007, p. 178), accurately sensed the contemporary zeitgeist of delayed motherhood in calling Winnicott's 'good enough' mother into question. Susan Kraemer's (1996) work asked for 'more subjectively complex descriptions of mothering within psychoanalytic literature.' Baraitser and Noack (2007, pp. 177–178) appraised Klein, Winnicott, Mahler, Bion and Benjamin as all equally problematic in their presentation of an idealized, psychologically savvy mother who must be resilient enough to survive motherhood to be able to bring about non-pathological adaptation in the infant. As we look in vain for such a perfect mother, we must ask: how can any woman who has barely survived her own critical mother complexes feel ready to help an infant survive childhood in such a way as to not be critical of its mother – who is now herself.

Lisa Cosgrove (2003, p. 94–95) draws on Kristeva's theory of identity (Kristeva, 1986, p. 98) to offer an 'emancipatory potential' for psychological research to investigate 'how ideologies of motherhood function to regulate subjectivity' (Cosgrove, 2003, p. 95) in far too normative a way. Cosgrove, after Moi (1985) and Weir (1996), calls for a mother that isn't occupied with overcoming the negative concepts of psychoanalytic literature, but is able to be a subject in her own right, with maternal desires and ambivalences that cannot be attributed to her desire to overcome a lexically 'phallic economy' of words – 'repudiating', 'merged', 'omnipotent', 'phallic', 'death-mother', 'witch', and (in time, possibly no longer) the 'phallic mother'.

Humanizing patriarchy's masculine archetypes complements and heals the wounds inflicted by the patriarchal Mother Monster (Woodman, 1990). An infant or child can have many effects on a mother, some humanizing, while others may leave a void. Mothers are not always perfect, but that doesn't stop the expectation that they should be, as I have learned through media's representation of late motherhood. Perhaps that is a part of what needs wrestling with alongside delayed motherhood; the pressure to be perfect.

New paths for individuation arise through immersion into enduring the *night sea journey* 'for the sake of later advantages on the path ...' (Hillman 1972, p. 284). This perspective could be a narrative of a journey culminating in midlife pregnancy. Often it is a destination that eclipses maternal pre-occupation and subjectivity, feverish and compelling as a priori over all other priorities, eclipsing conscious awareness of the soul seeking a new reason for life. Midlife is the time to pursue new goals. Simply stated '... becoming what you already are ... but now more deeply and more consciously' (Stein, 2010, p. 177) can so very easily be swept up in the goal of making a new baby without asking 'why?'. In this book we ask the question.

## Good and Terrible

The idea of the good and terrible mother (woman) did not originate in Neumann's (1955) work. It goes back further to the story of first woman, Lilith (Vogelsang, 1985; Koltuv, 1986, p. 87; Hurwitz, 2009, pp. 31–32), and its relevance to women who wish to understand how longstanding patriarchal views of the feminine impact them at every stage of life. Women who unconsciously delayed motherhood became inclined toward self-doubt and social anxiety in regard to younger mothers, while the media amplified these affects in shaming reportage as will be examined further in the next chapter. This kind of media reporting on late motherhood may be responsible for the emerging confessional, subversive voice in literature on motherhood (Felski, 1989; Wolf, 2001; Slater, 2001; Quiney, 2007) which has become a dichotomous voice of resistance against the interruptive nature of motherhood in accord with the submission of a pre-emptive demand of biological destiny. Adjacent to this idea I found unconscious resistance to be a feature of delayed motherhood as an archetypally inspired developmental echo of Jung's (1972, p. 25) earlier observation of the daughter who wanted to be 'anything but like mother' to create an interface with bio-technology as the 'interference' with nature's processes to impose a new form of medical patriarchy on older women. It is not uncommon for women to think of a pregnancy as a means to calm fears about becoming older alongside a wish to 'rejuvenate' (Pattis Zoja, 1997, p. 110) through procured generative identity. The issue of interruption, seen through

Bianchi's (2012, pp. 39–40) observation of the female body as riddled on such a path, must be newly reconsidered as part of the re-imagined feminine hero who is able to withstand domination and sublimation rituals (Benjamin, 1988). In turn these culturally indigenous oppositions led to right–wrong fears in all of the participants. At every point in their journey, all the participants were facing a *complexio oppositorum*, mirroring the inner argument and resistance they had learned from their familial relationships, which later became a harsh super-ego. There were also many junctures of an *enantiodromia* in which they met a turning away from earlier points of identity within a pattern of 'trans-generational transmission of female violence and destruction' (Leusinger-Bohleber, 2007, p. 326) such that 'sexual passion carried the risk of existential dependence on their love partner and of eventual deception and abandonment by him' [and sometimes, her] (ibid., p. 324). Throughout modern history, women have conducted an increasingly ambivalent relationship to childbearing (Apfel and Keylor, 2002, p. 87). Benedek (1952) went as far to speculate an unconscious choice of infertile men as marriage partners was a means to defend against pregnancy. Furthermore, awareness of such theories impacted self-reporting on preference tests to include questions suggesting causal relationship between culturally defined feminine performance and infertility (Benedek, 1952). Whether we call it a complex to do with Mother or Medea, when it takes on both personal and cultural proportions, it may be more difficult to get hold of because it is embedded within the ideas, language, beliefs, mores and social clock (Neugarten, Moore and Lowe [1965]1996) of normative expectations within every structure that supports cultural and collective experience of interaction. Late motherhood may be considered a symbolic equation of early unrequited love with parental objects that 'remains unconscious [such that] repetition occurs without understanding, [and] a pattern is established for an endless cycle of repetitive, non-generative activity' (Conforti, 2003, p. 94). Delayed motherhood has emerged in a bio-technological age as another form of power, control and resistance, in the process of becoming a modern symbol, juxtaposing life and death, creativity and destruction. 'The attainment of female identity is a process of repression and restraint, "based largely on pain and humiliation"' (Flax, 1990, p. 145; Rubin, 1975, pp. 188, 197).

> The culmination of this process is the 'domestication of women'; women learn to live with their oppression. The family is the source of women's oppression because under patriarchal domination it is the agency in and through which women and men are engendered – replicating men who dominate, women who submit.
> *(Rubin, 1975, pp. 188, 197)*

Initially, it was my belief that delayed motherhood was fuelled by an unconscious desire to upend the status quo of this relationship between genders. This superficial hypothesis gathered momentum and deepened as the study unfolded in the following pages.

## References

Apfel, R.J. and Keylor, R.G. (2002). 'Psychoanalysis and infertility: myths and realities', *The International Journal of Psychoanalysis*, 83(1), pp. 85–104.
Baraitser, L. and Noack, A. (2007). 'Mother Courage: reflections on maternal resilience', *British Journal of Psychotherapy*, 23(2), pp. 171–188.
Barone-Chapman, M. (2007). 'The hunger to fill an empty space. An investigation of primordial affects and meaning-making in the drive to conceive through repeated use of ART', *Journal of Analytical Psychology*, 52(4), pp. 389–541.
Beebe, J. (1992). *Integrity in Depth*. College Station, Texas: Texas A&M University Press.
Benedek, T. (1952). 'Infertility as a psychosomatic defense', *Fertility and Sterility*, 3(6), pp. 527–541.
Benjamin, J. (1988). *The Bonds of Love: Psychoanalysis, Feminism, and the Problem of Domination*. New York: Pantheon Books.
Benjamin, J. (2004). 'Beyond doer and done to: an intersubjective view of thirdness', *The Psychoanalytic Quarterly*, 73, pp. 5–46.
Bianchi, E. (2012). 'The Interruptive Feminine: Aleatory Time and Feminist Politics'. In H. Gunkel, C. Nigianni and F. Soderback (eds), *Undutiful Daughters: New Directions in Feminist Thought and Practice*. New York: Palgrave Macmillan.
Bion, W.R. (1962). *A Theory of Thinking*. London: Routledge.
Chodorow, J. ([1978]1999). *The Reproduction of Mothering*. Berkeley, CA: University of California Press.
Conforti, M. (2003). *Field, Form and Fate Patterns in Mind, Nature and Psyche*. New Orleans: Spring Journal Inc.
Cosgrove, L. (2003). 'Feminism, postmodernism and psychological research', *Hypatia*, 18(3), pp. 85–112.
De Beauvoir, S. (1949/1972). *The Second Sex*. Harmondsworth: Penguin.
Felski, R. (1989). *Beyond Feminist Aesthetics: Feminist Literature and Social Change*. Cambridge, MA: Harvard University Press.
Flax, J. (1990). *Thinking Fragments: Psychoanalysis, Feminism and Postmodernism in the Contemporary West*. Berkeley, CA: University of California Press.
Friese, C., Becker, G. and Nachtigall, R.D. (2006). 'Rethinking the biological clock: eleventh hour moms, miracle moms and meanings of age-related infertility', *Social Science & Medicine*, 63, pp. 1550–1560.
Gilligan, C. (2013). *Joining the Resistance: Psychology, Politics, Girls and Women*. Cambridge, MA: Harvard Graduate School of Education.
Gilligan, C., Lyons, N.P. and Hanmer, T.J. (1989). *Making Connections: The Relational Worlds of Adolescent Girls at Emma Willard School*. Cambridge, MA: Harvard University Press.
Hillman, J. (1972). (ed.), *The Myth of Analysis: Three Essays in Archetypal Psychology*. Evanston, IL: Northwestern University Press.
Hollway, W. (2006). *The Capacity to Care: Gender and Ethical Subjectivity*. Women and Psychology Series, ed. Jane Ussher. London and New York: Routledge.
Hurwitz, S. (2009). *Lilith – The First Eve: Historical and Psychological Aspects of the Dark Feminine*. Einsiedeln: Daimon Verlag.
Jung, C.G. ([1928a]1990). 'The Persona as a Segment of the Collective Psyche in The Relations Between the Ego and the Unconscious'. In *Collected Works, Vol. 7. Two Essays on Analytical Psychology* (2nd edn). London: Routledge & Kegan Paul.
Jung, C.G. ([1930–1931]1991). 'The Stages of Life'. In *Collected Works, Vol. 8. The Structure and Dynamics of the Psyche* (2nd edn). London: Routledge & Kegan Paul.

Jung, C.G. ([1932]1997). *Visions. Notes on the Seminar given by C.G. Jung in 1930–1934, Vol. 99*. Princeton, NJ: Princeton University Press.

Jung, C.G. (1972). 'The Mother Archetype'. In *Four Archetypes: Mother, Rebirth, Spirit, Trickster*. London: Routledge.

Koltuv, B.Black (1986). *The Book of Lilith*. York Beach, ME: Nicolas Hays, Inc.

Kraemer, S.B. (1996) 'Betwixt the dark and the daylight of maternal subjectivity: mediations on the threshold', *Psychoanalytic Dialogues*, 6, pp. 765–791.

Kristeva, J. (1984). 'Julia Kristeva in conversation with Rosalind Coward'. In L. Appignanesi (ed.), *Desire*. London: ICA Documents: 23. Quoted in Allison Weir, *Sacrificial Logics: Feminist Theory and the Critique of Identity*. New York: Routledge (1986), p. 182.

Kristeva, J. (1986). *The Kristeva Reader*, ed. T. Moi. New York: Columbia University Press.

Leusinger-Bohleber, M. (2001). 'The "Medea fantasy": an unconscious determinant of psychogenic sterility', *The International Journal of Psychoanalysis*, 82(2). pp. 323–345.

Merleau-Ponty, M. (1968). *The Visible and the Invisible*. Evanston, IL: Northwestern University Press.

Miller, C.C. (2018). 'The U.S. fertility rate is down, yet more women are mothers', www.nytimes.com/2018/01/18/upshot/the-us-fertility-rate-is-down-yet-more-women-are-mothers.html. Accessed 20 January 2018.

Moi, T. (1985). *Sexual/Textual Politics: Feminist Literary Theory*. New York: Methuen.

Nelson, A.M. (2004). 'A qualitative study of older first-time mothering in the first year', *Journal of Pediatric Health Care*, 18(6), pp. 284–291.

Neugarten, B., Moore, J.W. and Lowe, J.C. ([1965]1996). 'Age Norms, Age Constraints, and Adult Socializations'. In D.A. Neugarten (ed.), *The Meanings of Age: Selected Papers of Bernice L. Neugarten*. Chicago, IL: University of Chicago Press, pp. 24–33.

Neumann, E. (1955). *The Great Mother: An Analysis of the Archetype*. New York: Pantheon Books.

Paris, G. (2007). *Wisdom of the Psyche: Depth Psychology After Neuroscience*. Hove and New York: Routledge.

Parker, R. (1995). *Mother Love/Hate: The Power of Maternal Ambivalence*. London: Basic Books.

Parker, R. (1997). 'The Production and Purpose of Maternal Ambivalence'. In W. Hollway and B. Featherstone (eds), *Mothering and Ambivalence*. London: Routledge, pp. 17–36.

Parker, R. (2005). *Torn In Two: The Experience of Maternal Ambivalence*. London: Virago.

Parker, R. (2010). *The Subversive Stitch: Embroidery and the Making of the Feminine*. London: IB Tauris.

Pattis Zoja, E. (1997). *Abortion: Loss and Renewal in The Search for Identity*. Trans. Henry Martin. London and New York: Routledge.

Pew Research Center, Social & Demographic Trends (2018). 'U.S. Women More Likely to Become Mothers, But Are Doing So Later in Life', http://www.pewsocialtrends.org/. Accessed 20 January 2018.

Powell, S. (1993). 'Electra: the dark side of the moon', *Journal of Analytical Psychology*, 38(2), pp. 155–174.

Quiney, R. (2007). 'Confessions of the new capitalist mother: twenty-first-century writing on motherhood as trauma', *Women's Cultural Review*, 18(1), pp. 19–40.

Rubin, G. (1975). 'The Traffic in Women: Notes on the "Political Economy" of Sex'. In R. Rapp Reiter (ed.), *Toward an Anthropology of Women*. New York: Monthly Review Press.

Seligman, E. (1985). 'The Half-Alive Ones'. In A. Samuels (ed.), *The Father: Contemporary Jungian Perspectives*. London: Free Association Books.

Showalter, E. (1992). *Sexual Anarchy: Gender and Culture at the Fin de Siècle*. London: Virago Press.
Simonsen, K. (2012). 'In quest of a new humanism: embodiment, experience and phenomenology as critical geography', *Progress in Human Geography*, 37(1), pp. 10–26.
Singer, T. and Kimbles, S.L. (2004). 'Introduction'. In T. Singer and S.L. Kimbles (eds), *The Cultural Complex: Contemporary Jungian Perspectives on Psyche and Society*. New York: Brunner-Routledge.
Slater, L. (2003). *Love Works Like This: Travels through a Pregnant Year*. London: Bloomsbury.
Smajdor, A. (2009). 'Between fecklessness and selfishness: is there a biologically optimal time for motherhood?', *International Library of Ethics, Law, and the New Medicine*, 43, pp. 105–117.
Stein, M. (2010) *Jung's Map of the Soul: An Introduction*. Chicago, IL: Open Court.
Swartz, S. (2013). 'Feminism and psychiatric diagnosis: reflections of a feminist practitioner', *Feminism & Psychology*, 23(1), p. 41.
Vogelsang, E.W. (1985). 'The confrontation between Lilith and Adam: the fifth round', *Journal of Analytical Psychology*, 30(2), pp. 149–163.
Weir, A. (1996). *Sacrificial Logics: Feminist Theory and the Critique of Identity*. New York: Routledge.
Welldon, E.V. (1988). *Mother, Madonna, Whore: The Idealization and Denigration of Motherhood*. London and New York: Karnac.
Winnicott, D.W. (1968). 'The use of an object and relating through identifications'. In D.W. Winnicott, R. Shepherd and M. Davis (eds), *Psycho-Analytic Explorations*. Cambridge, MA: Harvard University Press.
Wolf, N. (2001). *Misconceptions: Truth, Lies and the Unexpected on the Journey to Motherhood*. London: Chatto & Windus.
Woodman, M. (1990). *The Ravaged Bridegroom: Masculinity in Women*. Toronto: Inner City Books.
Young-Eisendrath, P. (1984) *Hags and Heroes: A Feminist Approach to Jungian Psychotherapy with Couples*. Toronto: Inner City Books.

## Further Reading

Baring, A. (2013). *The Dream of the Cosmos: A Quest for the Soul*. Wimborne: Archive Publishing.
Barone-Chapman, M. (2014). 'Sulphur Rises From The Blackened Body'. In D. Mathers (ed.), *Alchemy and Psychotherapy: Post-Jungian Perspectives*. London: Routledge.
Barone-Chapman, M. (2016). 'Trickster, Trauma and Transformation. The Vicissitudes of Late Motherhood'. In E. Brodersen and M. Glock (eds), *Jungian Perspectives on Rebirth and Renewal*. London and New York: Routledge, pp. 189–204.
Benjamin, J. (1996). 'In defense of gender ambiguity', *Gender and Psychoanalysis, Vol. 1*, pp. 27–43.
Campbell, P. (2011). 'Boundaries and risk: media framing of assisted reproductive technologies and older mothers', *Social Science & Medicine*, 72(2), pp. 265–272.
Chesler, P. (2009). *Woman's Inhumanity to Woman*. Chicago, IL: Lawrence Hill Books.
Douglas, M. (1966). *Purity and Danger*. Abingdon: Routledge Classics.
Erikson, E. (1950). *Childhood and Society*. New York: W.W. Norton & Co.
Gilbert, S. (2015). 'Why women aren't having children', *The Atlantic*, https://www.theatlantic.com/entertainment/archive/2015/04/why-women-arent-having-children/390765/, 17 April 2015.
Khan, M.M.R. (1963). 'The Concept of Cumulative Trauma'. In M.M.R. Khan (ed.), *The Privacy of the Self*. Abingdon: Routledge, pp. 42–58.

Klein, J. and Sauer, M.V. (2001). 'Assessing fertility in women of advanced reproductive age', *American Journal of Obstetrics & Gynecology*, 185(3), pp. 758–770.
Klein, M. (1948). 'On the Theory of Anxiety and Guilt'. In *Envy and Gratitude and Other Words (1946–1963), (1975)* The Melanie Klein Trust. London: Hogarth Press.
Rich, A. (1976). *Of Woman Born*. New York: W.W. Norton & Co.

# 2
# FORGETTING, THEN REMEMBERING

Over the past fifty years, as biotechnology has stretched the age span of female reproduction, the desire for motherhood and its status has gone through many changes, including idealization, denigration, avoidance, and ambivalence until recently reaching new peaks of idealization once more. Newspapers and magazines have heralded the 'Death of the single girl' and 'Motherhood is the new sex' (Watson, 2009, Season 3) to promote the glamour and status of the procreative potential within a committed relationship. This represents a narrative shift on a collective level from the neurotic, at home mother of the 1950s (Spiegel, 2001) through the advent of birth control, to the current situation in which young women of a class can postpone babies in favour of opportunities for career advancement (Walkerdine, Lucey and Melody, 2001).

Polarities of idealization and denigration are at the epicentre of delayed motherhood. As a psychosocial phenomenon, underpinned by an aging population and the rise of bio-technology, we are able to forecast (Future Foundation, 2002; Dixon and Margo, 2006) that more women will continue to have a first child later in life and are less likely to have a larger family.

Postponing childbirth increases the gap between generations making for fewer generations born in any given time period. These figures are part of a larger story for the Western world, in what Van de Kaa (1993) identified as a 'Second Demographic Transition'. Defined as a decline in fertility and mortality, the SDT emerged in the 1950s with rising divorce rates, followed by lower birth rates and a disconnection between marriage and procreation (Lesthaeghe, 2010). Within the SDT, delayed motherhood has become institutionalized around medical care. In 2011, 48,147 women had IVF treatment compared to 32, 626 in 2005 (http://www.hfea.gov.uk/1269.html#1278/). The higher rate of female IVF treatment is related to reproductive ageing, alongside an increasing demand by older, less fertile women to bear children (Klein and Sauer, 2001).

Liefbroer (2005) found that the decision to have children was the result of benefit/cost weighting, drawing on Van de Kaa's (1993) identification of processes to do with modernization, secularization and individualization in Western societies thus reducing adherence to previously held concepts of normative choices. In parallel, individual autonomy, as both a goal and condition, is seen to have more value. A study, 'Childlessness in the UK' for the Economic and Social Research Council (ESRC), found 30 per cent of those intending to have children who were childless at age 30 remained childless at age 42. Highly educated women and men were considered more likely to achieve intended childbearing at older ages, whereas those of lower education who were childless at 30 stood a lower likelihood of becoming a parent (ibid., pp. 6, 11, 212). Partnership formation experiences were cited as one reason that childlessness is highest among those married after 30 and later separated. Most startling was the educational factor in the proportion of graduate women remaining childless (25 per cent) who were born in 1970 compared to women with below secondary qualifications (15 per cent) (ESRC, p. 14).

## Complexities

Initially, I defined the frame of late motherhood as a *pregnant pause* (Barone-Chapman, 2011, p. 188) to claim the psychosocial phenomenon not only as a narrative shift, but as a new creation myth in the making. As the research developed, a new place for the pregnant pause emerged within the midlife climax at the moment a woman began to reach for more unifying energy, simultaneously arousing, as if from nowhere, a traumatic memory from her early life, returning, to give her pause. The desire for a child can come on suddenly and begin to feel like a sacred duty necessary to uphold a relationship with the self. As a thematic principle the pregnant pause becomes both crucible and bridge in a life lived in two parts, first as Adam representing the area of work and identity, then later as Eve, matriarch of home and hearth, under the new patriarchal order. Within the trajectory of her early development, and later choices into adulthood, moving toward a relationship with other as midlife comes to climax, I discovered during my research that there are three phases of the pregnant pause which will we will see in the case histories that follow. What we are investigating are the unconscious processes necessitating the narrative shift to procreative identity, as a reparative motif from a one-sided, 'half-alive' ego-development, in non-essentialist terms (Seligman, 1985) at midlife. Jung (1940, para. 267) found the archetype of the child to be present most often when maturation processes became difficult to achieve, leading us to the question, 'What is the biological purpose of the archetype?' (ibid., para. 272). This teleology comes alive around explorations of delayed motherhood when a child is understood to be a redemptive, unifying symbol. For some, it can be reified through mothering, but actually the promise of the pregnant pause at midlife includes every notion of rebirth and creativity.

As a clinician, I have found the desire for motherhood has both an outer and inner sociology (Singer and Kimbles, 2004, pp. 4–5, 7) in the realm of individual experience within a context of the outer collective culture. Often, it is the fear of not having a maternal self that is most compelling past the time of midlife as the archetype of the 'mother', long held as the signifier of trans-generational comforts, traumas and other relational affects, weakens with no direct tutelage. The prospect of motherhood at midlife is not guaranteed, and this biological ceiling undermines all previous conceptions of biological imperatives. Delayed motherhood occupies a relationship to the past that is different from the past of younger mothers, as women who have delayed motherhood had to pass through the veil of cultural, societal and patriarchal expectations of what was considered to be 'good' and 'pure' for women (Douglas, 1966; Kristeva, 1982).

Late motherhood in midlife, for those who have not previously conceived or considered doing so, is not an accident, because it requires conscious agency, involving an unconscious purposeful forgetting of other, culture and the biological imperative that too often ensnares women until they *come of age* in and around the fourth decade. In part this may be due to what Bly (1997) described as *neoteny* (a very extended adolescent period). Becoming a mother is a form of initiation into a new consciousness that affects personal identity (Huws, 1982). It also comes with cultural expectations around stages of life (Jung, 1930–1931), and may be best understood as an inborn "social clock" (Neugarten, Moore and Lowe, 1965; 1996) that can impact the age of initiation into emerging identities, such as motherhood. Jung (1928a, paras. 243–253) called this formation of identity, to announce who one is in respect to community and culture, the persona. Later Erik Erikson (1950) referred to this on-going process as the development of a psychosocial identity with a purpose of limiting social anxiety by acquiring identifiable status in respect to others. However, the concept of the psychosocial in regard to identity formation went much deeper in Jung's concept of the persona, as 'a mask that feigns individuality … simply acting a role through which the collective psyche speaks' (Jung, 1928a, para. 245). The role paraded before the community evokes reactions on the part of the unconscious and these together form the seeds of individual development (ibid.). In the ever-changing human equation between the individual and the universal, Jung's opus matured into an interactive field between culture and cosmos (Baring, 2013). But now in this 'in between' space, 'the recovery of the Feminine invites a reorientation of consciousness: a receptivity not only to the events occurring in the external world, but to the long-ignored voice of the Soul' (ibid., p. 223).

In one sense, I am infusing into emerging social constructs a form of animism (Tylor, 1871) to Jung's interpretation of UFO sightings, which came into the collective consciousness after World War II, at a time when there were 'changes in the psychic dominants, of the archetypes … which bring about, or accompany, long-lasting transformations of the collective psyche' (Jung, 1958, para. 589). In effect, this phenomenon foreshadowed a new age that would see not only a rise in animism, but an unconscious rise in reliance on technology, the logos of science and in its shadow, the magical thinking that anything can and should be possible through science. Max Weber's (1947) phrase, 'disenchantment with the world' has application to the midlife longing to reach a higher purpose, through demystification of objects in the world as having life, to move into conditions in favour of scientific ways of making life. What delayed motherhood represents is not yet fully understood, though it is in the process of becoming symbolic of extending youth, joy, and overcoming past sorrows through the making of life after a soul death early in life.

Thus, we have the makings of a complex asking to be re-examined within the flux of midlife recapitulations. Unlike an individual complex that weakens once brought to consciousness, a cultural complex is more difficult to get hold of because it is embedded within the ideas, language, beliefs, and mores (Neugarten, Moore and Lowe, 1965) of every structure that supports personal and collective experience. While complexes may be attributed to a spectrum of cumulative trauma (Khan, 1963) in analytical literature, there is evidence they are also passed through longitudinal, familial and cultural ties (Symington, 2001; Belford Ulanov, 2014; Wirtz, 2014, pp. 153–157). Trauma can also become acculturated through more distant relationships. Most children move into adulthood through exposure to the wider culture of school, peers, village, region, nation and what is gleaned from interactions through cultural differences, experienced first-hand, through personal stories, as well those found in literature, film, on all media screens, including social media. What follows is a carefully selected group of research studies that have made their way into media perception of delayed motherhood. I review these in order for the reader to discover, not only the biases against older women seeking motherhood in midlife, but the challenges that face them every day of their motherhood. These are just some of the effects the *fourth state* (McChesney, 2015) can have on culture as an unrecognized political system, often seen simply as journalism. In the broadest sense, media has become how we are shaped by information, framed as news, gossip, social studies, trends, lifestyles, and how older first-time mothers are seen by media (Budds, Locke and Burr, 2013; Shaw and Giles, 2007; Hadfield, Rudoe and Sanderson-Mann, 2007).

## *Identity Influencers*

There has been a steady increase in articles offered by fertility experts warning women of the social and economic costs to late onset of motherhood after the age of 35 (Smajdor, 2009). The national press has regularly reported on some aspects of late motherhood in pejorative and damning tones. 'Fertility experts urge end to "selfish" late motherhood' (Foggo and Rogers, 2006) and 'Late motherhood as "big a problem" as teenage mums' (Templeton, 2006). Media framing of assisted reproductive technologies by Patricia Campbell has not only brought the focus to 'older mothers' who are postmenopausal, but the discovery that a discourse of risk emerges whenever technology and its users disrupt the stability of sociotechnical discourses leading to public re-examination of the technology and user in question to recreate a new debate focused on the associated risks. Campbell (2011, p. 270) cites the case of Ranjit Hayer as providing 'insight into the complex, broader debates surrounding ARTs. What is "natural" reproduction? What does it mean to be a mother or a father? What counts as a family? Whose knowledge and experience count in assessing technological risk?' As these and other questions become publicly debated, uncertainty and discursive tensions rise, destabilizing what has come to be seen as 'routine' use of assisted reproductive technologies (Campbell, 2011). What I am building up to in this discussion of media framing is how media reporting on late motherhood has affected older women through culture, in how they are viewed and related to.

Selfish equates to the 'having it all' narrative, implicating women's entitlement to what was previously seen as the male norm of having both career and a family. '"Feminist" anger against patriarchy has been wrongly interpreted as anger at the paternal principle ... The feminine revolution was not a rejection of the paternal archetype, nor was it an empowerment of the maternal principle. [It was] a revolt against a decadent monarchy; the ruling of one gender by another' (Paris, 2007, p. 144).

It is conceivable that Jung's clinical experience informed him of the erotic transference (Heuer, 2012), or *hieros gamos* (incest desire) concept within the notion of a *kinship libido* (Jung, 1946, para. 431) which went on to inspire a view of the web of familial relationships and biological relatedness, extending to the field of anthropological research and assisted reproductive technology only later considered apropos to the emerging relational changes in families and culture (Inhorn and Birenbaum-Carmeli, 2008). A review of recent media presentations on late motherhood below, examines and links the messages of media judgements to a woman's procreative trajectory. On a social and cultural level, the 'fourth estate' is implicated in a process of splitting the feminine into idealizing (younger baby making) and demonizing (older women) for late procreative desire. Shaw and Giles' (2009) investigation of the media's framing of older mothers in 'Motherhood on Ice?' found an adherence to the 'normative' narrative in regard to women's development. Alongside this discovery I found the notion of the 'perfect' mother continues to prevail in every fabled construction of motherhood. Adjacent to negative portrayals of older mothers, there was also a maternal, confessional auto-biographical body of literature which contributed to a trauma culture around the intimate subject matter of childbirth and mothering. It would not make for easy reading to any woman unfamiliar with labour and its aftermath.

Karen Henwood's (1993) study on 'Women and Later Life: The Discursive Construction of Identities within Family Relationships' paid particular attention to mothers and daughters accounts of their relationship and whether they were complicit or resistant to a 'femininity discourse' of relational mother–daughter closeness. Henwood found this closeness to be 'located within a socially or culturally organized framework for understanding which prescribes women's identity and conduct in terms set by gendered social institutions and relationships, such as those of "family life" where themes of complicity arise around endorsement or challenges to what is considered the "normative framework"' (Henwood, 1993, p. 306). One finding of note in Henwood's study was the long-standing assumption in social science (Young and Wilmott, 1957) that a shared feminine identity and gender role creates a 'unique closeness' between mother and daughter, which serves as a 'lynchpin' within the life of the family (Henwood, 1993, p. 310), even though traditional, gendered roles and institutions, by their own definitions, may no longer be held outside of the private domestic domain (ibid., p. 314). What makes Henwood's research relevant to delayed motherhood is her finding that older women 'are still defined primarily within traditional gender framework where women are either good or bad mothers and wives. Moreover, since older women no longer occupy a central reproductive function, there is a dearth of positive images of them and the social positions they can occupy' (Henwood, 1993, p. 316). One reason for this media portrayal is the view that women 'are 'choosing to have babies later in life, [leaving] them open to criticism that they are no longer taking full advantage of their biological window of opportunity in which they can safely conceive' (Budds, Locke and Burr, 2013, pp. 133). The perception that women can 'choose' to have babies anytime they want carries a patriarchal tone and tenor regarding the appearance of 'having it all' (ibid.). Gill (2007a) takes account of autonomy akin to a post-feminist sensibility, while Young-Eisendrath (1984) through the notion of sovereignty claims that such ideas are androcentric in their ignorance of the woman's experience, her social context and the nature of her female gender identity in context to traditional sex roles. There is evidence of a social construction to motherhood that must be taken into consideration when considering what media culture does with the idea of a woman having choices and sovereignty. The first of these is 'the age at which women become mothers reflects their socio-economic status' (Hadfield, Rudoe and Sanderson-Mann, 2007, p. 255). The second social construction is the way in which older mothers are portrayed in the media with their choice of time appearing to require justification, as if it were 'strange' given the many health risks (ibid., p. 258).

Another study, '"Having It All" No Longer: Fertility, Female Labor Supply and the New Life Choices of Generation X' (Vere, 2007) concerns itself with differentiating Generation X from the previous 'baby boom' generation (1946–1962). The study seeks to demonstrate how fertility decisions made earlier than a previous generation of recent college (university) graduates made a significantly reduced contribution to the labour force, and a reduced and possibly sustained decline in the female workers extrapolated to indicate 'a drag' on economic growth (Vere, 2007, p. 827). The data show a significant shift on the allocation of time between the experience of motherhood and participation in the work force, which peaked in 2000. The article uses the pejorative term 'have it all' to convey the combination of achieving motherhood and a 'high-powered career', with the latter definition of 'baby boom' achievement lacking defining differentiation. The context and impact of employment choices made by the baby boom generation are overlooked, even though these choices spurred the economic rise of the middle class in the US and Canada following World War II. The cumulative effect meant women had to create a family on 'two incomes' in order to survive and maintain what their own parents worked hard for them to achieve through higher education (Bell, 1976). What is important to note from this study is a trend of reversing declining fertility among higher educated women for those born in the mid-1960s (ibid., p. 824). However, it is significant that the data is in part relying on 'total intended fertility' to measure the freedom of Generation X to feel fecund.

The study '"Informed and Un-informed Decision Making" – Women's Reasoning, Experiences and Perceptions with Regard to Advanced Maternal Age and Delayed Childbearing: A Meta-Synthesis' (Cooke, Mills and Lavender, 2010) offers three items of interest within their research published in the *International Journal of Nursing Studies*, under the heading 'What is already known about the topic?' – 1. Delayed childbearing beyond 30 years of age is a global trend. 2. A quantity of methodologically limited studies have reported on maternal and neonatal risks with advanced maternal age by health professionals labelling older women as 'high risk'. 3. A dearth of qualitative research on this topic gives little understanding of women's experience and views.

The meta-analysis was synthesized into twelve papers originally culled from 2,686, on a similar basis to my own curious desire to learn what unconscious processes create a delay in procreative identity. Their findings showed the pursuit of education and career to attain independence and stability before motherhood was unlikely to change. The authors found the trend of delayed childbearing as a trend likely to continue, and in their minds, necessitating the need for informed reproductive decisions.

Following their analysis, the authors conducted what they believe to be 'the first UK qualitative study of women's views of delayed childbearing' (Cooke, Mills and Lavender, 2012, p. 37) and made the following conclusions:

- Women do not have ultimate choice or control over the timing of childbearing
- This is a new concept not found in existing literature
- While UK media analysis suggests women choose to delay having children due to education and career, this was opposed by participants
- Instead the participants taking part in the study claimed a 'complex interplay' of factors determined when they had a baby, which included relationship, stability, health and fertility
- Women perceived an element of chance was involved, as all the factors would need to be in place in order to have a baby at the selected time
- Delayed childbearing is rarely a conscious choice
- Some form of control is in place, but it is believed to be 'subconscious'
- Trend for increasing maternal age at time of first birth set to continue
- Health professionals have pre-conceived ideas why women delay and these need to be reassessed
- Clinicians need to understand the complexity of factors affecting women's decisions rather than working on assumptions
- Health professionals need to provide appropriate information with sensitive support in light of varying perceptions of risk

The study, '"I think motherhood for me was a bit like a double-edged sword": The Narratives of Older Mothers' (Shelton and Johnson, 2006) aimed to explore the transitional experience required in delayed motherhood. Interviewing five women over 30 prior to the birth of the first child, revealed a predominant tone of maternal ambivalence at the interpersonal level. The research highlighted the contradiction between societal idealizations of the 'perfect mother' against the hidden realities of motherhood, a theme also appearing in Almond (2010) regarding the state of motherhood as under some pressure with a mother having to be 'forever improving' herself or else she could harm the child. Shelton and Johnson's study emphasized a need to portray delayed motherhood as 'more realistic' to address a theme found in many of the women's stories: resistance and the undermining of dominant societal expectations about motherhood (Shelton and Johnson, 2006, p. 327). However, there has emerged another opposite position that the 'need' to have children is perpetuated by the myth that 'having children is the single most important thing a person can do with his or her life, and that not having children leaves people sad and empty' (See Gilbert, 2015, 'Why Women Aren't Having Children').

Working with progressive narratives of participants (Gergen and Gergen, 1986), I found theories of a developmental perspective to be a pervasive societal narrative (Lee, 2001) where certain goals should be achieved at various points in life. While the participants of these studies spoke in positive terms about their readiness for motherhood in terms of advanced age, 'the tone and metaphors used emphasized the prominence of a "double-edged" ambivalent storyline' (Shelton and Johnson, 2006, p. 327). Citing Berryman (2000) to underscore the view that delayed motherhood is more socially acceptable today, they ultimately concluded as follows:

> … the dominant developmental narrative positions motherhood as part of a natural progression in women's lives and the telling of a progressive narrative of maternal identity integration could be viewed as being central to ensuring that women live up to this developmental imperative.
> 
> *(Shelton and Johnson, 2006)*

## What is a Real Mum?

Three studies caught my attention to do with the experience of 'older motherhood' or 'late parenthood' or even being a 'real mum'. What these studies have in common is emergent new designations brought on by biotechnology in service to reproduction and procreative identity. The first, 'Older Motherhood and the Changing Life Course in the Era of Assisted Reproductive Technologies' (Friese, Becker and Nachtigall, 2008), is one of the few pieces of research that investigated the shape-shifting social currents and identities in the fallout of bio-technology, head on, as a shape shifter of the definition of old age. Their cohort of 79 women was seen to represent a new 'middle age' responding to 'changing social, cultural, physical and economic realities … potentially extending much later in the life course' (ibid., p. 65), and is consistent with the experiences of some of my participants when they talked about 'managing stigma' and 'normalizing older motherhood' (ibid., p. 70). Problem areas were identified in terms of whether the older mother would have another child, as well as choosing areas to live where the presence of older mothers was seen to be more normal. Other remedies against stigma were found through means such as altering their appearance, cosmetically and surgically, to present themselves socially as younger mothers.

The inference in the research is suggestive that doing what one can so as not to appear as the grandmother in future photographs goes hand in hand with de-stigmatizing looking like an older mother (Goffman, 1963). The authors, Friese, Becker and Nachtigall (2006, p. 72) reference a body of literature described as 'impression management and stigma' to account for the gap in experience between social identity and self-definition (ibid.; Miall and Herman, 1994; Snow and Anderson, 1994). Citing Goffman (1963) as the defining author on stigma, we get a view of a social process co-existing with interpretation of symbolic interactions to consider stigma as representing a discrepancy in the service of avoiding stigma. Other strategies observed in coping with age discrepancy were of a more psychological, socially defensive position of hyper-validating notions of exceptional status as and against 'impression management'. Both strategies allowed women to feel legitimate as the mother of a family (Becker et al., 2005), in terms of a self that happens to be an older mother (Travers, 1995).

In 'Late Parenthood Among Sub Fertile and Fertile Couples: Motivations and Educational Goals', Van Balen (2005) found more common ground between younger and older first-time mothers. The research concerned itself with two groups of women around the age of 30 and another at 40. Yet in the study, the implications were that women aged 20–25 felt they were not ready for a child and this coincided with the desire to enjoy life and career first, including establishing themselves financially (ibid., p. 276). First time mothers above the age of 35 were referred to as 'primiparas' (ibid., p. 277) which found first-time parents over the age of 35 more effective in family functioning to do with problem-solving and affective responsiveness (Kooij, Bukman, Hoek, Heineman and Tymstra, 2005). The primiparas, though displaying less of a traditional maternal role had a higher professional status and were more self-assured and independent. More importantly, this study also found that initially, voluntary childless women, could change their mind and come late to motherhood (Friese, Becker, and Nachtigall, 2006). The finding that older fertile women had less traditional reasons for motherhood and reported less femininity (Van Balen, 2005) places late motherhood in the realm of an individuation process (personal) at a time when modern science has been shifting toward the transformation of the collective psyche (Jung, 1958, para. 589), placing late motherhood at the vanguard of something important for both sexes.

The next study to consider the co-mingling of medicine and social science, comes from the prolific authors Friese, Becker and Nachtigall (2006) cited above in Van Balen (2005), 'Rethinking the Biological Clock: Eleventh-Hour Moms, Miracle Moms and Meanings of Age-Related Infertility'. This highly relevant study captures the 'eleventh hour' impulse for procreative identity in midlife, which can feel like the onset of a complex under which a woman has little or no control. It is often the case that a diagnosis of age-related infertility is the first time a woman discovers she is no longer still young. The 79 US couples conceiving post-donor oocytes (eggs) gathered from twelve different fertility centres were reported on along two narrative engagements. The first set of responses clustered around what the authors call, 'eleventh-hour moms' who discovered later in the process their only hope for conception was resorting to donated oocytes in order to have a chance of making their own baby with their opposite sex partner. The second group clustered around the author's other term, 'miracle mom', reflecting the narrative of women who were biologically older and who mostly knew using their own eggs would not yield them a pregnancy to term. Unusually for medically trained researchers, the term 'symbolic' has been used as carrying more meaning than the act or thought itself, regarding the elusive awareness of diminished ovarian reserves, for too long rooted in the language of 'old eggs' rather than menopause, which has more social stigma. These observations reflect the internecine problems for women in midlife around ageing and time. 'Women described a condensation, shortening, or curtailment of their reproductive years that was experienced not only as premature aging but as having lost time or being in a state where precious time was constantly slipping away. For some the lost time implied waste: in time, opportunity, or eggs' (Friese, Becker and Nachtigall, 2006, p. 1554), and by extension, self-blame.

My observation is that women can all too often be relied upon to self-blame in their social interactions, often leaving them with little space required for the present, in whatever form it arrives. In midlife, the goal of making a baby may also transform into a sacred duty to the self, with high feeling-toned affect. Other endeavours and occupations lose their brilliance in the fourth decade, demonstrating an *unconscious determination* (Jung, 1955a, paras 355–406). Within a clinical setting this affect would be seen as a crucial part of regression for the purpose of individuation (Jung, 1946, paras 445–449) and has become a *symbol of transformation* (Jung, 1911–12/1952a, paras 300–418,) when 'the libido that is withdrawn so unwillingly from the "mother" turns into a threatening serpent, symbolizing the fear of death – for the relation to the mother must cease, *must die,* and this is almost the same as dying oneself' (Jung, 1911–12/1952b, para. 473). The 'return to the mothers' (Stein, 2010, p. 177) in this example, and in many others where the 'new king of consciousness' is attempting to be birthed, we find an opening to the unconscious, becoming conscious. When the desire for a child in the second half of life carries a drive to conceive at all costs, we may become curious about what traumatic influences have previously caused a woman's desire to become pregnant to be split off until now (Jung, 1955b, paras. 203–229). We observe the attempt to re-integrate as a frantic gesture of repair with little concern for the addictive nature of repeated IVF (Barone-Chapman, 2007). Sudden transformation raises the possibility of an early relational disturbance, with an inhibiting or prohibiting affect, which may have been preventing 'the trauma [to] be "forgotten", and "remembered" instead of being always present' (Cavalli, 2012, p. 598). The term trauma here has relevance to 'any experience that causes the child unbearable psychic pain or anxiety' (Kalsched, 1996, p. 1). At this juncture of discovery my attention turned toward finding an ethical methodology that would honour the ways in which psyche heals through *remembering* and forgetting, regardless of age or gender.

The parameters of the *pregnant pause* and the field affects surrounding this by-product of bio-technology, have produced an atmosphere around delayed motherhood filled with conflict and resistance, as yet they are not clearly understood widely between the realm of history and teleological purpose (see 'pregnant pause' in Definitions).

# References

Almond, B. (2010). *The Monster Within: The Hidden Side of Motherhood*. Berkeley, CA: University of California Press.

Baring, A. (2013). *The Dream of the Cosmos: A Quest for the Soul*. Wimborne: Archive Publishing.

Barone-Chapman, M. (2007). 'The hunger to fill an empty space: an investigation of primordial affects and meaning making in the drive to conceive through repeated use of ART', *The Journal of Analytical Psychology*, 52(4), pp. 389–541.

Barone-Chapman, M. (2011). 'Pregnant Pause: Procreative Desire, Reproductive Technology and Narrative Shifts at Midlife'. In R. Jones (ed.) *Body Mind and Healing After Jung: A Space of Questions*. London and New York: Routledge, pp. 174–191.

Belford Ulanov, A. (2014). *Knots and Their Untying: Essays on Psychological Dilemmas*. New Orleans, LA: Spring Journal Inc.

Bell, D. (2008). 'The coming of the post-industrial society', *The Educational Forum*, 40(4), pp. 574–579.

Berryman, D.L. (2000). 'Riding the winds of change', *Journal of Leisure Research*, 32(1), pp. 7–11.

Bly, R. (1997). *The Sibling Society*. New York: Vintage Press.

Budds, K., Locke, A. and Burr, V. (2013). '"Risky business": constructing the "choice" to "delay" motherhood in the British press', *Feminist Media Studies*, 13(1), pp. 132–147.

Cavalli, A. (2012). 'Transgenerational transmission of indigestible facts: from trauma, deadly ghosts and mental voids to meaning-making interpretations', *Journal of Analytical Psychology*, 57(5), pp. 597–614.

Cooke, A., Mills, T.A. and Lavender, T. (2010). '"Informed and uninformed decision making" – Women's reasoning, experiences and perceptions with regard to advanced maternal age and delayed childbearing: A meta-synthesis', *International Journal of Nursing Studies*, 47(10), pp. 1317–1329.

Cooke, A., Mills, T.A. and Lavender, T. (2012). 'Advanced maternal age: Delayed childbearing is rarely a conscious choice. A qualitative study of women's views and experiences', *International Journal of Nursing Studies*, 49(1), pp. 30–39.

Dixon, M., and Margo, J. (2006). *Population Politics*. London: Institute for Public Policy Research.

Douglas, M. (1966). *Purity and Danger*. Abingdon and New York: Routledge & Kegan Paul.

Erikson, E. (1950). *Childhood and Society*. New York: W.W. Norton & Co.

Berrington, A. (2015). 'Childlessness in the UK', ESRC Centre for Population Change Working Paper 69, September 2015, http://www.cpc.ac.uk/publications/cpc_working_papers/pdf/2015_WP69_Childlessness_in_the_UK.pdf, 6 April 2016.

Friese, C., Becker, G. and Nachtigall, R.D. (2006). 'Rethinking the biological clock: eleventh-hour moms, miracle moms and meanings of age-related infertility', *Social Science & Medicine*, 63(6), pp. 1550–1560.

Friese, C., Becker, G. and Nachtigall, R.D. (2008). 'Older motherhood and the changing life course in the era of assisted reproductive technologies', *Journal of Aging Studies*, 22(1), pp. 65–73.

Future Foundation (2002). *Saving for a Foot on the Property Ladder*. London: Future Foundation. Press release available at http://journalist.egg.com/aboutegg/newsreleases/news2003/pressrelease/?id=2909648

Gergen, K.J. and Gergen, M.M. (1986). *Narrative Form and the Construction of Psychological Science*. Washington, DC: American Psychological Association.

Gill, R. (2007a). 'Postfeminist media culture: elements of a sensibility', *European Journal of Cultural Studies*, 10(2), pp. 147–166.

Goffman, E. (1963). *Stigma: Notes on the Management of Spoiled Identity*. New York: Simon & Schuster.

Hadfield, L., Rudoe, N. and Sanderson-Mann, J. (2007). 'Motherhood, choice and the British media: time to reflect', *Gender and Education*, 19(2), pp. 255–263.

Heuer, G.M. (2012). 'A most dangerous – and revolutionary – method: Sabina Spielrein, Carl Gustav Jung, Sigmund Freud, Otto Gross, and the birth of intersubjectivity', *Psychotherapy and Politics International*, 10(3), pp. 261–278.

Huws, I. (1982). 'The concretization of women: A rite of self-initiation with the flavour of a religious conversion process', *Women's Studies International Forum*, 5(5), pp. 401–410.

Inhorn, M.C. and Birenbaum-Carmeli, D. (2008). 'Assisted Reproductive Technologies and culture change', *Annual Review of Anthropology*, 37, pp. 177–196.

Jung, C.G. (1946). 'The Naked Truth'. In *Collected Works, Vol. 16. The Practice of Psychotherapy* (2nd edn). London: Routledge & Kegan Paul, 1993.

Jung, C.G. (1911–12/1952a). 'Symbols of the Mother and of Rebirth', *Collected Works, Vol. 5. Symbols of Transformation* (2nd edn). London: Routledge & Kegan Paul, 1995.

Jung, C.G. (1911–12/1952b). 'The Dual Mother', *Collected Works, Vol. 5. Symbols of Transformation* (2nd edn). London: Routledge & Kegan Paul, 1995.

Jung, C.G. (1928a). 'The Persona as a Segment of the Collective Psyche', *Collected Works, Vol. 7. The Relations Between the Ego and the Unconscious* (2nd edn). London: Routledge & Kegan Paul, 1990.

Jung, C.G. (1930–1931). 'The Stages of Life', *Collected Works, Vol. 8. The Structure and Dynamic of the Psyche* (2nd edn). London: Routledge & Kegan Paul, 1991.

Jung, C.G. (1940). 'The Psychology of the Child Archetype', *Collected Works, Vol. 9i. The Archetypes and the Collective Unconscious* (2nd edn). London: Routledge & Kegan Paul, 1990.

Jung, C.G. (1955a). 'The Aetiology of Neurosis', *Collected Works, Vol. 4*.

Jung, G.G. (1955b). 'A Review of The Early Hypotheses', *Collected Works, Vol. 4*.

Jung, C.G. (1958). 'Flying Saucers: A Modern Myth', *Collected Works, Vol. 10. Civilization in Transition* (2nd edn). London: Routledge and Kegan Paul, 1991.

Kalsched, D. (1996). *The Inner World of Trauma: Archetypal Defences of the Personal Spirit*. London: Routledge.

Khan, M.M.R. (1963). 'The Concept of Cumulative Trauma'. In M.M.R. Khan (ed.), *The Privacy of the Self*. New York: International Universities Press, pp. 42–58.

Klein, J. and Sauer, M.V. (2001). 'Assessing fertility in women of advanced reproductive age', *American Journal of Obstetrics & Gynecology*, 185(3), pp. 758–770.

Kooij, L., Bukman, A., Hoek, A., Heineman, M. and Tymstra, T. (2005). 'Women's opinion on the use and offer of ovarian reserve testing: a first step towards a wide ranged social discussion. *Journal of Psychosomatic Obstetric Gynecology*, 26(3), pp. 205–209.

Kristeva, J. (1982). *Powers of Horror: An Essay on Abjection*. New York: Columbia University Press.

Lee, C.S. (2001). 'The use of narrative in understanding now cancer affects development: The stories of one cancer survivor.' *Journal of Health Psychology*, 63(3), pp. 283–293.

Liefbroer, A. (2005). 'The impact of perceived costs and rewards of childbearing on entry into parenthood: evidence from a panel study', *European Journal of Population*, 21(4), pp. 367–391.

Lesthaeghe, R. (2010). 'The unfolding story of the second demographic transition', *Population and Development Review*, 36(22), pp. 211–251.

McChesney, R.W. (2015). *Rich Media, Poor Democracy: Communication Politics in Dubious Times*. New York: The New Press.

Miall, C. and Herman, N.J. (1994). 'Generic Processes of Impression Management: Two Case Studies of Physical and Mental Disability'. In N.J. Herman and L.T. Reynold (eds), *Symbolic Interaction: An Introduction to Social Psychology*. Dix Hills, NY: General Hall, Inc.

Neugarten, B.L., Moore, J.W. and Lowe, J.C. (1965). 'Age norms, age constraints, and adult socialization', *American Journal of Sociology*, 70(6), pp. 710–717.

Seligman, E. (1985). 'The half-alive ones'. In A. Samuels (ed.), *The Father: Contemporary Jungian Perspectives*. London: Free Association Books.
Shaw, R.L. and Giles, D.C. (2007). 'Motherhood on ice? A media framing analysis of older mothers in the UK news', *Psychology & Health*, 24(2), pp. 221–236.
Shelton, N. and Johnson, S. (2006). '"I think motherhood for me was a bit like a double-edged sword": the narratives of older mothers', *Journal of Community & Applied Social Psychology*, 16(4), pp. 316–330.
Singer, T. and Kimbles, S.L. (2004). *The Cultural Complex: Contemporary Jungian Perspectives on Psyche and Society*. London and New York: Routledge.
Smajdor, A. (2009). 'Between fecklessness and selfishness: is there a biologically optimal time for motherhood?', *International Library of Ethics, Law, and the New Medicine*, 43, pp. 105–117.
Snow, D.A. and Anderson, L. (1994). 'The problem of identity construction among the homeless'. In N.J. Herman and L.T. Reynolds (eds), *Symbolic Interaction: An Introduction to Social Psychology*. Dix Hills, NY: General Hall, Inc.
Spiegel, L. (2001). 'Media homes then and now', *International Journal of Cultural Studies*, 4(4), p. 385.
Stein, M. (2010). *Jung's Map of the Soul: An Introduction*. Chicago, IL: Open Court.
Symington, N. (2001). *The Spirit of Sanity*. London: Karnac.
Travers, A. (1995). 'The identification of self', *Journal for the Theory of Social Behaviour*, 25(3), pp. 303–340.
Tylor, E.B. (1871). *Primitive Culture*. London: John Murray.
Van Balen, F. (2005). 'Late parenthood among sub-fertile and fertile couples: motivations and educational goals', *Patient Education and Counselling: Social and Cultural Factors in Fertility*, 59(3), pp. 276–282.
Van de Kaa, D.J. (1993). 'The Second Demographic Transition Revisited: Theories and Expectations'. In G.C.N. Beets *et al.* (eds) *Population and Family in the Low Countries 1993: Late Fertility and Other Current Issues*. Lisse: Swets and Zeitlinger, pp. 81–126.
Vere, J.P. (2007). '"Having it all" no longer: fertility, female labor supply, and the new life choice of Generation X', *Demography*, 44(4), pp. 821–828.
Walkerdine, V., Lucey, H. and Melody, J. (2001). *Growing Up Girl: Psycho-Social Explorations of Gender and Class*. Basingstoke: Palgrave.
Weber, M. (1947). *The Theory of Social and Economic Organization*, trans. A.M. Henderson and Talcott Parsons. New York: Oxford University Press.
Wurtz, U. (2014). *Trauma and Beyond: The Mystery of Transformation*. New Orleans, LA: Spring Journal Inc.
Young-Eisendrath, P. (1984) *Hags and Heroes A Feminist Approach to Jungian Psychotherapy with Couples*. Toronto: Inner City Books.

## Further Reading

Barone-Chapman, M. (2014). 'Gender legacies of Jung and Freud as epistemology in emergent feminist research on late motherhood'. In L. Huskinson (ed.) *The Behavioural Sciences in Dialogue with the Theory and Practice of Analytical Psychology*. Basel and Beijing: MDPI.
Jung, C.G. (1911–12/1952a). 'Symbols of the Mother and of Rebirth', *Collected Works, Vol. 5. Symbols of Transformation* (2nd edn). London: Routledge & Kegan Paul, 1995.
Jung, C.G. (1956). 'Definitions', *Collected Works, Vol. 6. Psychological Types* (2nd edn). London: Routledge & Kegan Paul, 1989.

# 3
# A METHOD OUT OF MADNESS: ETHICS

What is determined to be masculine or feminine behaviour, expression, and choices, continues in post Jungian psychotherapies as a question regarding development, even when these are attached to archetypes (Douglas, 2000; Rowland, 2002). The biological difference in women with an implied imperative to reproduce opens the depth question of a woman's unconscious use of her body as a means of separation, individuation and psychic growth (Pines, 1993, p. 83). Delayed motherhood in a bio-technological age may be yet another form of power and control (Oppenheim, 1991; Showalter, 1992; Swartz, 2013). Contrasting consideration of motherhood in a technological age we have Jung's (1932) Visions Seminars originally presented in the 1930s to his students, as the early working through of his ideas on the 'contra-sexual within' (anima and animus), drawing from his own experience of what a lack of procreativity could arouse in a woman.

> ... then you get into a special kind of hell ... For a woman there is no longer any way out; if she cannot [does not] have children, escape into pregnancy, she falls into hellfire ... she discovers that she is not only a woman, she is a man too.
>
> *(Jung, 1932, p. 794)*

Brooke (1991) defended Jung's seeming neglect of the body, not as a schizoid psychology, but because Jung's approach to psyche '... subsumes the body so that the body merely tends to remain [un-themed] in his work. He assumes it as the "natural face of mind (a Merleau-Ponty expression"' (Roger Brooke, 25 January 2008, IAJS Discussion List).

Raphael-Leff's (2007) inquiry into femininity, the unconscious, gender and generative identity, in a bio-technological age, argues that a basis of psychoanalytic theory in place throughout Freud's life was the limitation of femininity and masculinity on original bisexuality. She lays claim to Freud's bisexual fluidity concept as ultimately eroded by occluding 'reification of body-based dichotomies' leading to multi-layered views of fantasies/relational configurations/identifications proffered by Harris (1991), Dimen (1991), Benjamin (1996) and Sweetnam (1996). Raphael-Leff further frames Freud's notion of bisexuality through the dichotomy of conscious unity twinned with unconscious diversity to Person (1999) based on Goldner's (2005) notion of culture as authorizing agent. Her synthesis of 'sex' as an accommodation between chromosomes present at birth, and gender as a self-categorizing of a psychosocial construct (Raphael-Leff, 2007, p. 500) produces new categories for 'gender role' and 'sexual orientation': *'Embodiment'* (femaleness/maleness), *'Gender Representation'* (femininity/masculinity) and *'Desire'* (sexuality). Organically this becomes understandable only when we consider Freud's earliest repudiation of the feminine (Schaeffer, 2010, p.129) against Jung's tendency to appropriate the feminine as a man's anima while projecting the masculine as woman's animus as a detriment to her character (Wehr, 1988; Cowan, 2000; Douglas, [1990]2000). Can Jungian feminist literature ever be on a par with mainstream feminism? David Tacey (2010, p. 308) finds it far 'from mainstream feminism …'. Jung's dichotomous idealization of the feminine as a man's anima while denigrating the masculine in a woman (animus) as a character flaw, creates a problematic for the researcher who wishes to use Analytical Psychology as the theoretical basis for emergent *feminine/feminist* psychosocial dilemmas, until coming onto his alchemical works. Jung's mytho-poetical views, theories, imaginations, and proclivities regarding the feminine, along with Freud's fluid notion of bisexuality, are both offered as evidence; acceptance of the feminine as different but equal, remains a long-standing difficulty for both genders, which may be the underpinnings of both an intra-psychic and inter-subjective cultural phenomena within a *pregnant pause* (Barone-Chapman, 2011, p. 188). I therefore frame delayed motherhood as a way through a patriarchal paradigm, not as a quick way out of it. A feminist view of the psychosocial aspects of a woman becoming a mother, for the first time (Hollway, 2016) becomes more complicated as she ages. My search for a whole view of psyche's discontents on motherhood at midlife, paralleled how the female body had been dis-included in culture parallel to how women can suddenly find they are *out of time* for procreative identity. I had to dig down, because much of the literature had been buried in older, earlier works. But thanks to media pressure, current social movements and the increasing number of older women having first-time babies, the time had come to re-visit, re-vision and re-connect with a subject that leaves many women embarrassed at not being able to have their own biological baby.

## Time Out Of Time

When a complex is activated by, for example, a memory or word, associations to that stimulus will take longer to process because there are more affect-laden memories attached to the 'file' of associations. In studies, such as those in Jung's

Word Association Experiment (Jung, 1904–09), the time it takes to reach a response to the stimulus (Jung, 1905) can take as much as sixty seconds or more. When compared to the years of repressing a desire to procreate, time is relative to the degree of unconscious processes working within the personal and collective complex. When an affect-laden complex kicks off, time changes. Psychological reality replaces biological time. Time is lost. Activities take longer. Immediate requirements are overlooked, forgotten or turned into pathology. Though the personal and collective unconscious is not easily differentiated (Huskinson, 2010, p. 82), the sphere of culture, operating at the personal level, provides the lens through which a changing relationship to motherhood is investigated in this book. Without inclusion of time within the Jungian canon on the identification of complexes, there would not be enough tangible evidence other than affect. Affects alone are not complexes, unless the affects observed may be said to form a pattern.

Yvette Weiner's (1996) exploration of two dimensions of time within the psychotherapeutic process brings an understanding of time at midlife as the convergence of Chronos and Kairos. Chronos, the god of linear time, with both destructive and constructive aspects, and Kairos, the god of the opportune moment, come together to compel seizing the opportunity to do what has not already been done. Paul Tillich (1965) is credited with naming Kairos as 'an opening in time, pregnant with the promise of meaning' (Stein, 2007, p. 87). Assisted Reproductive Technology stops linear time to create an opportune moment for a pregnant pause. Chronos and Kairos bring on a *'memoire involuntaire'* in order for something unique to happen. To the naked eye, a pregnant pause comes on as passionately as first love, with all the high feeling tone effects of a complex that has been suddenly activated after years of being suppressed.

Murray Stein finds the uniting of the time-bound ego and the timelessness of the Self, to be necessary for initiation into the spiritual realm where one may 'put existential anxiety to rest' (Stein, 2007). Stein finds the midlife period to be a point in time where many do gravitate toward initiation into the spiritual but emphasizes the spiritual as being beyond the comprehension of ego consciousness and outside social intent. Initiations therefore fall into two categories: intentionally calculated and purposeful or arising spontaneously from unprompted impulses. He describes entry into the time of midlife as if it was a geographical 'liminal' space between two points in space and time, announced through loss, defeat, mourning and death. This eruption of the unconscious brings forth what has been previously rejected, cast aside or barely considered in our fast-forward, modern Western life, in order to sow the seeds of the future. The experience of liminal space can be likened to psychological floating bringing an awareness of impulses ordinarily unattended to in periods of great stability. In an earlier volume, *In Midlife*, Stein's (1983) chapter, 'Return of the Repressed,' focuses on those impulses which for reasons that know no explanation, can be distinguished from the 'acting out' defences of denial, repression and projection, through 'conscious wish fulfilment' of the Self (Stein, 1983, pp. 79–81. The unconscious, acting upon the conscious, is viewed as a signal of what one needs to feel complete. This section of *Midlife* must be read with appreciation that since 1983 women's lives are no longer divided by nurturing first, and personal desire, later.

## Learning From Participants

On discovering that women who delayed motherhood have been secretly harbouring conflict and resistance to dominant societal expectations within the 'normative framework' (Henwood, 1993, p. 306), the gender issue emerged as an argument against fundamental inequality. More often than not, there was a distinct memory of a more privileged male sibling within the family, while the mothering of the female child was recalled as receiving more anxiety than care. Other forms of hegemony include struggles in choices in education, sport, and career. It must be noted that patriarchy does not always have a penis, nor do feminists always come with a vagina. The Berlin Institute for Population and Development have corroborated these narrative observations in the publication of statistical data revealing that the higher the gender equality, the higher the birth rate (The New York Times, 2013). There has been scepticism surrounding the freely adopted theories within empirical studies without consideration of their impact on women. Feminist vocabulary, ignored in early modern studies, is today more elaborate and subsequently more prominent, outside of those traditions that focus on historiographical material meant to privilege social history (Dialeti, 2018). Early scholarly pieces found in books and journals thirty years ago used 'patriarchy' as a 'key system undergirding society in many times and places' (Wiesner-Hanks, 2018), coming out of radical feminism. Weisner-Hanks finds that 'scholars of women and gender either fail to use the word [patriarchy] altogether or refer to it only obliquely, doubting the value of patriarchy as an analytical framework or dismissing it as depressing or essentialist.'

One of the first Jungian analysts to question the masculine psychologies of Jung and Freud, James Hillman, (1972, pp. 291–292) finds in Freud (1937a, p. 219) a definition of the conditions under which an analysis may end, based upon the achievement of 'feminine inferiority' finding it to be 'the root of repression and neurosis ... bringing about both our psychic disorders and method of analysis aimed at these disorders'.

> ... one reaches the "bedrock," the place where analysis could be said to end, when the "repudiation of femininity" both in a man and a woman has been successfully met. In a woman the repudiation of femininity is manifested in her intractable penis envy; in a man his repudiation does not allow him to submit and be passive to other men.
>
> *Freud (1937a, p. 219)*

Thus, the repudiation of femininity is suggested to be biologically founded and part of the natural psychical world (Hillman, 1972, p. 292) whereas for Hillman, 'the end of analysis coincides with the acceptance of femininity'. Hillman takes on the 'bedrock' of misogyny by undermining its basis on the 'biological aspect of the female' finding instead a psychological basis of an 'Apollonism' as the 'bedrock' of the 'first-Adam-then-Eve' perspective. This Apollonic archetype seeks physical form through 'an objective and detached selfhood, a heroic course of … quest and search … above all the ego-Self as its carrier, and analysis as its instrument' (Hillman, 1972, p. 293). Putting aside the relational aspect of the feminine acculturates life in two parts, 'First Adam-then-Eve'; creation is out of the head of Zeus. From just a small glimpse into Freud's thinking of the feminine through one of his last writings in Vienna, it may be possible to see the necessity of feminist thought to salvage Psychoanalysis from Freud's complaint that 'psychology cannot solve the riddle of femininity' (Freud, 1933a, p. 149). For Jung, the analytic process reached its ultimate goal in conscious bisexuality through the alchemical image of the *coniunctio*; the conjunction (Jung, 1954b; Hillman, 1972; Samuels, 1989; Barone-Chapman, 2014b). Rowland, (2002, p. 145) redeems Jung for feminists by analysing his work as a whole, and in particular on alchemy, where there is 'recognition of the limitations of heterosexual opposition … what is cast out, what is structured as an abject body, must be reconfigured *within*'.

The feminine as an aspect of men and the masculine as an aspect of women became tangled up in Jung's reflections between biological bodies, the embodiment of archetype and effects of culture and the collective unconscious. This is no different to what happens to anyone when the principle of 'masculine' and 'feminine' is concretized as first Adam, then Eve. A false adaptation to compensate for psychic wounds to sexual identity, aroused by conformity to cultural stereotypes can confound gender, sublimating the feminine such that men find they want babies and women are afraid to have them (Barone-Chapman, 2014b). Usefully, Verena Kast (2006, p. 118) draws from Jung's *Mysterium Coniunctionis* (Jung, 1954d) to demonstrate how fluid the notion of masculine and feminine has been throughout Jung's explorations, reaching in his final book the notion 'that the animus compensates for female consciousness' (Jung, 1954d), to which Kast adds, 'Anima and animus can be seen as representing the unconscious at any given moment … often discovered in the form of projections onto other persons' (Kast, 2006, p. 119).

While aspects of Analytical Psychology have been relevant, I found feminist inspired psychoanalytic views to make two halves of analytic history a whole view of psyche's discontent with patriarchal views of the feminine. Analytical psychology has a proud history of finding truth in the cosmos through archetype and image 'rooted in the unconscious as transcendent of knowledge' (Rowland 2002, p. 143) while Swartz (2013, p. 41) reminds us 'Feminism has a proud history of interrogating the truth claims of psychiatric science, and of foregrounding the ways in which the machinery of psychiatric diagnosis and treatment has been used to obscure or amplify the psychological effects of patriarchies', for which she credits Chesler (2005), Smith (1990) and Ussher (1991). In particular, in reviewing psychiatric diagnosis from a feminist perspective, Swartz (2013) gives credit to Jessica Benjamin's (1998) work concerning the long history of patriarchal domination where feminists have challenged Freudian psychoanalytic diagnostic premises and opened up new ideas on the formation of female identity such that experiences as mother, sister, wife, or daughter can no longer be automatically synonymous with a lack of agency. Freud and Jung's views became evidence of patriarchy as background, while extension of feminist inspired psychoanalytical thinking, Queer theories and Creation Myths allowed new meanings of the embodied feminine to emerge through a recapitulation of a union of opposites as a union of epistemology and ethos. 'The essence of Jung's mid-life theories, altered by modernity and eclipsed by female advancement, remain replicable and paradigmatic outside of essentialist gender performance' (Barone-Chapman, 2014a, p. 41).

The use and relationship to the 'feminine' in all its variations, including 'femininity' emerged as the 'last straw' turning Freud and Jung from sparring partners on 'universal principles' to 'warring opposites'. Both men were caught in the prejudices of patriarchal culture to do with rights, roles and conduct of women in relation to men, pleasure and becoming a mother, until the mother–son incest taboo provided grounds for their ultimate parting of ways (Anthony El Safar, 1994, pp. 46–47).

The assumptions of heterosexuality and gender certainty has been problematic for the classical Jungian canon when masculine and feminine are concretized. Despite my and other Jungian analysts' criticisms of 'gender certain' contra-sexual opposites, the archetypes of anima and animus, continue to appear in dreams to reveal shadow aspects of those parts of the self that are unknown, unwanted and un-integrated. As principles of both agentic and allowing energies, seeking conscious integration in men and women, they are useful to dismantle gender performance from procreative identity, and sexual desire as a pre-requisite for the embodied feminine. As I journeyed through participants' association networks, dreams and inter-subjective affective fields, the ineffable longing was a wish for transcendence and love.

I stand in the centre of this psychosocial phenomenon as one who could not consider motherhood until I was in the fourth decade of life. In effect, I am making the definition of feminine feminist research as having aspiration for political and social change according to Mies (1991), 'the personal is the political and the political is the personal.' Recognizing 'the effect of the patriarchal animus on generations of women', Jungian analyst Clare Douglas ([1990]2000, p. xviii) examined the outmoded aspects of Jung's theories including the ephemeral, contaminated, and biased, to find the kernel of theory with 'the possibility of freeing women and the feminine from the very patriarchal formulations that surround them' (ibid., p. x).

Jung demonstrates the essence of our psychosocial dilemmas best in describing his view of opposites followed by the literal symptom he observes when these are not in their 'right order'.

> … woman's conscious is characterized more by the connective quality of Eros than by the discrimination and cognition associated by Logos. In men, Eros … is usually less developed than Logos. In women on the other hand, Eros is an expression of their true nature, while their Logos is often a regrettable accident.
>
> *(Jung, 1948, para. 29)*

'Women's fear of men's attacks on their bodies but also ... denigrating social systems that reinforce a second-class status ... devalue what it means to live through a feminine point of view' (Alexander Stewart, 2009, p. 96), and comprise the dangers, horrors and defilements that have been described and examined by both Kristeva (1982) and Douglas (1966). Their frame of prohibitions leading to the abjection facing the feminine if it is not pure, puts us into the space occupied by the character Clarice Starling, as portrayed by Jodie Foster in the film *Silence of the Lambs* which has been described as a 'new heroic journey of the feminine' (Alexander Stewart, 2008, p. 96). Within 'a set of feminine ethics ... [to] create hope for the safety of a feminine presence in our society', Clarice defies conventional wisdom on what is safe for a woman in a man's world, by not behaving like a man who fears for his survival. Instead, Clarice chooses to trust what the feminine has to offer, 'her inner forces, for example, trusting in intuition, in revealing herself and interacting on the level of intimacy' (Alexander Stewart, 2008, p. 99). These traits invoke fear for her and of her, a greater threat to her survival than Hannibal Lecter himself, including 'searches for meaning from the way his actions make her feel' (Alexander Stewart, 2009, p. 104; Barone-Chapman, 2014a, p. 51).

## In Search of the Feminine Hero

The feminine hero may be different from the heroine in my observations. The heroine comes up believing it is safe to be female because her nurturing early environment made it so. Throughout her development she does not cower at real life challenges, even those threatening her with domination and sublimation rituals (Benjamin, 1988).

> The fact remains, however, that the masculine bound to an obsolete patriarchal tradition experiences the emergence of the feminine as a threat. To disarm the masculine of its patriarchal fear of the feminine is thus crucial to releasing the creative dynamics of partnership. Equally the oppression of the feminine within a patriarchal tradition renders the masculine shaped by that tradition as its natural enemy. It is therefore also necessary to disarm the feminine of its fear of the patriarchal masculine in order to release the dynamics of the new relationship.
> *(Woodman, 1990, p. 16)*

The women who engaged me to listen to their stories were attempting to suspend fear of the patriarchal masculine they had experienced with their mother's animus to be able to access motherhood, albeit much later than some, in order to enter into a new kind of relationship outside of patriarchal domination.

These feminine heroes had to learn how to have a relationship to their body, the root of having what Jung called a Self (Plaut, 1998, p. 282). But the feminine body can often be interrupted through 'punctuations' of menstruation, penetrative intercourse, becoming pregnant and breastfeeding, rhythms resonating with vulnerability (Bianchi, 2012, pp. 39–40). It can take time to make or find a self/Self if it hasn't been installed in early childhood through conducive social interactions (Zinkin, 2008). An unconscious relationship to her body difference from the masculine counterpart, including her vagina, womb, breasts and ovaries, may indicate her feelings are as an unknown aspect of self, which have made her unavailable for relationship or procreative identity until how she appears to others, how she fears she will be used/not used, no longer betrays her loss of integrity through some kind of violation (Beebe, 1992), even one of abjection, but emerges in synthesis toward the primary task of finding integrity within herself. The dichotomous struggle to achieve equality in political, social and economic fields between the sexes only to abandon the struggle in the sexual realm, confuses the need to uphold sexual difference (Schaeffer, 2010, p. 139). In this dichotomous state we may see into the ingredients for an individuation process: psychic-physical tension with the potential for a union of opposites. 'Creativity springs from the resolution and the reconciliation of opposing psychic forces within an individual' (Seligman, 1985, p. 83).

Here then lies the ethical methodological junction, where feminist inspired Psychoanalysis and feminist leaning Analytical Psychology join up to design a feminist ethos to access intra-psychic associations and inter-subjectivity as a research model. Commencing with the gender neutrality of Merleau Ponty's (1968, p. 263) non-dualist understanding of corporeality as the body in an environment, later affiliated to feminist and post-colonial thinking regarding critical potentials of phenomenology as embodiment and embodied experience (Simonsen, 2012), I sought to develop an ethical subjectivity in my methodology where the subjective and affective spaces of the body contain living meaning. In this space action/lack of action is an ever flowing both/and articulation of emotions 'simultaneously passive and active' (ibid., p. 17).

> ... the bodies' situatedness in intersubjective fields and socio-corporeal hierarchies not only bring about incorporation and sedimentation, but also a rise to personal experiences of fragility and vulnerability. The flesh is vulnerable to material as well as symbolic pain ... bodies are marked by others, such that different bodies are recognized and categorized, disciplined and excluded.
> *(Simonsen, 2012, p. 37)*

Reflexivity as a way of being with affectivity is not limited to feminism or feminist topics, though it is perceived to be central to feminist research (Tickner, 2005). When inter-subjectivity and reflexivity have a central role, reflexivity becomes a sympathetic introspective self-scrutiny for self-analysis within the researcher (England, 1994, p. 82). As psychosocial research draws more from the consulting room, a researcher's reflexivity of affective states becomes a cohort in meaning making. But here the very use of the word *feminist* too easily connotes the patriarchal line of what the feminine does that is different from the masculine, automatically en-*gendering* a predictive androcentric subject. Can women do credible feminine feminist research without putting them or their subject under patriarchal interrogation? To engage with this 'reality' requires a relationship to psyche capable of manifesting observable phenomena from the borderlands of consciousness, where the truth of image, perhaps of God, enables her to find for herself what makes her desire for motherhood feel profoundly liberating. From years of examining her roles as daughter or sister unable to believe she could become an autonomous partner/wife and mother, she commences the very rudiments of feminist psychoanalyst Jessica Benjamin's (1988) project of reconciling inter-subjectivity with intra-psychic theory. In reformulating the classic Freudian Oedipal model of father-son dominance followed by revolt, Benjamin (ibid., p. 134) found '… the identification and closeness with the mother must be traded for independence; it means that being a subject of desire requires repudiation of the maternal role, of feminine identity itself.'

## Queering Patriarchy and the Feminine

A complex develops out of processes of an archetype at the centre of psychic development, which this book seeks to bring together, with the question – is delayed motherhood a revolt against domination of the biological imperative to reproduce sooner rather than later? This is an ethical question to do with non-normative sexual behaviour, which is where Queer theory began its linguistic life before moving into gay and lesbian caucuses, then feminist politics and academic institutions, in parallel to rising awareness of AIDS (Jagose, 1996) before turning on gender itself as an encasement of an 'oppressive system of classification – both heterosexuality and homosexuality … as artificial categories' (Young, 1992, p. 29). But as recently seen in politics in the United States and elsewhere, feminism and the politics of difference (Young, 1990a; 1990b) remain at the forefront of gender discussion as women seek to de-gender equality. For the majority of women I spoke to about delayed motherhood, this subject area remained a crucial element of their unconscious anger, born of sibling rivalry, tracking them through their adult choices in the world of work, which they were struggling to bring to awareness, as passionately as they could, because it seemed that in order to bring new life into the world, they knew instinctively, new life had to be re-birthed in them, as well. The timing of the research fit into this transition in a deeper way than just donning a mask. In this way, Queer undermines notions of feminine, masculine and eclipses both the conflict and union of opposites, something Jagose (ibid., p. 107) describes as 'holding open a space whose potential can never be known in the present.'

What we may be seeing is the upside-down re-making of individuation in mid-life for women challenging the characterization Jung observed in his day when women began integrating the repressed masculine in later life. For women who are not railroaded by economics into early pregnancy, the agency to 'embrace … one's own development' (Young-Eisendrath, 1984, p. 87) is a postmodern step change involving an embrace of the feminine as nurturer later in life. The meaning and purpose of motherhood at midlife may be a natural alchemical response to early archetypal disappointment.

Archetypal and human experience co-conspire in the making of a complex. Both ingredients are necessary for psychic development, leading us to a slightly different ethical question, *is delayed motherhood a revolt against domination of the biological imperative?* From Judith Butler ([1990]1999) there followed the idea that both heterosexuality and homosexuality is an 'oppressive system of classification' (Young, 1992, p. 29). These works and others contributed to destabilizing prior notions of subject formation through observation of the disparity between identity and performance. In Butler's analysis of linguistic processes, the conditions of precipitating emergence (*Entstehung*) of a subject and their identity could not be reduced to a historical moment as fact any more than fabrication (Young, 1992, p. 15). Queer is evasive, skirting the signifiers, what it includes or refers to cannot be pinned down easily (Abelove, 1992, p. 20). 'Queer is a relation of resistance to whatever constitutes the normal' (Jagose, 1996, p. 99) the 'open mesh of ... excess of meaning where the constituent elements of anyone's gender, anyone's sexuality aren't made (or *can't* be made to signify monolithically)' (Sedgwick, 1993, p. 8).

We are considering Queer as a theoretical and *non-predictive-performance* condition as an emerging new signifier of normative behaviour for women who consciously or unconsciously, (indeed that is the ultimate arbiter, nature or nurture) to delay motherhood. Queer undermines notions of feminine, masculine and eclipses both the conflict and union of opposites, something Jagose (1996, p. 107) describes as 'holding open a space whose potential can never be known in the present'.

In feminist inspired literature, I found the physical body of the woman who had lost time during her most fertile years through conflicting messages from the unconscious, between ego and self. In short, I came to see Jung and Freud as reproducing what has been long standing in civilization, the split between feminine denigration and idealization, and have used these theorist's words as evidence of patriarchal privilege as the screen through which each man analysed female patients (Appignanesi, 2009).

Freud's method of studying and amplifying the content of the unconscious found focus on the patient's personal history structured by manifestations of psychosexual history seen through concepts such as repression and repetition compulsion, which Jung referred to as the reductive method, preferring to concentrate on universal symbols of the collective unconscious to find primitive aspects of psyche according to the teleological principle where symptoms carry a symbolic function of meaning for transformation, thereby making it a prospective method; together their individual work forms a whole view of psychic life (McFarland Solomon, 2003). Yet both these backward and forward perspectives, one concretized and the other mythologized, were pre-occupied with the feminine in mutable and evolving expression, repression and emergent integration of the masculine, as the basis of bisexuality prohibited by nineteenth-century culture and society, prompting a need to incorporate consideration of Queer non-normative performance and androcentric time into this examination.

Delayed motherhood in a bio-technological age is a pause out of time – requiring a non- pathological ethical position for non-participation in essentialist notions of feminine performance.

I believe the work of Jung and Freud was the beginning of a longer work on the reproduction of misogynistic culture. In the remarkable findings in literature on women and gender I set out an ethos and epistemology to finding a research methodology that could circumvent ego issues of power, control, defence, separation and repair. To achieve this, I had to let the older mother speak herself, to make associations to things she could not otherwise speak about, and to dream the dreams that might point the way. The subject matter has led me to a method of researching the unconscious.

## Out Of Madness

Since the introduction of the unconscious to modern clinical understanding with Charcot's (1882) observation that paralysis was a split-off autonomous capacity to form spontaneous ideas separate from the ego, developing over a significant period of time (Ellenberger, 1970, p. 149), an element of doubt has remained as to whether any individual, man or woman, could be relied upon to knowingly, consciously be in command of the unconscious at any given moment. Doubt became the ethical benchmark. To discover if there was a connection between delayed motherhood to personal and collective unconscious complexes, I began with interpretive phenomenological analysis (IPA) as a method of inquiry, which was designed (Smith, 2003; Smith, Michie and Quarrell, 2000) to make room for a high level of feeling toned-affects, on a subjective level, which strangely mimicked analytical dialogue in the consulting room. I first observed high feeling toned affects in women who were sub-fertile, while conducting mind-body workshops at a fertility clinic. I never expected research participants to tell me why they had delayed procreation. What we wanted to establish was whether the valence of a malingering unconscious complex had formed to influence their seeming opposition to procreative identity earlier in their lives. From a wide arena of relational inter-subjective affects through to stimulation of associative networks, sifting down to links found within dream material, I wanted to understand how their experience of midlife aroused them to act with a reproductive response. As a result, the aetiology of delayed motherhood has become more three-dimensional: intra-psychically, relationally and culturally. A woman's relationship to the personal and the collective is an exploration of factors invoking a double imperative: a woman's rising desire for motherhood at midlife against the biological pre-emptive role of motherhood and how it may have changed in an age of biotechnology. Implicit is the cultural status of mating and partnership vs. autonomy and independence, and whether children are a natural outcome of a primary relationship. But also, to learn if their status has eclipsed adult relationship relegating children to an acquisitioned status or 'partner substitute'. Here then, is the question to the answers found in the following pages: *Is delayed motherhood connected to a personal area of conflict and what does it reveal about cultural complexes and those of the collective unconscious toward womanhood?*

# References

Abelove, H. (1992). 'Some Speculations on the History of "Sexual Intercourse" During the "Long Eighteenth Century" in England'. In A. Parker, M. Russo, D. Sommer and P. Yaeger (eds), *Nationalisms and Sexualities.* New York: Routledge, pp. 335–342.

Alexander Stewart, J. (2009). 'Feminine Hero'. In V. Apperson and J. Beebe (eds), *The Presence of the Feminine in Film.* Newcastle upon Tyne: Cambridge Scholars Publishing.

Anthony El Safar, R. (1994). *Rapture Encaged: The Suppression of the Feminine in Western Culture.* London: Routledge.

Appignanesi, L. (2009). *Mad, Bad and Sad: A History of Women and the Mind Doctors from 1800 to the Present.* London: Virago.

Barone-Chapman, M. (2011). 'Pregnant Pause: Procreative Desire, Reproductive Technology and Narrative Shifts at Midlife'. In R. Jones (ed.), *Body, Mind and Healing After Jung: A Space of Questions.* London: Routledge.

Barone-Chapman, M. (2014a). 'Gender Legacies of Jung and Freud as Epistemology in Emergent Feminist Research on Late Motherhood'. In L. Huskinson (ed.) *The Behavioural Sciences in Dialogue with the Theory and Practice of Analytical Psychology,* Basel and Beijing: MDPI.

Barone-Chapman, M. (2014b). 'Sulphur Rises From The Blackened Body'. In D. Mathers (ed.), *Alchemy and Psychotherapy.* London: Routledge.

Beebe, J. (1992). *Integrity in Depth.* College Station, TX: Texas A&M University Press.

Benjamin, J. (1996). 'In defense of gender ambiguity', *Gender and Psychoanalysis,* 1, pp. 27–43.

Benjamin, J. (1998). *Like Subjects, Love Objects: Essays on Recognition and Sexual Difference.* New Haven, CT: Yale University Press.

Bianchi, E. (2012). 'The Interruptive Feminine: Aleatory Time and Feminist Politics'. In H. Gunkel, C. Nigianni and F.Soderback (eds), *Undutiful Daughters: New Directions in Feminist Thought and Practice.* New York: Palgrave Macmillan.

Brickell, C. (2005). 'Masculinities, performativity, and subversion: A sociological reappraisal', *Men and Masculinities,* 8(1), pp. 24–43.

Brooke, R. (1991). 'Psychic complexity and human existence: a phenomenological approach', *Journal of Analytical Psychology,* 36, pp. 505–518.

Butler, J. ([1990]1999). *Gender Trouble.* New York and London: Routledge.

Cadwallader, J. (2009). 'How Judith Butler Matters', *Australian Feminist Studies,* 24: 289–294.

Charcot, J.M. (1882). 'Sur les divers états nerveux déterminés par l'hynotisation chez les hystériques', *Comptes-Rendus hebdomadaires des séances de l'Académie des Sciences,* XCIV (I), pp. 403–405.

Chesler, P. ([1972]2005). *Women and Madness.* New York: Palgrave Macmillan.

Cowan, L. ([1994]2000/2003). 'Dismantling The Animus'. *Reflections on Psychology, Culture, Life.* www.cgjungpage.org

Daley, S. and Kulish, N. (2013) 'Germany Fights Population Drop', *The New York Times,* 13 August. https://www.nytimes.com/2013/08/14/world/europe/germany-fights-population-drop.html.

Demme, J. (Dir.) (1991). *The Silence of the Lambs.* Strong Heart/Demme Production, Orion Home Video.

Dialeti, A. (2018). 'Patriarchy as a category of historical analysis and the dynamics of power: the example of Early Modern Italy', *Gender & History* 30(2), pp. 33–342.

Dimen, M. (1991). 'Deconstructing difference: gender, splitting, transitional space', *Psychoanalytical Dialogues,* 1(3), pp. 335–352.

Douglas, C. ([1990]2000). *The Woman in the Mirror.* Lincoln, NE: iUniverse.com Inc.

Douglas, M. (1966). *Purity and Danger.* Abingdon: Routledge Classics.

Dow Magnus, K. (2006). 'The unaccountable subject: Judith Butler and the social conditions of intersubjective agency', *Hypatia*, 21(2), pp. 81–103.
Ellenberger, H.F. (1970). *The Discovery of the Unconscious: The History and Evolution of Dynamic Psychiatry*. New York: Basic Books/Perseus Books Group.
England, K.V. (1994). 'Getting personal: reflexivity, positionality, and feminist research', *The Professional Geographer*, 46(1), pp. 80–89.
Freud, S. (1933a) 'New Introductory Lectures on Psycho-Analysis'. In J. Strachey et al. (eds), *The Complete Works of Sigmund Freud*. London: The Hogarth Press and the Institute of Psychoanalysis, SE 22, pp. 3–182.
Freud, S. (1937a) 'Analysis Terminable and Interminable'. In J. Strachey et al. (eds), *The Complete Works of Sigmund Freud*. London: The Hogarth Press and the Institute of Psychoanalysis, SE 23, pp. 211–253.
Glocer Fiorin, L., and Abelin-Sas Rose, G. (eds) (2010). *On Freud's 'Femininity'*. London: Karnac.
Goldner, V. (2005). 'Ironic Gender, Authentic Sex'. In L.K. Toronto et al. (eds), *Psychoanalytic Reflections on a Gender-free Case: Into the Void*. London: Routledge.
Gunkel, H., Nigianni, C., and Soderback, F. (eds) (2012). *Undutiful Daughters: New Directions in Feminist Thought and Practice*. New York: Palgrave Macmillan.
Harris, A. (1991). 'Gender as contradiction', *Psychoanalytic Dialogues*, 1, pp. 197–224.
Henwood, K.L. (1993). 'Women and later life: the discursive construction of identities within family relationships', *Journal of Aging Studies*, 7(3), pp. 303–319.
Hillman, J. (1972). 'On Psychological Femininity'. In J. Hillman (ed.) *The Myth of Analysis: Three Essays in Archetypal Psychology*. Evanston, IL: Northwestern University Press.
Hillman, J. (1972). (ed.) *The Myth of Analysis: Three Essays in Archetypal Psychology*. Evanston, IL: Northwestern University Press.
Hollway, W. (2016). 'Feminism, psychology and becoming a mother', *Feminism & Psychology*, 26(2), pp. 137–152.
Huskinson, L. (2010). 'Analytical Psychology and Spirit Possession: Towards a Non-Pathological Diagnosis of Spirit Possession.' In B.E. Schmidt and L. Huskinson (eds), *Spirit Possession and Trance: New Interdisciplinary Perspectives Continuous Advances in Religious Studies*. London and New York: Continuum.
Jagose, A. (1996). *Queer Theory: An Introduction*. New York: New York University Press.
Jung, C.G. (1904–1909). 'Studies in Word Association'. In *Collected Works, Vol. 2. Experimental Researches*, 2nd edn. London: Routledge & Kegan Paul, 1992.
Jung, C.G. (1905). 'The Reaction Time Ratio in the Association Experiment'. In *Collected Works, Vol. 2. Experimental Researches*, 2nd edn. London: Routledge & Kegan Paul, 1992.
Jung, C.G. (1932). *Notes on the Visions Seminar, Vol. 2*, 2nd edn. London: Routledge, 1998.
Jung, C.G. (1948). 'The Syzygy: Amina and Animus'. In *Collected Works, Vol. 9ii. Aion. Researches into the Phenomenology of the Self*, 2nd edn. London: Routledge & Kegan Paul, 1989.
Jung, C.G. (1954b). 'The Personification of the Opposites'. In *Collected Works, Vol. 14. Mysterium Coniunctionis*, 2nd edn. London: Routledge & Kegan Paul, 1981.
Jung, C.G. (1954d). 'Adam and Eve'. In *Collected Works, Vol. 14. Mysterium Coniunctionis*, 2nd edn. London: Routledge & Kegan Paul, 1981.
Kast, V. (2006). 'Anima/animus', B. Whitcombe (trans.). In R.K. Papadopoulos (ed.), *The Handbook of Jungian Psychology: Theory, Practice and Applications*. New York and East Hove: Routledge.
Kristeva, J. (1982). *Powers of Horror: An Essay on Abjection*. New York: Columbia University Press.
Mathers, D. (ed.) (2014). *Alchemy and Psychotherapy: Post-Jungian Perspectives*. London and New York: Routledge.

McFarland-Solomon, H. (2003). 'Freud and Jung: an incomplete encounter', *Journal of Analytical Psychology*, 48(5), pp. 553–569.
Merleau-Ponty, M. (1968). *The Visible and the Invisible*. Evanston, IL: Northwestern University Press.
Mies, M. (1991). 'Women's Research or Feminist Research? The Debate Surrounding Feminist Science and Methodology'. In M.M. Fonow and J.A. Cook (eds), *Beyond Methodology-Feminist Scholarship as Lived Research*. Bloomington: Indiana University Press.
Morrison, T. and Macleod, C. (2013). 'A performative-performance analytical approach: infusing Butlerian theory into the narrative-discursive method.' *Qualitative Inquiry*, 19(8), p. 566.
Oppenheim, J. (1991). *'Shattered Nerves': Doctors, Patients, and Depression in Victorian England*. Oxford: Oxford University Press.
Person, E. (1999). *The Sexual Century*. New Haven, CT: Yale University Press.
Pines, D. (1993). *A Woman's Unconscious Use of Her Body*. New Haven, CT and London: Yale University Press.
Plaut, F. (1998). 'What Do I Mean by Identity?' In I. Alister and C. Hauke (eds), *Contemporary Jungian Analysis*. London: Routledge.
Raphael-Leff, J. (2007). 'Femininity and its unconscious "shadows": Gender and generative identity in the age of biotechnology', *British Journal of Psychotherapy*, 23(4), pp. 497–515.
Rowland, S. (2002). *Jung: A Feminist Revision*. London: Polity Press.
Samuels, A. (1989). *The Plural Psyche*. London: Routledge.
Schaeffer, J. (2010). 'The Riddle of the Repudiation of Femininity'. In L. Glocer Fiorini and G. Abelin-Sas Rose (eds), *On Freud's 'Femininity'*. London: Karnac.
Sedgwick, E.K. (1993a). *Tendencies*. Durham, NC: Duke University Press.
Seligman, E. (1985). 'The Half-Alive Ones.' In A. Samuels (ed.), *The Father: Contemporary Jungian Perspectives*. London: Free Association Books.
Showalter, E. (1992). *Sexual Anarchy: Gender and Culture at the Fin de Siècle*. London: Virago Press.
Simonsen, K. (2012). 'In quest of a new humanism: Embodiment, experience and phenomenology as critical geography', *Progress in Human Geography*, 37(1), pp. 10–26.
Smith, D. (1990). *Conceptual Practices of Power: A Feminist Sociology of Knowledge*. Boston, MA: Northeastern University Press.
Smith, J.A., Michie, S. and Quarrell, O. (2000). 'Genetic testing for Huntington's disease: an interpretative phenomenological analysis of candidates' perceptions of risk and decision-making processes.' *Journal of Medical Genetics*, 37, SP21.
Smith, J.A. (ed.), (2003). *Qualitative Psychology: A Practical Guide to Research Methods*. London: Sage.
Stein, M. (1983). *In Midlife: A Jungian Perspective*. Woodstock, CT: Spring Publications.
Stein, M. (2007). 'On Modern Initiation into the Spiritual: A Psychological View'. In T. Kirsch, V.B. Rutter and T. Singer (eds), *Initiation: The Living Reality of an Archetype*. London and New York: Routledge.
Swartz, S. (2013). 'Feminism and psychiatric diagnosis: Reflections of a feminist practitioner', *Feminism & Psychology*, 23(1), p. 41.
Sweetnam, A. (1996). 'The changing contexts of gender between fixed and fluid experience', *Psychoanalytic Dialogues*, 6(4), pp. 437–459.
Tacey, D. (2010). Book Reviews: Introduction to the Fay Book Series in Analytical Psychology reviews. *Journal of Analytical Psychology*, 55, pp. 300–312.
Tickner, J.A. (2005). 'What is your research program? Some feminist answers to international relations methodological questions', *International Studies Quarterly*, 49(1), pp. 1–21.
Tillich, P. (1965). *Ultimate Concern*. New York and London: Harper & Row.
Wehr, D. (1988). *Jung & Feminism: Liberating Archetypes*. London: Routledge.

Weiner, Y. (1996). 'Chronos and Kairos: two dimensions of time in the psychotherapeutic process', *Journal of the British Association of Psychotherapists*, 30(1), pp. 65–85.
Weisner-Hanks, M. (2018). 'Forum Introduction: Reconsidering Patriarchy in Early Modern Europe and the Middle East', *Gender & History* 30(2), pp. 320–330https://onlinelibrary.wiley.com/doi/abs/10.1111/1468-04424.12365
Woodman, M. (1990). *The Ravaged Bridegroom: Masculinity in Women*. Toronto: Inner City Books.
Young, A. ([1972]1992). 'Out of the Closets, Into the Streets'. In K. Jay and A. Young (eds), *Out of the Closets: Voices of Gay Liberation*. London: Gay Men's Press.
Young, I.M. (1990a). *Throwing Like A Girl and Other Essays in Feminist Philosophy and Social Theory*. Bloomington: Indiana University Press.
Young, I.M. (1990b). *Justice and the Politics of Difference*. Princeton, NJ: Princeton University Press.
Young-Eisendrath, P. (1984) *Hags and Heroes: A Feminist Approach to Jungian Psychotherapy with Couples*. Toronto: Inner City Books.
Zinkin, L. (2008) 'Your self: did you find it or did you make it?' *Journal of Analytical Psychology*, 53(3), pp. 389–406.

## Further Reading

Hillman, J. (1996). *The Soul's Code: In Search of Character and Calling*. New York: Random House.
Papadopoulos, R.K. (ed.) (2006). *The Handbook of Jungian Psychology: Theory, Practice and Applications*. New York and East Hove: Routledge.
Schmidt, B.E. and Huskinson, L. (eds) (2010). *Spirit Possession and Trance: New Interdisciplinary Perspectives Continuous Advances in Religious Studies*. London and New York: Continuum.
Ussher, J.M. (1991). *Women's Madness: Misogyny or Mental Illness?* New York: Harvester Wheatsheaf.

# 4
# INTERSUBJECTIVE SPACES

My goal was to reach the objective level of psyche, through amplification of intersubjective psychodynamic material and a network of associations unconsciously held in clusters of feeling and ideas linked in the unconscious. In order to learn how the trend of delayed motherhood may have been formed within the family of origin, culture and society and how this may be changing how women view what is possible, at every life stage, my own reflexivity had to come to the forefront.

In time, I discovered my own unconscious processes became more interested in broader questions and my list of questions turned into a frame of discovery, a lamp in the dark between my own considerations of a bio-technological solution for delayed motherhood and the many other realized solutions chosen by research participants. Also, in time I found feelings of gratitude for the way the maternal operated in my psyche to be able to have a distance from the object of my curiosity. All of this led me to a clinically informed methodology within a Jungian framework to discover how the 'child' archetype induced transformation through the catalytic use of the Trickster archetype.

Jung heavily weighted the analyst's 'own hurt that gives him (her) the measure of [their] power to heal' (Jung, 1951, para. 239) rather than a 'clean hands' perfection. Invoking the myth of Asklepios, or 'wounded physician' as a healer with an incurable wound, required a deepening of the CT as the mediating healing power. This would mean CT became both a symptom of the patient's transference as well as the unconscious transferring of the patient's symptoms to the analyst (Jung, 1929, para. 163–164). Jung suggests it is the destiny or fate of the analyst to be psychologically infected by the patient (Jung, 1946, para. 365) and this should be expected. The archetype of the wounded healer, in Jungian terms, is the activation of a parallel wound in the analyst she is able to work through, which gives her the method by which to interpret (speak/heal) the patient (analysand). This is how Jung came to emphasize the analyst's vulnerability rather than clean hands perfection, in order to deepen the countertransference. 'It is his <her> own hurt that gives him <her> the measure of his <her> power to heal' (Jung 1951, para. 239). By invoking the myth of Asklepios, Jung weights the analysts' connection to her own wound to mediate the healing power of bringing unconscious contents to consciousness. Not only is it an empathic response, it is an acute awareness of the way in and through the abyss of painful unconscious contents. I take into this research all my attempts to remedy an abyss of life and death experiences later redeemed through my own training analysis that was able to transcend the literality of life and death. That is why I have chosen a research model that most closely 'simulates' the metabolizing processes of the consulting room.

My interest in the unconscious originates in the journey of my own analysis in preparing to become a Jungian Analyst and later working with patients, who have taught me how difficult it is to know the unconscious in isolation. A relation to other is necessary as a catalyst to awareness of one's inner being, which over time can lead to relationship with the self. While this certainly suggests a constructionist view of psyche, a developmental perspective is only part of the material I will be working with. To work with another human being's unconscious has required a conscious relationship to my own feeling toned affects within the inter-subjective space of receiving in order to perceive the effects of another. These affects are referred to as transference and countertransference, and they demand asking 'How is what I am feeling related to how the participant is feeling?' as a way of reflectively using myself to see into the subject. The Jungian approaches to countertransference (Sedgwick, 1994) originated from Freud's (1917) theory of identification in which 'how the apparently isolated subject constantly assimilates what is outside itself [not seeing how it] casts a shadow in two directions' (Benjamin, 1998, p. 79). It is mainly concerned with the ego's duality to at once identify with the other while denying the uncontrollable nature of otherness with a concomitant need for recognition, which arouses simultaneously the feeling of being negated (ibid.). 'In his descriptions of analysis as a "dialectical" or "reciprocal" process between equal parties, Jung ... [likens] the combining of two chemical substances ... [to] ... the alteration of each element and the creation of a new third compound' (Sedgwick, 1994, p. 12). A Jungian analyst expects to be infected by the patient. To apply this same principle to a research method means there needs to be a similar chemistry of attraction/repulsion between researcher and subject in order to identify the felt lived experience of the participant.

## First Meetings

In the first phase of the research I utilized clinically informed Interpretive Phenomenological Analysis (Smith, 2003) which was designed to allow the participant a space to transfer and induce in me an experience of what Freud (1914) referred to as a repetition compulsion, to an experience of what she had experienced in her life. In other words, insight into a repetition compulsion is primarily based on the hermeneutics of suspicion that how the participant uses me is a route to how they may have been used, and so does not rely solely on discourse alone. Behaviour matters as well. In this study, I interpreted this experience through a process of amplification to discover how inter-subjective dynamics were aroused and perpetuated over time to become complexes in one or more of the three spheres of personal, cultural and collective unconscious existence.

In employing a clinical Jungian Analytical position, within IPA, I am doing IPA differently than Professor Jonathan Smith originally envisioned based on an extended psychoanalytical understanding of the 'felt experience of a double Hermeneutic'. What remains true to his original vision is the structural process of three levels of analysis in aid of discovering if superordinate themes applied across the stories of all participants. Here I began with three columns to the right side of the transcript printed out on A3 paper. In the first column I made note of all affects I had observed in the participant. In the second column, I focused on the intersubjective space of transference and countertransference. I sought to discover what was being pushed into me and what my subjective feelings told me about their emotional state. In effect, I was operating as a mirror of the participant's affects. Transcripts were read 5–10 times and analysed line by line. The initial read of the proofread transcript involved notating anything with any degree of potential relevance or consequence. In the second column, an initial level of interpretation developed after several reads following on from their affects and phenomenon in the intersubjective field. These emerged into superordinate themes. Each transcript held these themes uniquely until all the IPA analysis could be completed and crosschecked across the participants for emerging themes related to the whole of the story of the research.

Each transcript was analysed to discover what super-ordinate themes were present. This began with numbering each line of text and applying these to any write-up of the material where a participant needed to be quoted, and wherever her words served as testimony to her experience. These line numbers developed into a system of cataloguing the testimony according to initial/line/page number. These citations led to interpretations which were useful for keeping track of how stories shifted and turned (see Chapter 5). When all the super-ordinate themes were identified from each woman's transcript, they were crosschecked among all the participants. Only those themes shared with at least three other participants were put forward into the findings of Super-Ordinate Themes. From this analysis a final dynamic thematic picture was developed, awaiting the results of the next phase of research.

A long look into the trajectory of late motherhood as a phenomenon of modernity has involved designing the research in such a way as to provide the puzzle pieces involved in building dialogical, empirical and dream evidence of the transformation of trauma into a procreative solution. The synthesis of IPA as a means to observe closely the inter-subjective field of affective communication followed by the Word Association Experiment's association networks tested the reliability of the discursive method. The two methods began to speak to each other, as if one was finishing the sentence of the former. While there may be those Jungian Analysts who believe the WAE should be given on its own, without any prior methodology, by including the Clinically Informed IPA method beforehand, I was assessing whether the participants would be able to reasonably sustain a lengthy endeavour such as the WAE, to ensure their own well-being and psychological safety.

What makes some women want babies when they are more fertile, while others prefer to wait until their fertility is on the eve of disappearance, appears on the cultural horizon as a tension of opposites between adherence to traditional female roles and modern emancipating influences, made possible through biotechnology. The more agency and autonomy that is consciously available to a woman, the more non-uterine activity takes precedent in conscious thought, where time is of less concern. How each woman negotiates individual needs in the present against anticipated but unknown future events creates space for new expression within gender norms. From this consideration the methodology I have utilized has the capacity to explore what the horizontal plane of socio-biological culture can tell us about the vertical plane of the collective unconscious.

The eight women who participated in this research ranged from 36 to 52 years old, with one woman who became a mother at 31 believing she had delayed in comparison to her peers. The recommended participant size for a study using Interpretive Phenomenological Analysis (IPA) is six participants to prevent the data from becoming unwieldy (Smith, 2003). I extended the participant group to eight to allow for a 20 per cent rate of drop out, given the highly affective field that can remain around the topic of delayed motherhood for some time. It must be noted that not all the women could afford ART privately, and their inclusion in this study represents a cross-section of participants with means and those without.

Therefore, the women varied in class, education and professional background, the majority was white, except for one who was of mixed race. Only one was non-British, an expatriate from a former British colony. During the almost three years it took to conduct the research, financial reversals took place for many of the women, from better to worse, and vice versa. Not all of them had been powerful, working women with great ambition. Some had higher education, some had none and only one had achieved a doctorate. Their occupations were chef, estate agent, corporate librarian, bookkeeper, catering manager, interior decorator, journalist, corporate scientist and university level academic. They were all able to reflect and feel something about their delayed motherhood. I chose to assign the informal title of 'Ms' whether they were legally married or not, out of respect for their dedication to establish a family and function in a role where they could care for the *other*. The formality of such a designation is within the tenor of analytical literature which includes case studies. But also, there is the matter of how birthing a child has, since antiquity, assigned a woman with an elevated status in passing from maidenhood to womanhood, akin to Persephone blossoming into Kore to become Hades' equal in the underworld. While some women were married, others were not. By assigning them the same neutral title, they occupied a level field of maturity outside of social status. The three case studies presented are representative of a composite of research participants coalescing in similarity and difference of age group, personal history, trauma culture, and psychological outlook. All names have been changed to protect privacy.

## Participants

After Phase 1 and Before Phase 2

### *Ms A Requests Special Meeting to Make Special Request*

Within the first 25 minutes:

- Explanation: Wants to return because she had some revelations.
- 'The penny has dropped'.
- 'I didn't find myself able to say quite a few things'.
- 'I still have this worry that I'm deadly and that I'm going to chase people away'.
- 'I think there's more than one reason why I couldn't say some of the things, but one of the reasons was that I was trying to say the right thing' (A2p1, 5–10).

**TABLE 4.1** Ms A Special Meeting

| *Affective Symptoms* | *Transf./CT* | *Super-ordinate Theme* |
| --- | --- | --- |
| Anxious | Do something for her | Not good enough |
| Will be rejected | Burdened, obligated | Need to be perfect |
| Wants to repair | I must forgive her? | Seeks redemption |
| Needs to buy me | Outrage/can't buy me | Make me whole again |
| See me I'm good | Good girl gets better | Need for reparation |

In the liminal space between the first and second phase of the research, Ms A discovered she was encapsulated in an affective field that made her ignore the masculine through denigration, which felt like a match to her family system of dynamics (ibid., 43–46) that she wanted to come in and discuss in the only place she felt she could ask for space to explore.

In our last meeting I had felt nervous and weary at her insistence that she would encourage anyone and everyone to keep trying for a baby through IVF. 'My hope for your research is that it gives hope to people like me' (Ap19, 62). Having a baby was a life or death deal for Ms A, in contrast to my observed experience that trying to make a baby past a certain point in life could be pushing a rock up hill. As with King Sisyphus, it can feel futile for a very long time. You might get the rock to the top of the mountain, but the cost to body and mind was likely to have an effect on unconscious parts of you. I wondered if perhaps her early narcissistic injury was imposing upon her and this was having a 'field affect' on my countertransference feelings, such that I felt what she was imposing in that moment. Yet at any point she could annihilate herself from the research, or worse, from the self she had built, if I wasn't able to join her, along with her community, a collective with whom she could celebrate her success at achieving motherhood (Ap13, 432–443). My anxiety for Ms A reflected her anxiety about making her needs known and accepted, carte blanche. The past came rushing into the present.

## The First Meeting 8 Years Later – Ms B

Within the first 25 minutes:

- Sedate, aloof, calm, unwilling to interact with questions from the semi-structured interview schedule.
- She worked hard to arouse my interest in her very clever, confident little boy.
- Lack of inter-penetrative effect became an affect unto itself.
- Movement, expression and amplification was flat and limited as if she might be afraid to give too much away.
- Only one over-riding affect, to maintain composure and control, appeared to link into her new-found identity as the mother of a very bright child.

**TABLE 4.2** Ms B Eight Years Later

| Affective Symptoms | Transf./CT | Super-ordinate Themes |
| --- | --- | --- |
| Clipped whispered voice | Expects critical mother | Secretive shame |
| Needs to appear all right | Fragile and tentative | Alone in parenting role |
| Amnesia about past | Frozen out of time | Dissociation |
| Fear of becoming mother | Feeling like her mother | Maternal wound |
| Bouts of depression | Feeling old | Wants to be younger Mum |
| Self-persecution | Shame – regret | Tortured false self |

At the time of the interview I felt there was more to her not having another child to do with mortification within a personal framework of logic and so pursued questions surrounding having the same egg donor (Bp3, 79–84) and how not having the same egg donor would have affected her and her children (B85, ibid.). Secretive, toxic shame underpinned her agentic reproductive processes. Since conceiving her first child the law has since changed regarding anonymity.

> … it was kind of unfair to get kind of … I got pregnant I think for the first time … at about 37–38 and that ended up in miscarriage and then it went on, and that was cruel, it was like fate was kind of saying, "I'm not giving you a chance" … I was ready for it and it would have been good because it wouldn't have been as late as I am now [to being a mum] … I would still be within the age of my peer group … that would have made all of the difference.
>
> *(Bp18, 540–546)*

Fate has indeed played upon her perception of how this aspect of her life has unfolded, following her into the place where talking about it became an act of bravery, which I could not have known before meeting her again so many years later.

## The First Meeting 8 Years Later – Ms D

Phase 1 Phenomena of Affective Communication
  We meet again on a new study now that she is a mother
  Participant wanted to speak out and opine
  Within the first 25 minutes:

- Launched into speaking about herself significantly from the moment she walked into the room.
- I needed to formally re-start the interview and précis the acute anxiety she had expressed before the recording started.
- First expressed anxiety – possible hyper-stimulation of ovaries could have a carcinogenic effect in the future – why take risk.
- Second expressed anxiety – she doesn't want any more children. (Dp1, 4–7)
- Affect laden persona due to loss of inherited maternal ideal from her Mother.
- Celebrates luck to have a second IVF child who is a boy.
- Context for her new maternal subjectivity, husband becomes the third child.
- 'I'm sure if my husband was married to someone else, he'd probably have more (children) but it really works well (with only two)!' (Dp1, 9–14).

**TABLE 4.3** Ms D Eight Years Later

| Affective Symptoms | Transf./CT | Super-ordinate Theme |
|---|---|---|
| Defensive | Wants things to be special | Vulnerability |
| In Charge of Unit | Awoke to non-uterine ambition | Power seeking |
| Gender trouble | Boys have more value | Adaptive patriarchy |
| Gender trouble | Girls are more trouble | Feminine problem |
| Tense dogmatism | Domination | Social authority hunger |
| Guilt | Self-centred | Rebellion |
| Lucky | Obsessive | Identity confusion |

From this trajectory of affect it was apparent to me something, possibly called motherhood, had a profound effect on Ms D. Things had not gone as perfectly as she envisioned when I first interviewed her for a previous study on repeated use of IVF (Barone-Chapman, 2007), a time when idealized motherhood was held up against a denigrated career as a working mother. Fear of developing cancer was presented as a good reason for not having any more children as the drugs involved had been known to cause older women problems. Her partner was presented as an extra child she needed to cater to, making him another justification. But it was her first-born daughter not being mentioned at all that gave me pause. Through this omission I began to sense the past was in the present through three layers of communication on gender bias.

These masks came on and off over the course of the two-hour Phase 1 interview to learn more about what made her narrative so different in this inter-subjective space from other participants. Ms Daimon, named so to acknowledge the hunger in her that could not be denied ... 'eventually it will out. It makes its claim. The daimon does not go away' (Hillman, 1996, p. 8). Ms D offered several different reasons for not wanting any more children, slowly building toward an affect laden communication.

> ... It's been a really weird learning curve for me ... I've discovered quite a lot about myself since I've had children which I really, I'm not saying I particularly like these, actually because I mean I do think that I'm a maternal person, but I thought I was really maternal you know, desperate to have children
> 
> *(Dp1, 15–17)*

My feelings were a mirror of what she may have been feeling and I wondered to myself if she was splitting between self-criticism and apprehension as to whether she could be as good a mother as her mother; a 'see-saw' of envious attack and envious idealization.

I noticed how her turn from our very first encounter where she idealized maternal preoccupation in anticipation of a new identity, albeit a match to her feelings about mother, had induced in me a perverse confusion about her. The affects between us aroused her need to let me know how difficult it was for her to claim a place that risked disapproval, can only be described as a *complexio oppositorum*, which inspires a change to an opposite identity, feeling and experience. Ms D found something that had lain hidden in her shadow, never fully coming to awareness until she discovered how children can take over a woman's life. This was an important moment for both of us. I became aware of how proto-shame (shame from shame; Maibom, 2010, p. 142) can infuse the intersubjective field with a double helix of fear, concomitant within delayed motherhood, both personally and culturally. Though I was not expecting this kind of epiphany, I felt grateful for it. Ms D was claiming maternal subjectivity and marking the limitations of maternal preoccupation. Despite all the important good things she was discovering for her well-being, she mis-read my agape as disappointment. The projection here was her way of giving me an insider's view of the relationship she had with an idealized person, likely her mother, with whom she rarely felt she could measure up. Her mis-read may have even made her daimon stronger. 'The reason we resist the myth of the Daimon, I believe, is that it comes clean. It is not disguised as empirical fact. It states itself openly as a myth. Furthermore, it challenges us to recognize our individuality as a birthright without the fallback pillow of Mother as comforting ground and archetypal support' (Hillman, 1996, p. 68).

## References

Benjamin, J. (1998). *Like Subjects, Love Objects: Essays on Recognition and Sexual Difference*. New Haven, CT: Yale University Press.
Freud, S. (1914). 'Remembering, Repeating, and Working Through'. In *S.E. Vol. 12*. London: Hogarth Press.
Hillman, J. (1996). *The Soul's Code: In Search of Character and Calling*. New York: Random House.
Jung, C.G. ([1929]1993). 'Problems of Modern Psychotherapy'. In *Collected Works, Vol. 16. The Practice of Psychotherapy* (2nd edn). London: Routledge & Kegan Paul.
Jung, C.G. ([1946]1993). 'The Psychology of the Transference'. In *Collected Works, Vol. 16. The Practice of Psychotherapy* (2nd edn). London: Routledge & Kegan Paul.
Jung, C.G. ([1951]1993). 'Fundamental Questions of Psychotherapy'. In *Collected Works, Vol. 16. The Practice of Psychotherapy* (2nd edn). London: Routledge & Kegan Paul.
Maibom, H.L. (2010). 'The descent of shame', *Philosophy and Phenomenological Research*, 80 (3), pp. 566–594.
Sedgwick, D. ([1994]2017). *The Wounded Healer: Countertransference from a Jungian Perspective*. London and New York: Routledge.
Smith, J.A. (ed.), (2003). *Qualitative Psychology: A Practical Guide to Research Methods*. London: Sage.

## Further Reading

Barone-Chapman, M. (2007). 'The hunger to fill an empty space: an investigation of primordial affects and meaning making in the drive to conceive through repeated use of ART', *The Journal of Analytical Psychology*, 52(4), pp. 389–541.
Freud, S. (1957). 'Mourning and Melancholia'. In *S.E. Vol. 14*. London: Hogarth Press, pp. 237–258.

# 5
# LIVING IN THE SHADOW

'For Jung, confession is the cure for psychic isolation – both from oneself and others. Repression and psychic concealment represent greater "sin" than that which is concealed' (Lambert, 1981, p. 29; Jung, 1931, paras 122–123). Women who delayed motherhood, I found, have something in common with a particular kind of mother who does not value her daughter sufficiently to encourage her sovereignty. While the patriarchal mother showed up early in all their lives, the three stories I have chosen to amplify show how the tensions of delayed motherhood occupy a cross section of women from many walks of life, including my eight participants. Though they all reveal facets of such a mother, they yielded the same solution to the fear of overwhelming authority; delay motherhood until you are old enough to hold your personhood. Each of the case studies from the initial interview setting aroused unconscious communication about what they had suffered, or were continuing to suffer, under the notion they had done something wrong. Delaying motherhood was the 'sin'. Compounding this union of personal and cultural influences was the emergence of a potential transcendent space between a woman's personal mother and the mother she thought she must be in order to qualify as mother material. While the personal mothering style each woman had received was influential in developing a maternal self, mother's style of partnering, including how she included father (or not) in the intra-psychic marriage formed by the parental relationship, was also significant in how each woman felt about being creative, procreative, sexual and female.

> We are all tellers of tales … to provide our scattered and often confusing experiences with a sense of coherence by arranging the episodes of our lives into stories … In order to live well, with unity and purpose, we compose a heroic narrative of the self that illustrates essential … Enduring human truths …
>
> *(McAdams 1993, p. 11)*

The subject of delayed motherhood has gathered cultural popularity. Many have written about it with little psychological appreciation for the epistemology and aetiology of a gendered complex circulating around the delay itself. What is important to keep in mind as you read the three stories and results, is how complexes of the collective unconscious are not considered pathological unless they are connected to a personal conflict and become installed too soon (Jacobi, 1974; Mathers, 2001, p. 164). Throughout I was asking, myself 'Is delayed motherhood a personal area of conflict with a connection to the cultural and collective unconscious?' Separating out the cultural/collective influence from those of the personal realm establishes the valence and gravity of a complex.

As I will soon discuss and demonstrate, the more emotion is present in the file of memories and experiences, the longer it takes to make a connection to the association and return to equilibrium in the present. To view affective communication solely as a defensive operation (Zepf, 2007, p. 106) misses the teleological purpose of habits, fears, avoidance, bodily symptoms erupting chronically or spontaneously, and in liminal space, through fast and slow decisions, responses, and include those that hide within associative networks. To be understood fully, affect is a survival operation in the present with a link to the personal past, connected to a cultural context rooted in the archaic level of the collective unconscious. Some affects have a 'numinous' – 'divine' or 'sacred' quality (Jung, 1937b, para. 448) because they raise particular contents to a higher degree of awareness causing other potential conscious contents to return to the dark recesses of the unconscious. Affects constellate around the nucleus of a complex. This nucleus is theoretically associated to particular archetypes as a symbolic representation of the complex. They can have an explosive quality as well as an imploding resonance, catching us off guard and taking over our understanding of our relationship to other and the self. These findings, from Jung's experiments with the Word Association Experiment, began to reveal a connection to mythological patterns that led him to begin identifying motifs he referred to as archetypes (Jung, 1904–1906; 1904–1909). Jung's associative method was not the free associations of Freud, which in the main linked back to earlier points in life. Jung was interested in looking forward (teleology), in verifying the link between affect, association and a subsequent change in energy. He began to build his ideas along similar lines to Janet's view of psyche's capacity to dissociate, as well as personal desire in him to reconcile religion and science through mythological ideas. From Jung's mythopoetic leanings, a form of anthropology was created over a lifetime of work through observing patterns of *archetypes*. These unseen felt images are understood to be the nuclei of a complex, acting as conductors between the divine and their human form. Together they give depth to the nature of embodiment on a transpersonal level of experience.

## The Long and Winding Road: A Maternal Self

The making of a maternal self appears as a journey through obliquity (Kay, 2011, p. 15). By this, I mean there was not a conscious, focused path toward procreation as a goal. The female body, as recalled in the narratives that follow, appear to have been neutered into performance of patriarchal values, creating both a fear of becoming a mother as well as the longing for it. In the conflicted journey toward development of a maternal self, there had been various representations of identity in relation to the 'other' until there was an awakening in the fourth or fifth decade that something had to be done to create a baby. Serial monogamy, and co-habitation, was no longer enough. Such unions could easily fail. Unconscious processes observed by Pines (1993) in a clinical capacity with fertility challenged women, found the repeated pattern of mother's role to be both controlling and withholding, as if the adult daughters did not yet have mother's permission to bear their own babies. Adjacent forays into developing a personal self, often taking a woman into arenas where the act of mothering was transferred onto peers, work projects, and colleagues, projected into causes or movements, had been displaced. Developmentally inspired obstructions included uncertainty regarding sexual and gender identity, most often seen through a disassociated relationship to the female body, as if the body was responding in collusion or rebellion, to messages learned earlier in childhood within the family (Pines, 1993, p. 79). 'What differs in development for a female, compared to development for a male, is that her environment is more centrally described by interpersonal relatedness and affect' (Eurich-Rascoe and Van de Kemp, 1997, p. 13).

Erikson's (1950; 1968) stages of identity may not apply to female classifications of identity and achievement (Belenky et al., 1986; Chodorow, [1978]1999; Friday, 1977; Gilligan, 1982; Gilligan et al., 1990; Miller, 1976). Strict delineations along the lines of finding basic virtues such as 'love' (aged 18–40), 'care' (aged 40–65) or 'maturity' (aged 65 plus) within predictable timeframes becomes fluid since delayed motherhood has become a powerful modern mainstay of reproduction and the manufacture of generative identity. In its wake, a neotany (Bly, 1996) has formed wherein time has expanded and extended the period of adolescence, not as a regression or retardation but as a social construction sustained through an unconscious reliance upon magical forces, such as the 'technological unconscious' (Rutsky, 1999). A shift in the collective to the look to the skies as a social phenomenon, marked a new period between humans and technology, suggestive of 'communion with supernatural forces, hypnotic or trance states, or other forms of openness to the ineffable complexities of a technological world' (ibid., p. 147). I am proposing, post the atomic bomb, the acceptance and rise of delayed motherhood has become a part of the historical continuum in the rise of a techno-logical unconscious (op cit.). As a symbol of the self, born in the caverns of the mind-body, they have been associated with physical disorders of a psychic origin (Jung, 1933, paras 291–293). Throughout this extended exploration I have observed how the effect of scientific medicine (e.g., IVF) can cut us off from experiencing the body through feelings and emotions (Redfearn, 1985).

## Case Study 1: To Denounce Destruction as the Feminine Hero

While she believed she started out intending to be a mother, becoming engaged to marry when she was 20 while still at university, somewhere between two to three years into the relationship Ms A remembered that something had happened.

> ... [we] were actually beginning to plan the wedding and I think I had the first of the control battles with my mother about the wedding and something inside me just went funny and I had this dream that I was getting into this wedding dress and I was in a state of total dread and fear. So I broke off the relationship. (Ap1, L4–7)

What struck Ms A the most about her twenties was her habit of having relationships for a certain amount of time and then for one reason or another she ended them. When her relationships were 'good' she thought about children but if they went 'wrong' children went out of her mind. She had three or four relationships that turned into being wrong. On the last of these, at 28, she had an epiphany.

> I realized that there was actually nothing wrong, the only thing that was wrong in the relationship was me ... it was only a vague feeling but I definitely knew there was something wrong with me, and it probably took me about 18 months or maybe two years to get into therapy but that was eventually what happened. (Ap1, L12–17)

After more than a decade in analysis, Ms A discovered what went wrong for her in relationship with male partners. Following her private analysis, she met the man who, after ten years of trying naturally and through IVF, fathered their first child through ovum donation when she was in her late forties. When we first met, her first child was three and a half years old. She was still besotted by him and relieved he was a boy. She breastfed him up until he was two and a half, and, thought this was down to what she described as 'separation issues' between them. The topic of gender came up again throughout our three years of contact. In that time Ms A had a second child, at 52, another boy, through another ovum donation from a different donor. She described her second boy as 'hot'. I imagined Freud nodding at how Ms A perfectly demonstrated his observation of how a woman can feel when she has delivered a male child. Some part of her wanted to be male, to be able to gloat proudly. Making a relationship to her own animus had been denied; mother was protecting herself from her child.

## The Maternal Self

What struck me most about her trajectory to finding a maternal self, was her struggle to find and hold onto a relationship with all things that might be considered feminine. 'Destructive' was the word she used to describe how relationships kept getting in the way of her becoming a mother.

> When I went to therapy, I think my therapist thought that I had had quite a bad childhood but that actually I had lots of destructive stuff inside, you know and that I'd kind of created my own bad object, and I'm sure that that was almost true. It is true, but it was when I said to her a few of the actual things

that my mother said that I think the whole therapy changed a bit because then I started thinking about actually the reality of some of it. (Ap3, L81–85)

Her description of anguish with mother and father was that she '… tried so hard to make them care' (Ap3, L103), but they seemed not to take her body seriously. Retrospective complaints included long-term anaemia not being investigated and being allowed to cycle on a road where other children had been killed. I felt she was attributing ambivalence to her living or not, to something bad inside her. Ms A had wanted to be a doctor; she was good at sciences, won prizes in chemistry and biology. At the point where she was about to give these subjects up her teacher pleaded with her to re-consider. Why did she feel she had to give them up?

I gave them up because my parents ignored it, they ignored everything (I did) except music. It was a ridiculous choice … a total waste of my years at university in terms of my academics, they also couldn't recognize my talent for French … I had French prizes also on the shelves. They also never came to one single athletics match and at 13 I was the best high jumper in the school and I loved it … (Ap6, L185–198).

Ms A met her long-term partner at 37 and remarked about her acceptance of him as 'not perfect, but we both feel we're lucky'. They went through four miscarriages. She valued the relationship for his availability to want children in their lives as much as she did. It was obvious from her narrative that Ms A had not felt like a human being for a long time (Ap8), and felt there was 'something broken' (Ap6, L265) that could not be healed by the feeling of being loved by someone with whom it 'felt right' until she was able to have their first child together, even though it was through ovum donation. '… I've killed so many children' (Ap6, 279) explaining she had something within her body '…so when I turned up as her first child, I immunized her against my sister and two other babies she lost' (Ap9, L293–295). A biological anomaly had left Ms A with the idea there was something about her that was dangerous and awful, believing mother blamed her for the losses, and later adopted a baby boy to complete the family. 'I left something that endangered the other babies' (Ap9, L310). What Ms A has had to face over and over again in relationship was the feeling her intimate other didn't care about her, which was a parallel to feeling her parents didn't care about her because her birth caused later deaths in utero (Ap10, L331). But with the father of the child she carried, she admitted, '… neither one of us is perfect, our relationship isn't perfect, but it feels so right' (Ap8, L267–268). Ms A has kept the fact of her child's birth through ovum donation from parental figures, explaining she never knew if she was going to be attacked.

At first, it seemed that the relationship Ms A had with her partner was an antidote to the difficult relationship with her parents, especially her mother. She talked about how they had both waited a really long time to 'find someone' (Ap8, L268–69), they were about the same age and neither had been married before. Her partner really wanted to have children and said, 'I knew by the way he said it, he really meant it, and that has mattered … it would be a lot harder if you knew it wasn't reasonably equal' (Ap8, L269–273). Ms A felt delight for her beautiful baby boy, believing he had become the stronger 'antibody' against a toxic childhood, giving her protection against a critical mother.

Ms A is not alone in regaling this child as a 'divine child'; she firmly believes the lack of familial genetics would break her father's heart if he were to find out. In this child Ms A's father sees the twin he lost when he was a small boy. Unconsciously, Ms A gave her first-born child the name of her father's lost twin. The child appeared to have given her something she did not have before; something good inside her that can produce good things for others. The loss of an erotic relationship with her partner came as more of a shock, and her ego was ill prepared for it. She talked about 'proudly breastfeeding my baby in public and that was the right thing to do anytime I could (laugh)' (Ap13, L418–419). This is in sharp contrast to the picture she painted of herself sitting on a train platform for some time thinking of jumping onto the tracks because of too many earlier miscarriages.

> I felt so persecuted … like I was being punished for something I hadn't done. I felt as if it was my mother getting at me you know, that's how mad I was … I did get a letter at one stage telling me that my desire to have a child was putting pressure on my partner … as if my financial contribution wasn't relevant … She didn't want me to have children. (Ap15, 477–483)

Ms A had enjoyed a high-powered job for many years, but as it became clear she could no longer rely on her own eggs to become pregnant, she began to work four days a week and then three while having fertility treatment. Her earning power was no longer the litmus upon which she measured her abilities. Suspecting a complex had been suddenly accessed from this highly persecutory field of self-doubt, I wanted to discover what she felt happened to her between childhood and adulthood, the 'in between place' paralleling why she had come back in to speak to me in the liminal space between Phase 1 and 2 of the research. It wasn't an accident, but a synchronous parallel of her adolescent wound in the present. She said she was anxious to return, because she had accessed 'new information'. Also, she wanted to make herself acceptable and valuable to me by offering to pay me for the interview time, because important, big feelings had arisen. In that moment, I understood what had happened to her in the potent teenage years when her parents adopted a male child. She had tried to meet mother's animus, but was rejected under patriarchal gender reasons. She had forgotten to mention her adopted brother in our first meeting.

Ms A herself formulated she had ignored the masculine through denigration, thinking this was a match to her family system of dynamics (Ap15 43–46). Yet, Ms A spoke about working hard to develop an acceptable work persona as a masculinized woman. But with the onset of motherhood, she discovered her sexual life with her husband was no longer what it had been (S2p2, 38–39). Delayed motherhood, for Ms A, began to take on the character position of rebellion through long standing gender issues. She recalled times when mother tried to get her to do feminine subjects like music and English Literature rather than her more favoured interest in sport and science.

Fear of emasculating her husband became a way of saying she fears she has emasculated herself in relationship to buried rage that could be considered a screen memory of what happened between her and mother. Yet men and male activities were put down in her family, robbing her of her physical abilities and scientific talents which manifested in a successful career in science before moving into a more serious relationship, on the way to bringing two children into the world in her late forties and early fifties.

It was no surprise to find the scientist in her could easily explain to me the 'natural killer cells' that went into her mother after she was born, preventing mother from becoming pregnant again. Her concretization, and reliance, upon the 'natural killer cells' as symbolic of the mother-daughter/partnering/procreating relationship was cracking under a life-long masculine persona for a disavowed feeling function. One of the most useful aspects of the 'natural killer cells' is its ability to help her separate out her problems from her mother's: 'No, rhesus is my mother's problem and the killer cells are mine. They are different, they are entirely different but we both ended up with immune systems which killed our babies (which sounds horrible) and in my case I switched that response on … I left something that endangered her other babies' (Ap9, 305–307, 310). Her body holds affects that both confirm and redeem her.

In the domain of parallel processes, I considered how her body acted as a mirror neuron of her psychological issue with her mother. It was as if mother wanted to prevent a union of masculine and feminine aspects and Ms A was fighting for them to reunite. Her body has been under the spell that she was more of a Lilith rather than an Eve. I was uncertain whether I was being asked to be mother or father, and realized I was standing in for both in her mind. 'I can see you know that there was a pattern in the family …' (Ap9, L36–37), attributes knowledge to me I did not have at that moment in time. There were often times in the first interview where I felt she was penetrative and wondered if she could let anyone in. While there were many evidences of attempting to face herself in the first interview, I often felt she was trying to get me on her side. Though seemingly an independent woman she wanted to be reassured. In effect she was trying to make me the better parent she had spent her early life doing with her parents. I saw and felt this in the way she was telling me her story; story telling was more important than her reflection. I found my responses mirrored her desire to penetrate me with the courage and wisdom of her experience so that through the intersubjective space of two, I was asked to penetrate and contain her through nominative interpretation of what she was saying (Ap8, L266–280). Such analytical interpretation is a way of consolidating metaphorical considerations between analyst and analysand to make a symbolic baby – something new, which can change the course of fate.

The research process had activated a hunger to see herself and be seen, as someone who was good, not bad. I wondered if she was protectively identified with mother about being a disappointment to herself, and to me, as if I would also be harsh and disappointing. The disappointment emerging between us was a *confession* that delivering her first baby hadn't taken away the feeling she had to kill off the feminine in order to get through the pain of living a lonely life for so long. She also hated feeling she had to kill off the masculine in her partner, just as her mother had done to her father. Once she achieved motherhood, she didn't want to copy what her mother had done, she wanted to find a way to bring previously opposing elements within her, back together. I wasn't there to provide therapy, only a space for her to ascend into that re-union through her own confession and elucidation (Jung, 1931, para. 122).

Identifying with something inside her that could kill off babies, would make her as powerful as Lilith and from this perspective she began to author a new personal creation myth from the chaos of a half-alive childhood. Delayed motherhood became a redemptive motif of the Hero and Heroine of the collective unconscious, who co-conspired, even encouraged, women to celebrate the creation of their own Divine Child. In some cases this" creative act" redeemed Ms A and many like her from the family of origin system, which was able to celebrate the masculine in a male, but not in a female. Considerable fury arose that cost Ms A good feelings about her ability to be a good female. This appeared at first to be a small price to pay as she imagined her mother did not want her to have children, therefore making her feel triumphant when she succeeded. An adhesive attachment to becoming the good mother in order to feel success as a woman, had not taken away all the pain of a denigrated gender identity. It seemed her many attempts and hard work were designed to make her feel lovable. I was therefore not surprised to learn some months later when I invited Ms A to return for Jung's Word Association Experiment, that she was pregnant again with her second child through ovum donation. She was 51 at the time, and we took every precaution to ensure the safety of mother and child.

## The 'Night Sea Journey' of Two Participants

Ten years before researching delayed motherhood I was analysing data in another research project to do with the phenomenon of women who had a hunger to fill an empty space (Barone-Chapman, 2007) that only a child could fill, through repeated use of IVF. In identifying the drive behind the need to conceive at all costs, I came into contact with the felt experience of childhood memories, the choices made during early adulthood and the fantasies of how a child would change their lives. The first theme was the importance of the relationship to mother and the quality of the mothering received in a woman's availability to become a mother at a time in her life when she is most fertile. The second theme was the crisis of identity that was aroused when the assumptive position of a right to be fecund suddenly becomes dispelled (Barone-Chapman, 2007). The data revealed how a fertility crisis creates a mask for a crisis of identity with links to the personal mother and the intra-psychic parental couple (archetypes) become installed as a model to emulate. I saw repeated infertility treatment as a transformative process necessitating repetition until something new had the potential to be birthed, beyond that of a healthy living baby (Barone-Chapman, 2007).

At the outset no one knows how long they will be subjected to repeated use of Assisted Reproductive Technology (ART) at the centre of cycles of hope and despair. For some this liminal place can last anywhere from a few years to as many as twelve, in my experience. The study concerned itself with women who had more than four attempts at IVF. The two women you will meet here were pregnant with their first child at the time, agreeing to return to participate on the subject of delayed motherhood. I felt the longitudinal experience would bring something very rich to understanding the making of a maternal self, especially around one of the research questions, 'How has the world changed toward you since becoming a mother?' In the two longitudinal stories that follow, we see into the making of a maternal self from the perspective of being the child of the 'disappointing death' mother who stultified her daughter. This is in sharp contrast to the 'too-good' mother's effect on a daughter who was 8–15 years younger than most of the participants I was working with at the time. The first may be viewed as leaving the maternal self far too late, for reasons that will become clear, while the second story was about the anxiety of keeping up with peers for identity purposes, or so it seemed at the time. Revisiting their earlier ideas of mother, motherhood, interests, hopes, memories of menarche, first sexual experiences, partnering history, adult choices and importantly – their hopes and expectations of life after their first child, has been useful in developing a plural understanding of what a longitudinal perspective of 'then' and 'now' can bring when viewed through Jung's lens of enantiodromia (Jung 1911–12/1952c, para. 581).

The success of getting past their first trimester of pregnancy after many delays and failed attempts was carried as gloom in the daughter of the 'disappointing death' mother while the euphoria in the daughter of the 'too good' mother was very high in feeling tone as a grand achievement. What had prevented them from getting on the journey to motherhood was relayed as if it had been a matter of life or death, raising my awareness of how difficult subject formation had been without having had a child. Their memories of the past were fresh and as yet untainted by their own transformation into having a maternal self. Fear and desire changed the complexion of their narratives between longing for an experience and the actual experience. Ultimately both participants underwent an enantiodromia on how they understood motherhood as something to manage through meaning and purpose after fear and desire had waned.

## Case Study 2: To Demonstrate Repair and Recovery is Possible

Affect needs other people in some form of relationship in order to be seen. The response from these 'others' over time and generations, whether conscious or unconscious, spoken of openly for kept in the closet (unconscious) only to spill out with other shames, is the best means we have of identifying longitudinal complexes.

Ms B's subsequent experience of motherhood showed her something about time she did not know as a daughter to her mother. She hadn't known if she could ever get her timing right for herself on any activity, until she began to follow the guidance of an author (Ford, 2001) who specializes in writing about maternal care for infants using time management as a guide for creating contented babies through consistent regular feeding and sleeping times. When she began telling the stories about how easy her son was to teach and train at each developmental marker (Bp5, L138–144), I became mesmerized by her confidence, capability and determination to have a positive influence on the child, and by extension to me. By the time she cited how easy potty-training was by the way she did it, contrary to the way her mother wanted her to do it (Bp5, B144–146), I briefly lost connection with the subject of toilet training her son and found myself back on the subject of 'getting pregnant' (Bp5, B147–148). Initially I felt I was becoming lost in her story/his story, mother/child preoccupation just as much she was. My thinking function became desiccated on some of the meaning making possibilities around potty-training details. This was due in large part to the more vibrant enthusiasm Ms B held for her son than I thought would ever be possible. What impressed me most was how she was able to relish the detail of necessary tasks involved in raising a child, despite her mother's continued criticism. I became immersed in the detail of Ms B's narrative, thus becoming part of her loss for 'leaving it too long' and not being able to have another child. Maternal preoccupations sat comfortably for Ms B now in a way she too had never thought possible. After the initial fright of not knowing what to do, she undertook some therapy and embraced the task. Any prior expectations (over eight years ago) of returning to work she may have had when we last met had vanished, and she could barely recall them. Her experience of doing motherhood well enough, better than her own mother, had drowned out the critical mother hammering on that she was useless at everything and mothering would be no different. 'I didn't have a natural affinity with babies. I didn't kind of look at a baby and coo … I thought babies were ugly … but what I have now realized is that your baby is different' (B7, 179–181).

## Unconscious Rebellion

After years of trying and never getting it quite right with her mother or herself, in her late forties, Ms B began her transformation into first-time motherhood. Now in her mid to late fifties, her former insecurity of having no identity if she did not work has been replaced by motherhood. She now knows herself more fully as a related and compassionate woman whose sympathies for children appear to have also repaired her own difficult memories with her mother.

M: 'So what do you think becoming a mother has done for you?'
B: 'Oh I think you become much more aware, or I have you know. You look at children in a completely different way … a much more sympathetic way …'
M: 'Does that extend to people or is it …?'
B: 'Yes I think it does extend to people, but I also wonder … I'm no longer working in a stressful job and I have a much less stressful life.'

M: 'Yes. I remember you saying you weren't going to be a stay at home mother, you were going back to work ... you were going to show your mother. Do you remember that?'
B: 'I mean I haven't ... I do a bit of charity work ... which is quite fun ... I would quite like to go back to some kind of work but on the other hand I don't want to go back to work and not see Leo, because you know having got this far I just want to enjoy him ... it's such a short time and soon he'll be up and gone' (Bp7, 195–209).There were times during the interview when I could not believe this was the same woman I had met years earlier. Had I not witnessed her highly affective BC (before child) state while pregnant, I would not have seen how she could grow into a confident woman. No longer was she in contact with her earlier pain to do with a contest with mother over her own fundamental goodness as mother's first-born. Since having some cognitive behaviour therapy (CBT) she came to find new views about fearful places in context of being an older mother. This was a work in progress as she anticipated the future.

In loosening her grip on her former identity as a high-powered businesswoman, motherhood had given Ms B a new psychological frame, enabling a larger sense of what could have been, in her childhood. It was almost as if she had always been a mother, and she corroborated this as true (Bp9, 271–276). Her own mother crossed this Janus gate when she was still quite a young woman. Little B hadn't yet understood the ferocity of regret. This kind of narrative and amnesia was a way of making sense out of something that doesn't make sense. In many ways this is the reparative fabric between past and present woven together in the belief that what she is doing is the right thing for *her* child. But the allusion came slightly undone when she considered when I asked, 'What would you be doing now if you had not become a mother do you think, and what would that role look like?' 'I have no idea, but I expect I might have been in the Priory' (an institution for rehabilitation from addictions) (laughs) (Bp10, 301–303).

Experiencing her laughter was important for me to see as I came to understand how she has surpassed the longitudinal affects of her mother, along with the continual shame she felt for not doing something important at the right time. It wasn't the right time for her mother to have had her at 21 – it spoiled her long honeymoon – and then when she was 51 she conceived, but it was too late in her mind, to have another child. She's too late to join the party of school mothers who have been young enough to go on to having the second and third baby. Her whispered tones led me to hear her remorse. '... being older is a disadvantage' (Bp2, 52–53). 'I think it's just that you adapt less well ... On the plus side you've got more time. You're not dashing off to do other things ... the biggest minus is the fact that I'm one of the oldest mothers in the class, if not the oldest parent. And I've become a bit secretive about my age because I don't want to be seen as a freak – I don't want my son to see me that way' (Bp2, 55–59). Her toxic relationship with being too late to motherhood was in part fatigue after numerous miscarriages and IVF attempts over eight years. This experience co-conspired with those of her mother, solidifying some anxiety about how she appeared in comparison to other women.

I was led to understand this son had saved Ms B, helping her to mature into a more well-rounded human being. If she hadn't had a child, she imagined her life would have gone from bad to worse. Ms B went on to explain how she learned to do things for her him through remembering what wasn't done for her. A part of her salvation was in having a son who did everything in his development on time (Bp5, 138–144) and who is not at all like her, she told me. She no longer remembers worrying if she would be like her mother or that the child would be like her. She realized the love she always longed for (Bp11, 323–330) was within her grasp as she showed her child what love looked like, so he could respond in kind. This is precisely what she had hoped for when we first met, while still pregnant, during the previous study. For Ms B, her child had become 'that someone who would think I was wonderful' and in all ways, it seemed she had won a victory that could last a lifetime.

## Case Study 3: To Demonstrate a *Complexio Oppositorum* Can Happen to Anyone

Ms D was eight to twelve years younger than other research participants I spoke to. I've included her here for reasons of longitudinal symmetry alongside Ms B but also, because Ms D truly believed she had been too late to motherhood at 31. Her friendship group had children seven to ten years earlier than she and her partner.

When I first met Ms D, her enthusiasm for being pregnant went hand in hand with becoming, for her child, the same kind of mother as her own idealized mother.

> I mean going back to how she was as a mother, she was very good. We knew – you know – we knew where we were the whole time, we had a very structured childhood, but I never ever – can think of an unhappy time … (D20, 10).

Ms D's maternal idealization had a solid foundation but began to suggest that though married, she still had difficulty in separating from mother. It was Ms. D's relationship and feelings for her mother that allowed her to hear mother's alarm bells that she wasn't falling pregnant quickly or easily. Though seemingly ambivalent about becoming pregnant at that time, she sought a conversation with mother, not her partner, to help her work out how to become pregnant. For Ms D, mother is a bountiful resource for identification. Her primordial affects left her little choice in the world other than to be just like mother. Being able to have a baby completed the picture of having her life constructed in the same way as her mother's. In the following she recounts how she imagined her future when she was a child:

> Yes, it was definitely – definitely that I would have children … I've always thought when I was married that I wouldn't be working. And that's why – but I think as a child you see it in simplistic terms. And you know my

parents – well my mother didn't work so, you know (gestures toward herself to include herself) (Dp19, L17).

Ms D reported being an abysmal disappointment to both her parents regarding her academic performance to the point where they were quite worried about her future. She referred to herself as being 'bone idle' (Dp23, L2).

I don't want to be a career girl, I didn't want that … you know, you eat, live and breathe your job. I mean I love, love what I do, but I'm not built like that (Dp 37, L6).

Before delivering her first child, as a participant in my earlier research (Barone-Chapman, 2007), not wanting to be a 'career girl' occupied her as a symbolic equation to not being able to reproduce, which became more terrifying, in terms of whether she would be able to be successful at something, ever.

People who do have careers that are trying IVF, or have problems with conception, at least they've got, at least they always have their careers to fall back on, I mean where was I going to fit into society? (Bp 37, L11).

Here then was the core of the fertility crisis continuing to unravel, neatly summed up as the need to fit into society. But to which society did she belong?

## Enantiodromia is Ageless

In the first study, I thought Ms D's attachment and dependence upon mother for continued nurturance would be challenged when she had her first baby. I also thought the fertility crisis was attempting to help her form an identity that gave her permission to separate from mother and establish some autonomy. I predicted there was every possibility that the fear and anxiety of work and non-uterine activity, which was not fully dealt with as part of the fertility crisis, would somehow appear once again, perhaps in mid-life, or around forty. I was off in my calculations by two years.

Forward to eight years later, Ms D was back in to discuss delayed motherhood and was bursting to speak from the heart the moment she came in. Confession and elucidation were bursting to be heard. As a result, I had to ask her to pause for a moment, to start recording, and repeated what she had just said as she walked in the door. Out came the passion: she didn't want to be one of those 'stay at home mothers' (like her mother) who would be boring to be sat next to at dinner parties. Once she had the children, she discovered other needs were there to be nurtured.

M: … a couple of things you mentioned casually over tea … one was the worry your ovaries had been hyper-stimulated … The other was you definitely didn't want any more children? (DL 4–7, p.1).

Ms D had not considered taking a different position to motherhood than her own mother had displayed. She learned in time that motherhood is not a qualifying status outside of the world of women. Ms D had proven she could develop in the world of women and be part of something larger than herself through a community and friendships. But if she had more than two children, she would compromise her pursuit of other pleasures and would become dull and boring as she felt she had become in the early days with her first-born. Her daughter came into the world with more need of Ms D's new, untested, mothering skills. The experience gave her time to think about what would make her happy. She decided on having just one more child to see if it would bring her back to a place of being able to enjoy motherhood.

With the second child, a son, she was not shocked and dismayed as she was with the first. She readily conceived with one of the harvested eggs and had an easy delivery. To cement her decision to curtail more children, she donated the rest of her frozen eggs to research. During the course of the interview she held my attention as to whether she had made the right decision, and perhaps something hadn't yet settled for her about this. A fragment within her maternal ambivalence was unravelling before my eyes. I wondered what it was in her development that installed the need to become oppositional, perhaps to appear 'interesting' rather than boring. Ms D talked as if she was an 'older mother' already by alluding to past failed attempts of IVF in her late twenties. I was never able to find in Ms D an equal measure to the early life traumas of other women afflicted by the Mother Monster archetype, women who had delayed motherhood a further ten to eighteen years. I kept reminding myself that all experiences felt as trauma are of equal importance to those who have lived through it.

> I mean we, out of my friends, are in a huge minority actually having only two children. Most of our friends have four, three or five … I guess with IVF you're less likely to have a boy … so I feel hugely blessed by that. You know he (partner) needs a lot of looking after as well, and it just works great for our unit … If my husband was married to someone else he'd probably have more (children) but it really works well, the dynamics work well! (D9–14, para. 1).

It wasn't long before Ms D began to reveal cracks between the kind of life she had idealized for herself when she was first pregnant and the reality of motherhood two children later. Especially remarkable was all that she learned about herself in the process of *maternal individuation* (Parker, 2005, p. 24). She did not know at the time how normal she was in her wish to claim more of her own life and projected her shame outward in my direction as transference phenomena.

> I've realized there are other things that are important to me I'm not prepared to sacrifice. By having two I can be a good mum but also satisfy those bits as well, which sounds terribly selfish (D9, 19–22).

Ms D may have been maternally preoccupied before giving birth, becoming ambivalent with the first birth, but she has since found a means of not being like mother, through her development of maternal subjectivity, allowing her to have an experience of a separate self. The 'bits' she refers to are her desire to have 'complete sort of control of things' as a priority, that 'puts the house in order, with time to run it efficiently with a live-in nanny' (D9, 24–27).

> … and I think all the women that I know have the same problem. That being a mum is not your identity, being who I am is the fact that I am a designer, not a mummy (D47–49).

Mother and marriage have left something of a *pentimento* on Ms D's experience of herself. It is the voice that can feel the selfish sitting beside feeling lucky. She knew she was not as good at mothering her daughter as she was with her son. This may be another early phase of an unconscious parody to mother as well. A theme that resurfaces in the chapters that follow. In the end, her attempt to find the career girl she previously thought she wasn't, became the mitigating re-balance she needed to feel able to be in life, motherhood and marriage. The caveat was: without feeling suffocated by the other, any other, who needed her.

## A Complex View of Mother and Eros

Taking an expanded view of Jung's complex understanding on mother's position in the daughter's psyche, especially in a daughter who is in no rush to relinquish this position in favour of motherhood, included taking a view of another dimension on time. Jung's observations on whether or not the maternal instinct has been acculturated from mother has a bearing on the development of a maternal self. It was Jung's view that if Eros became *canalized* (narrowly focused) exclusively along the lines of a maternal relationship, not only would father be kept out of a relationship with the daughter, her own developing maternal instinct would be wiped out completely and this would lead to an over-development of Eros through an unconscious incestuous relationship with the father (Jung, 1954a). In this Electra Complex, father remains a foreign, unattainable love object. Alongside this schema, Jung also observed what a complete idealized projection onto mother would have on a daughter's own maternal capacities, keeping her maternal instincts unconscious and Eros remaining as a shadow element, while her mother holds sway over those domains. The demands of motherhood, responsibility, personal relationship and erotic invitations could well arouse feelings of inferiority, compelling a retreat to a mother who represents everything that is unattainable for the daughter (Jung, 1954a). In many ways this was where I first met Ms D.

The desire for procreation at midlife occupies an inter-subjective field between the individual woman and the collective culture in which she lives. Jung linked the formation of complexes to the psychological aspects within the mother-daughter relationship. He saw this psychological closeness as giving rise to a 'peculiar uncertainty as regards time ... a conviction of being outside time, which brings with it a feeling of immortality' (Jung, 1941, para. 316). Fascinated by the mother and the mother-daughter relationship Jung's 'The Psychological Aspects of the Kore' drew significant implications from the Demeter-Kore myth. 'Kore' refers to Persephone's transformation after her abduction into the underworld while her mother, Demeter searches the world to bring her back to a life as a daughter. But Persephone, while in the underworld eats a pomegranate seed offered by her captor, Hades. Once she takes the 'seed' from Hades she can no longer return to mother as a maiden and her name is changed from Persephone, beloved daughter of Demeter, to Kore, Queen of the Underworld. Jung believed his analysis of the Demeter-Kore myth showed the influence of the feminine on psyche outweighed that of the masculine, whose role was only as a seducer or conqueror (Jung, 1941, para. 309). 'For a woman, the mother typifies her own conscious life as conditioned by her sex' (Jung, 1934a, para. 192). Jung's definition of 'Mother' (see below) occupies two positions; 1. She is an inherited structure within the unconscious, and 2. 'She' is the prototypical definition of an archetype. If a daughter is kept in an adolescent phase of development, permission to procreate is implicitly withheld, as the mother archetype has not been 'humanized' or installed (Mathers, 2001), into her own being. Unable to mother herself, this eternal daughter, (Puella), unconsciously waits for the father to return in the form of a male other. Unable to find the man within, the Animus who would serve her in a heroine's quest to 'fight the dragons' of childhood, puberty and mid-life (Neumann, 1954) she struggles to bring her body back to mind. '... the "mother" is also the matrix, the hollow form, the vessel that carries and nourishes, and it thus stands psychologically for the foundations of consciousness' (Jung, 1934b, para. 344).

Jung's time riddle, 'a woman lives earlier as a mother, later as a daughter', implies the mother later lives on through, and in the daughter, in a process of projective identification. The unconscious experience of these ties produces the feeling that her life is spread out over generations – the first step towards the immediate experience and conviction of being outside time, which brings with it a feeling of immortality. An individual life is reduced to a type of pattern; indeed, it becomes the archetype of a woman's fate in general. This view suggests that a woman's relationship to mother is crucial to the development of a maternal self.

In 'The Psychological Aspects of the Mother Archetype' (Jung, 1954a) Jung amplifies the bipolar aspects of the mother complex in a daughter as leading to either a 'hypertrophy of the feminine side or its atrophy'. The former leading to the maternal instinct while the 'negative aspect' manifests in a woman is described by Jung as having one goal only – childbirth (ibid., para. 167). This begins to suggest an unconscious use of the body to compensate for maternal failure that Jung (1972, p. 115) found in conjunction with an infantilized role for the husband, who held 'secondary importance; he is first and foremost the instrument of procreation, and she regards him as an object to be looked after'. Jung finds the daughter of such a mother and father to substitute a dominant maternal instinct with an over development of Eros. The problem with this type of daughter is that she 'knows what she does not want but is completely at sea as to what she would choose as her fate' (ibid., p. 119). Demeter stands in for the possessive mother who stands in the way of daughter's separation from her by way of other unions and procreation. In her clinical practice, Pines noted that in women who were fertility challenged, 'they sustain a deep narcissistic wound and regress to a basic body image and state of mind in which they feel unsatisfied by their sexual partners and unsatisfactory to them, as they had once felt to their mothers' (Pines 1993, p. 183). Mother's role as a controlling and withholding *force majeure* produces adult daughters who did not yet have permission from their mothers to bear their own babies. Pines links the repeated desperate attempts at fertilization, despite earlier failures, to an envy of their own mother, pushing them to continue to attain their ego ideal of a maternal self. Samuels (1989, p. 77–78) observed that the double bind many women find themselves in, feeling a 'sense of failure at fulfilling neither the ancient nor the modern womanly ideal... heavily [colours] the woman's images of femininity and gender identity ... [since] Motherhood is absolutely equated with womanhood.' In modern culture 'mother' is often a signifier of the repressed, in part because many archetypal aspects of the feminine Self 'come to life' at midlife as part of individuation. At that stage of life, a baby becomes a living symbol of an emerging new identity, with the promise of futurity.

As Kradin remarks, 'some myths foster the child's optimal separation from parental influence, and others tend to hinder development.' The difference between optimal versus hindrance is what creates intra-family myths with far reaching consequences. The child's ability to mature through unconscious archetypal transference of feeling (projection) onto the parents, allowed or denied, sets the course for future relationships. The process of individuation must include the ability to form and maintain relationships, secure stable work and create a family of her own in adulthood, or remain puerile in support of parental immortality (Kradin, 2009, p. 217).

Learning to find an individuated maternal self could include consciously doing the opposite of everything mother did or did not do for the woman when she was a child. It is possible and remains to be shown whether procreative identity and the desire to feel fecund is postponed until a gravitational pull toward an 'other' allows/inspires a process of un-doing, un-learning to re-invent partnering and parenting roles. Maternal deprivation, disappointment, even cumulative trauma, appears to fuel each woman's experience of delayed motherhood. When the past re-emerges in the present as a shadow desire to be a better mother it appears as a struggle through positions of ambivalence, subjectivity and preoccupation. The birth of a new way by not being like mother begins to appear on the horizon of this book as a super-ordinate theme.

In summation, I am putting forward the hypothesis that delayed motherhood is not solely a product of biotechnology or 'career narcissism' but a larger longitudinal force passed on from mother to daughter to do with cumulative trauma (Khan, 1981, pp. 42–58), through breaches in the 'protective shield' between primary caregiver (mother) and daughter (child) (Khan, 1981, p. 47) preparing the ground for 'ego distortion and disturbance of psychosexual development ...[depending on] what type of failure of environmental provisions' (Ibid.) were present or absent. In wider cultural and collective considerations this primordial relationship prepares or detracts from the ability to function in the struggle with 'indigenous' cultural assumptions about the female body being ordained for motherhood aroused by an aspect of the feminine, identified by Jung (1972, p. 24) as resistance; the woman who wants to be 'anything but like mother'. This possibility is explored throughout the remainder of this book.

## References

Barone-Chapman, M. (2007). 'The hunger to fill an empty space. An investigation of primordial affects and meaning-making in the drive to conceive through repeated use of ART', *Journal of Analytical Psychology*, 52(4) pp. 389–541.
Belenky, M.F., Clinchy, B.M., Goldberger, N.R. and Tarule, J.M. (1986). *Women's Ways of Knowing: The Development of Self, Voice, and Mind*. New York: Basic Books.
Bly, R. (1996). *The Sibling Society: An Impassioned Call For The Rediscovery of Adulthood*. New York: Vintage Books.
Chodorow, J. ([1978]1999). *The Reproduction of Mothering*. Berkeley; Los Angeles, CA and London: University of California Press.
Erikson, E. (1950). *Childhood and Society*. New York: Norton & Co.
Erikson, E. (1968). *Identity: Youth and Crisis*. New York: Norton & Co.
Eurich-Rascoe, B.L. and Van de Kemp, H. (1997). *Femininity and Shame: Women, Men, and Giving Voice to the Feminine*. Lanham, MD: University Press of America.
Ford, G. (1999). *The Contented Little Baby Book*. London: Vermilion.
Friday, N. (1977). *My Mother, Myself*. New York: Dell.
Jacobi, J. (1974). 'Complex/Archetype/Symbol'. In *The Psychology of C.G. Jung*. New York: Bollingen Foundation Inc., Princeton University Press.
Jung, C.G. (1904–1906). 'The Association of Normal Subjects', C.G. Jung and F. Riklin. In *Collected Works, Vol. 2. Experimental Researches* (2nd edn). London: Routledge & Kegan Paul, 1992.
Jung, C.G. (1904–1909). 'Studies in Word Association'. In *Collected Works, Vol. 2. Experimental Researches* (2nd edn). London: Routledge & Kegan Paul, 1992.
Jung, C.G. (1911–12/1952c). 'The Dual Mother'. In *Collected Works, Vol. 5. Symbols of Transformation* (2nd edn). London: Routledge & Kegan Paul, 1995.
Jung, C.G., (1931). 'The Problems of Modern Psychotherapy'. In *Collected Works, Vol.16. The Practice of Psychotherapy* (2nd edn). London: Routledge & Kegan Paul, 1991.
Jung, C.G. (1933). 'The Meaning of Psychology for Modern Man'. In *Collected Works, Vol. 10. Civilization in Transition* (2nd edn). London: Routledge & Kegan Paul, 1991.
Jung, C.G. (1934a). 'A Review of the Complex Theory'. In *Collected Works, Vol. 8. The Structure and Dynamics of the Psyche* (2nd edn). London: Routledge & Kegan Paul, 1991.
Jung, C.G. (1934b). 'The Practical Use of Dream Analysis'. In *Collected Works, Vol. 16. The Practice of Psychotherapy* (2nd edn). London: Routledge & Kegan Paul, 1993.
Jung, C.G. (1937b). 'The Lapis-Christ Parallel'. In *Collected Works, Vol. 12. Psychology and Alchemy* (2nd edn). London: Routledge, 1992.
Jung, C.G. (1941). 'The Psychological Aspects of the Kore'. In *Collected Works, Vol. 9i. The Archetypes and the Collective Unconscious* (2nd edn), London: Routledge & Kegan Paul, 1990.
Jung, C.G. (1954a). 'Psychological Aspects of the Mother Archetype'. In *Collected Works, Vol. 9i. The Archetypes and the Collective Unconscious* (2nd edn). London: Routledge & Kegan Paul, 1990.

Jung, C.G. (1972). *Four Archetypes: Mother, Rebirth, Spirit, Trickster*. London: Routledge & Kegan Paul.
Kay, J. (2011). *Obliquity: Why Our Goals Are Best Achieved Indirectly*. London: Profile Books.
Khan, M.M.R. (1981). *The Privacy of the Self: Papers on Psychoanalytic Theory and Technique*. London: The Hogarth Press and The Institute of Psycho-Analysis.
Kradin, R. (2009). 'The family myth: its deconstruction and replacement with a balanced humanized narrative', *Journal of Analytical Psychology*, 54(2), pp. 217–232.
Lambert, K. (1981). *Analysis, Repair and Individuation*. London: Karnac.
Mathers, D. (2001). *An Introduction to Meaning and Purpose in Analytical Psychology*. London: Routledge.
McAdams, D.P. (1993). *The Stories We Live: Personal Myths and the Making of the Self*. New York: The Guilford Press.
Miller, J.B. (1976). *Toward a New Psychology of Women*. Boston, MA: Beacon Press.
Neumann, E. (1954). *The Origins and History of Consciousness*. London: Maresfield Library.
Parker, R. (2005). *Torn in Two: The Experience of Maternal Ambivalence*. London: Virago.
Pines, D. (1993). *A Woman's Unconscious Use of Her Body*. New Haven, CT: Yale University Press.
Redfearn, J. (1985). *My Self, My Many Selves*. London: Karnac.
Rutsky, R.L. (1999). *High Technē: Art and Technology from the Machine Aesthetic to the Posthuman*. Minneapolis, MN: University of Minnesota Press.
Samuels, A. (1989). *The Plural Psyche: Personality, Morality and the Father*. London: Routledge.
Zepf, S. (2007). 'The relationship between the unconscious and conscious – a comparison of psychoanalysis and historical materialism', *Psychoanalysis, Culture and Society*, 12(2), pp. 105–123.

## Further Reading

Gilligan, C. ([1982]1993). 'Introduction. Letter to Readers, 1993'. In C. Gilligan, *In a Different Voice: Psychological Theory and Women's Development*. Cambridge, MA: Harvard University Press, pp. ix–xvii.
Jung, C.G. (1928b). 'The Psychological Foundations of Belief in Spirits'. In *Collected Works, Vol. 8. The Structure and Dynamic of the Psyche* (2nd edn). London: Routledge & Kegan Paul, 1991.

# 6
# MEETINGS WITH THE UNCONSCIOUS

I frame the term 'trauma' in this chapter in a particular psychoanalytic fashion, crediting Donald Kalsched (1996, p. 1) for drawing on many authors in order to understand 'any experience that causes the child unbearable psychic pain or anxiety. For an experience to be "unbearable" means that it overwhelms the usual defensive measures which Freud (1920b, p. 27) described as a "protective shield against stimuli."' Trauma of this magnitude varies from the acute experiences of child abuse prominent in current literature, to the more 'cumulative traumas' of unmet dependency needs that mount up with devastating effect on some children's development (Khan, 1963), including the more acute deprivations of infancy described by Winnicott as 'primitive agonies', the experience of which is 'unthinkable' (Winnicott, 1974). The distinguishing feature of such trauma is what Heinz Kohut (1977, p. 104) called '"*disintegration anxiety*" an unnameable dread associated with the threatened dissolution of a coherent self' (Kalsched, 1996, p. 1). To this anxiety we may add the fear of being abandoned, unloved, or not kept in mind as a child, perceiving it hasn't performed to parental requirements to make the parent 'look good' to others. Psychoanalysis uses the term *cathect* to describe the hijacking of good things from the child (or any other) for narcissistic aim and ambition.

Jung saw the collective unconscious as a part of psyche, formed through inherited 'collective representations', a term he borrowed from Levy-Bruhl originally defined by Huber and Mauss on the subject of comparative religion (Jung, 1938, paras 88–90). Jung claimed these representations to be a 'second psychic system' (Jung, 1938, para. 90) pre-existing within everyone to synthesize conscious and unconscious elements. But it is the archetype of the child that 'paves the way for a future change of personality' (Jung, 1940, para. 278), placing it within the individuation process as a synthesizing of conscious and unconscious elements. In the Middle Ages an identification with the complex went by another term – possession (Jung, 1934a, para.

204). Jung pays considerable attention to the 'unpleasant' nature of a complex, though they are 'ubiquitous', they are not something to 'be met in the street and in public places' (Jung, 1934a, para. 209). Possession (Huskinson, 2015) of the ego by such an autonomous complex was considered crucial to maintaining mental health (Jung, 1931c, para. 925; p. 98) if the ego is capable of experiencing the possession without identifying with the unconscious.

A complex is identified through the structure of thought, language, affects, body responses, dreams, and in very serious cases, decompensating hysterical symptoms. Complexes do not exist in the mind, body or unconscious, but in the totality of psyche where observed phenomena functions like Trickster. A feature of delayed motherhood, when considered through the lens of early trauma, is how the psyche splinters to safeguard against developmental events and inter-penetrative exchanges that could signal further disappointment. With the help of the Trickster archetype, the traumatized child within the adult will go to great lengths to obscure attention to inter-subjectivity, repetitive patterns, highly charged affects – including time collapsing and lengthening. The meaning and purpose of enactments, as we will see in some of the cases, comprises not hearing/not remembering, transference and counter-transference phenomena that has been dissociated, but also unconsciously asking to be met within a humanizing relationship; 'see me, feel me, touch me' with understanding. When a complex is strong, the ego experiences little freedom to choose wisely. The necessary ambivalent creative processes of Trickster include normative thieving ways, pointing the way toward the irrational third or transcendent function to create the new. Although he may be the master of double-binding manipulation and paradox (Beebe, 1981), in alchemical considerations, Trickster is also the midwife and bearer of redemptive unifying symbols, foreshadowing the new king of consciousness, also known as a new idea. Jung's writing suggested women had, prior to the approach to the fourth decade, an 'unused supply of masculinity' that needed to become 'active' (Jung, 1930–1931, para. 782). In my observation, many of the women entering a *pregnant pause* (Barone-Chapman, 2011) at midlife have been engaging with the masculine at the expense of the feminine, and so the recapitulation required may be different than it is with women who have not delayed motherhood. 'What is the biological purpose of the archetype?' (Jung, 1940, para. 272). The question comes alive around explorations of the *pregnant pause*, in considering "the pre-conscious, childhood aspect of the collective psyche" (ibid., para. 273) with strong implications about futurity, one's own generativity and that of the human race. How will social media, movements and marches prepare the way for future generations to live and work beyond gender bias?

## Jung's Word Association Experiment

The Word Association Experiment (WAE) (Jung, 1904–1906) brought Carl Jung to the attention of Sigmund Freud who declared the method proof of the unconscious. Through the use of the WAE (Jung, 1904–1909; Meier, 1984) Jung found the basis upon which unconscious complexes could be identified as split-off psychic fragments existing semi-autonomously. As a psychological instrument the WAE bypasses rationale consciousness to more genuinely reflect what happens between two people engaged in dialogue, rather than an interview with questions and answers formed in sentences (Jung, 1934a).

Over 100 years later, Carl Jung's Word Association 'method' has continued to be considered into the 21st century on diverse research topics such as cognitive processes in implicit learning (Shin, Lee, Han and Rhi, 2005); re-examination of complexes forming outside of biographic conditions (Petchkovsky, et al., 2013); and measurement of changes in patient's initial complex set up in psycho-therapeutic work (Vezzoli, Gressi, Tricarlco, and Boato, 2007); and Jung's work on word association in relation to psychological approaches with application to schizophrenia (Silverstein, 2014).

The WAE consists of 100 words, many as short or two-letter form to which a participant makes an association while the time taken to make the association is measured by a stopwatch within a tenth of a second. The organization of the 100 words is segmented as the first 50, and the second 50, while the median time is determined within each group in order to gauge a measure of response for each segment overall.

The procedure of eliciting associations to the 100 words is conducted in two rounds. The first round established the associated word. The second round measures whether there has been a successful recall of the first associated word and over what length of time, above the median. Other complex indicators such as stereotypes, false reproductions, problems of hearing, comments made, are also noted as well as whether the participant tired over time. Results from the test are primarily the reaction disturbances spontaneously revealed through the lapse in timed responses to a word. More on this is amplified below.

The 100 words originally chosen by Jung were changed from their original German into English. The translations were taken from Vol. 2 of Jung's *Collected Works* (Jung, 1904–1906, para. 440) translated by Leopold Stein in collaboration with Diana Riviere, which Jung would have approved prior to publication. In preparing the list of 100 words for a worksheet to be read aloud during the WAE, an anomaly occurred. I repeated two versions of the emotion 'fear'. On one line I had the word 'fear' and further along its corollary, 'to fear'. This was not totally down to human error, but my own unconscious fear that I might not be able to get the co-ordination right between the left hand to mark the time while the right hand was starting and stopping the stopwatch purchased for this purpose. My own fear about getting this procedure right in advance of conducting the WAE, interfered with my accuracy in listing the words correctly, and could have been picked up later by the participants as their fear, to create a double helix of fear. This anomaly demonstrates both the significance of unconscious processes in the production of test results and the inter-subjective realm between self and other.

Running the Word Association Experiment was done twice with a 20-minute break between the first 100 words and the repeat of the 100 words. In some uses of the WAE the break can be an hour, a few days, or a week. I chose 20 minutes based on participant's time availability for this research. In the first round with the 100 words, the researcher asks for the first word that comes to mind, without reflection, noting the response and any non-verbal reactions. Reaction time is measured by starting the watch the moment after speaking the stimulus word. If the person starts to answer, and the researcher stops the watch, but the person starts again, the researcher doesn't change the watch time, but notes the additional factors. The WAE involves registering responses and timing reactions to these 100 words, pausing for a period of time, in this case 20 minutes, and repeating the 100 words to measure accuracy of memory and the presence of complexes again. From these second measurements of time and other reactions, the time is translated into fifths to find the median number of words where there are as many response times above as below the median. The median is calculated separately for words 1–50 and 51–100, and scores for each word were also calculated into fifths. Reactions are measured in terms of the time it takes to respond to a word and whether the associated word is accessed in the second round of 100 words accurately. More than .03 seconds to respond to a word is indicative of more 'complex' activity one could imagine as a 'larger file of information' that must be looked at thoroughly before a participant can clearly access an association

The WAE is a highly sensitive instrument for revealing unconscious thoughts and feelings, or 'complex indicators'. These are referred to as 'reaction disturbances' and most obviously may take the form of large gaps of time around some words but not others. There is also misunderstanding of words, falsification of memory, stumbling over words, changing the answer, playing with meaning, contrariness and responses that are meant to be rhymes or opposites, such as 'white' responding to 'black', which may reveal another kind of defence of the self (Kalsched, 1996, p. 41–42). Each are recorded as a complex indicator. These indicators include:

- Prolonged reaction-time
- Failure to respond
- Failure to reproduce/incorrect reproduction
- Perseverations
- Multiple reaction words
- Repetition of stimulus word
- Repetition of earlier responses
- Unusual use of words/foreign words
- Alliterative effects ('klang' associations)
- Slips of tongue
- Not hearing stimulus word correctly
- Movements, gestures, tremors
- Disrupted breathing patterns
- Vocalizations: exclamations, laughter, stammering, etc.

## Analysis of WAE Results

One aspect of the method of analysing and scoring the WAE includes looking for clusters of high reaction times and the perseveration of disturbance over several responses, to see how complexes wax and wane throughout the association method, and plotting them out graphically, if necessary, to illustrate how the words are activating a complex. At core, the WAE uses measurements of time to identify complexes. When a complex is activated by a word, associations to that word will take longer the more affect-laden memories are attached to it. In studies where this methodology has been used, the reaction time can range as much as 60 seconds. Compared to the years of repressing (disassociating from) a desire to procreate, time is relative to the degree of unconscious processes working within the personal, cultural or collective complex. When an affect-laden complex kicks in, time changes. Psychological affective reality replaces chronological time. Immediate requirements are overlooked, forgotten or deemed to be part of a dissociated state. Activities take longer. Though the personal and collective unconscious is not easily differentiated (Huskinson, 2010, p. 82), the phenomena of culture, operating at the personal level is the lens through which a changing relationship to motherhood is investigated here. Without inclusion of time against the identified median, identification of a complex is without tangible evidence other than with affect. Affects alone are not complexes, unless the affects observed may be said to form a pattern referred to as perseveration, because they persevere over the course of time within the WAE.

As a psychological instrument, the WAE bypasses the rational conscious mind to more genuinely reflect what happens between two engaged in dialogue, rather than an interview with questions and answers formed in sentences (Jung, 1904-1906). Jung suspected it would be possible to view a complex by identifying how speech patterns were altered, affected, by unconscious disturbance. Through the Word Association Experiment (Jung, 1904–1909; Meier, 1984) Jung found the basis upon which unconscious complexes were originally identified as split-off psychic fragments existing semi-autonomously. When a complex is activated it releases highly charged feeling toned affects. The term constellated is often used to describe how 'an outward situation releases a psychic process in which certain contents gather together and prepare for action' (Jung, 1918, para. 198). When this happens, the ego is no longer in control of consciousness or the body. Complexes are products of all types of positive and negative experiences in the personal realm, to do with family, school playgrounds, play groups, as well as emanating from cultural conditioning that comes from the total of all the messages from the collective on these experiences. Stein (1998, p. 49) views complexes as 'what remain in the psyche after it has digested experience and reconstructed it into inner objects.

The results that follow are based on Jung's (1904–1909; 1918) Word Association Experiment (WAE), and dream journals kept before and after participants undertook the WAE. Affects included enactments, such as participants showing up late or forgetting their appointment to participate. This demonstrates the large affective field around the WAE.

## Ms A WAE Results

Fifteen months after meeting Ms A for the first time, she came back a third time, not to say what she could not say in the first interview meeting, but to undertake the WAE and demonstrate she was fully pregnant at almost 52 years of age. Overall, Ms A

72  Meetings With The Unconscious

| Time 1 | Time 2 | Stereotypes | False Repro. | Disconnect | Repeated | No. CI |
|--------|--------|-------------|--------------|------------|----------|--------|
| 20 | 25 | 19 | 31 | 5 | 16 | 138 |

**FIGURE 6.1** Ms A and Jung's Word Association Experiment

delivered very fast responses, appearing to tire a lot in the second half of the test, explainable due to her pregnancy, which may account for so many false reproductions (errors). Ms A had a total of 138 complex indicators, the second highest of all six WAE participants, indicating someone who was in her own world at that point in time, slightly dissociated from reality.

The totality of the WAE appeared as a feeling struggle for Ms A to pay attention to her reactions and associations. In Part 1 of the test she had 20 Complex Indicators (CI) and 11 False Reproductions (FR), which together with Part 2 came to 31, suggesting some tiring over time. Even though the majority of her time reactions stayed close the median of 7, just above or below, it may be fair to say she was fighting to keep her feeling states from taking over. Looking over the numbers I had the feeling she was attempting to break a wild horse with concentrated, wilful speed and effort. Getting it 'right' rather than failing seemed to be the point. This made her association networks appear to be reverberating inside and outside of her. Again, this could be a function of pregnancy in full bloom at advanced age, but I sense the phenomena was part of her tenacity to prove she could hold on to want she wanted. I sensed she wanted to prove she had stamina, consistent with other quarrels to prove her worthiness for any endeavour she would choose. I wondered if presenting the persona of the bountiful mother at an advanced age was wearing her down. Ms A had some early childhood guilt around a biological malfunction that made further pregnancies impossible for her mother. Magical thinking allowed her to conflate mother's losses to her own miscarriages, which she felt responsible for, using the phrase, 'killing off my own pregnancies'.

| word | Response | 2nd word | Time | Fifths |
|------|----------|----------|------|--------|
| head | sore | ache | 1.23 | 6 |
| long | sore | stalk | 0.97 | 5 |
| to ask | for more | for more | 2.32 | 12 |
| to cook | badly | well | 1.69 | 8 |
| ink | well | well | 1.12 | 6 |
| angry | Yeah! | yes | 1.93 | 10 |
| to swim | Tommy | Tommy | 2.34 | 12 |
| journey | knapsack | rucksack | 3.49 | 17 |
| tree | climb | climb | 1.29 | 6 |
| pity | me | me | 1.62 | 8 |
| mountain | climb | climb | 1.12 | 6 |

**FIGURE 6.2** Early Perseveration Through Repetition

A pattern of repeated response words in the chart above (Figure 6.2), whether as responses to stimulus words or recalled words commenced with 'Sore', 'Well', and 'Climb' in Part 1 of the WAE. Taken in turn, 'Sore' was her response to the first stimulus word 'Head' and was later associated to her longstanding issues with mother which made her feel 'sore in the head'. The same word, 'Sore' was also the associated word a mere seven words later to the stimulus word 'Long' and was again associated to long standing issues with mother, followed by an incorrectly recalled word, 'Stalk'. The response word 'Well' came as the incorrect recall to the stimulus word 'To Cook', notably after her first association as 'Badly' indicating a desire to transform her doubt and poor view of herself. Quickly following were two more uses of 'Well' first as an association, and then as correct recall to the stimulus word 'Ink'. Ink in itself creates a stain no matter where it lands, but for Ms A it seems the stain landed in her, which I can only describe as 'the psyche' as a totality of mind, body, spirit, and soul. Immediately after the next stimulus word was 'Angry' to which she could only reply 'Yeah' and 'Yes' with great emphasis. 'Journey' comes shortly after the stimulus word 'Angry' to which she replied in the affirmative both times. Looking just above the word 'Angry' there is a cluster of responses all using the word 'well' and this word also appears as a response in the second half of the WAE. Given Ms A's biological relationship to 'killer cells' it appears the word 'Well' may have become a way of soothing herself that she does many things 'well' to take care of herself, including cooking and sleeping. But there is another kind of use of well, appearing as a stereotype in response to 'Ink', acting as a completion of the word, and in effect, a glib response to defend against feelings of never doing anything well, nor being well enough to procreate when she was ready to do it. In WAE terms the effect of an affect is what kicks off a complex and may be seen through perseverations within response times.

Her desire to be well enough so that she can have a family is evidenced in the repeated response and associated word 'Climb' which occurs twice as a correctly recalled word to her first associations. In the first instance she was responding to the stimulus word 'Tree' and in the second 'Mountain', both offering an indication of how large a task she feels she has undertaken. In between these two stimulus words there is a small cry to the stimulus word 'Pity' simply stated and correctly recalled with 'Me'. In Part 2, Ms A had 25 Complex Indicators (CI) and 20 False Reproductions (FR), again her response times were riding just above and below the median of 9. The higher median indicating she may have become a little tired as the test wore on, born out by twice as many significantly higher response times.

In the chart below (Figure 6.3), the first elevated response at 28 is to the stimulus word 'To fear' which Ms A associated to 'Waves' but was later incorrectly recalled with the second response of 'Lots'. These connections to being overwhelmed by the uphill 'Climb' to reach her goal of making a family that would repair the problems she had with mother do not do justice to her potency, drive and determination. The second elevated response at 33 to the stimulus word 'Door' is a reference to threshold experiences later associated to several IVF disappointments, which are masked by mundane associations of 'Clip' and the incorrectly recalled

74    Meetings With The Unconscious

| Word | Response | Second Word | Time | Fifths |
|---|---|---|---|---|
| Frog | Start | Money | 1.59 | 8 |
| to Part | Hair | Hair | 1.52 | 8 |
| Glass | Window | Fork | 1.62 | 8 |
| to Quarrel | Fiercely | Fiercely | 1.63 | 8 |
| to Fear | Waves | Lots | 5.71 | 28 |
| Door | Clip | Step | 6.52 | 33 |
| to Sleep | Well | Well | 2.16 | 11 |
| to Abuse | Fork | Fork | 1.95 | 10 |

FIGURE 6.3 Waves of Fears and Tears

word 'Step' which stand in for multiple shocks. These two very large blips are cushioned amongst response times that straddle the median slightly above and below, as we saw in Part 1 of the WAE. The narrative here begins with stimulus words 'Frog' and 'To Part', responded to with 'Start' and 'Hair', respectively. These act as catalysts, which take some time to implode. The first is an association to an inner fable, a wish to transform herself from a frog to a princess growing as a wish unfulfilled into the second association which brings up the bad memories of mother cutting her hair to make her look like a boy, one of many seemingly small traumas. There is a second story however in the second half of the WAE (when pregnant with the second baby) that has everything to with a second chance coming out of more seemingly small hopes, dreams, shocks and unbridled venom. I sense she is facing what is driving her to push herself to the limit. With the stimulus words and associations cited in the chart above, the complex really comes into bloom with 'Glass' and 'To Quarrel' two words that are connected to her fight with mother and her wish to abuse her for all the years of maternal deprivation and insinuation that Ms A was 'a killer' of babies because she left 'killer cells' in mother's womb. The incorrectly recalled 'Fork' is repeated again, this time correctly recalled to the stimulus word 'To Abuse' as a final response word.

'Fork' also had associations to 'needle'. She said she had hundreds of forks in her house because she likes feeding people. The fork image in her mind is related to a memory of watching a popular television programme called 'Midsomer Murders' where someone was killed with a pitchfork. She remembered linking this dramatic scene to what she would like to do to her mother. But to understand what kicked off the first response of fork, we need to go back to the stimulus word 'Glass' which she associated to a window breaking when the pitchfork was utilized in her association to a television drama, for us to understand her unconscious symbolic equation. Thinking about murderous rage toward mother reminded her she was not allowed to be angry and often had to think about stabbing food which later developed into a liking to cook. Aggression towards mother was also linked to mother having a second child, as she is now a mother expecting a second child. She remembered being three years old and mother breastfeeding her younger sister, but also giving her a sewing kit with real needles to play with. She recalls mother only started to hit her after her younger sister arrived. She said, 'Mother was unrepentant of how mean and uncaring she was to me'.

Though the word 'hair' had been repeated in one other place, I had the benefit of Phase I of the clinically informed Interpretive Phenomenological Analysis (IPA) interview to remind me of mother's need to cut Ms A's hair, wilfully, as if she was Delilah cutting down a potent Sampson-daughter because she was good at sport and drama. Haircuts became, throughout her life, associated to mother spoiling something good in Ms A as if to retaliate for having spoiled mother's womb. Taken together, the complex pattern from the WAE puts on display its own narrative between stimulus word and association, the former is the spark that lights up the latter. The corresponding *prosaic narrative interpretation* of what Ms A's perseverations were trying to convey in her WAE responses might be understood as this:

> My mother sat on my head and so my head is sore
> Whether I climb a tree or I climb mountain, always I want more.
> I ruined my mother's womb
> Here I am stuck I'm in her tomb.
> If I ask you for more will you pity me well
> If you ask me for more you'll send me to hell.
> Hear me well I part the waves with my hair
> I quarrel fiercely, should you dare.
> Don't clip my wings or shut the door
> I know what a fork is for.
> Be careful with your log,
> I wasn't meant to be a frog.
> Watch me step through fears and tears.

After the WAE, Ms A felt very tired. Her thoughts and feelings seemed to have torn her in two between the past and present. She kept associating back to a time when she had a lot of 'tower dreams' – dreams where tall buildings were significant. She wondered if she was more down to earth in her life now that she had a child with another on the way. She said she used to feel separate and removed from life. There was melancholy.

76  Meetings With The Unconscious

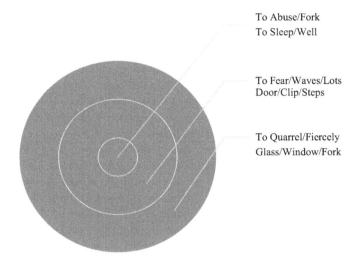

**FIGURE 6.4** Circumambulation of a Complex

Later, Ms A wanted to do further work on her rage at her mother, as seen in her WAE associations to the word 'fork', which included having a spiteful retaliatory response. Consistent with her earlier request for a second visit to pay me, the Trickster archetype continued to seek a therapeutic response from me as a way of getting me to help process her spiteful, retaliatory response to mother. Although I agreed to give her more time, I focused on opening up some emotional space to allow her to do the reflection work by herself. After the second baby came, Ms A sent me a birth announcement and let me know her mother was now more present in her life and she felt relaxed, even glad about it.

## Ms B WAE Results

Ms B was absent-minded about when we were doing the WAE and could not keep up with the thread of emails. Confirmation by me on the day before it was scheduled resulted in her finding her mobile mailbox full and unable to receive further messages.

When we spoke at 9:20 am on the morning of the WAE she asked, 'What did you want me to do with the dreams? I don't dream'. As it turned out she had written some things down from her dreams and asked if she could bring them. Dreams became confused in her mind, as did the day and time of meeting for the WAE. 'Does she or doesn't she dream, will she or won't she turn up?'. When I wrote this in my notebook, Ms B was already a half an hour late. I telephoned to see when she would be arriving and she apologized, 'I'm running late everywhere this morning'. I felt her anticipation of the WAE had already produced a large affective field.

In Figure 6.5 below, numbers recorded in fifths, under Time 1 and Time 2, represent the length time over the median for Ms B to find an association to the

| Time 1 | Time 2 | Stereotypes | False Repro. | Disconnect | Repeated | No. CI |
|---|---|---|---|---|---|---|
| 56 | 50 | 0 | 16 | 1 | 0 | 124 |

**FIGURE 6.5** Ms B and Jung's Word Association Experiment

stimulus word. The higher the number over the median, the longer the time it takes for a participant to work through the internal file of associated data to find the word that feels right. Ms B had the highest length of time among all participants to associate to stimulus words. In Part 1 of the test, Time 1 measured all responses over the median of 20. In Part 2 of the test, Time 2 measured all responses over the median of 13.

The lower number in Part 2, 'Time 2' of the WAE suggests that after some initial anxiety over attending and experiencing the WAE, Ms B was able to relax a bit more in the second half of the test. While it may have taken her longer to find the right, and later the correct word, she had one of the lowest numbers of falsely reproduced words at 16. The dissociated way she could not keep in mind the arrangements to do the test, aroused empathy in me as I saw her work extremely hard to show she could get things right, and this affect showed me that was the point of getting her answers 'right'. The WAE awakened the need: 'I want to put things right in my life'.

Thinking about my experience of Ms B eight years ago and then over the clinically informed Phase 1 interview, I can see how she would want to keep her mind ticking over to keep herself mentally fit for her son. Her life before attempting to conceive after the age of 38 was not successful until she was 47. The delay in part was due to her not wanting to quit her job and settle down. She was enjoying her freedom and her life. Another way of describing this turning point in her life could be stated as: Pride comes before a fall. This becomes most meaningful in the chart below when we consider her highest response time to a stimulus word took 22.85 seconds, which when translated into fifths takes on a value of 114 against a median of 20. The stimulus word attached to this recorded time was 'Pride' which she correctly reproduced as 'Feeling Good'. My sense is that Ms B struggled with feeling good about being in her fifties while her son is still so young, while her new friends at the school gates are working on the second and third baby. I sense Ms B remembered, with some melancholy, feeling good about herself, before she realized she was running out of time to make a child.

Once more there is a pattern that emerges with its own narrative between stimulus words and associations relating to each other. But in the case of Ms B, it is as if one is a problem and the other an empty space where the only solution is to submit to fate. There is no fight or hope left. The corresponding *Thanatos narrative interpretation* of what Ms B revealed consistently throughout the exploration, including clinically informed Interpretive Phenomenological Analysis (IPA), WAE and dream journals, might be understood in this way:

# 78 Meetings With The Unconscious

| Word | Response | Second Word | Time | Fifths |
|---|---|---|---|---|
| Death | Dying | Dying | 10.74 | 54 |
| Table | Desk | Desk | 13.25 | 66 |
| Pride | Feeling Good | Feeling Good | 22.85 | 114 |
| to Swim | Floating | Floating | 13.91 | 70 |
| to Sin | Wrong-doing | Faults | 18.86 | 94 |
| Rich | Wealthy | Poor | 16.85 | 84 |
| to Pray | Church | Church | 14.33 | 72 |
| to Fall | Drop | to Drop | 16.63 | 83 |

FIGURE 6.6 Narrative of Despair

Death would be easier than to feel myself slowly dying
a fate worse than death, forever crying.
We sit at the table as if colleagues at our desks.
When I'm with him, I only felt good doing burlesques.
Never did I suspect I was avoiding feeling sad
Never wanted to make my man a dad.
Busy swimming upstream I floated my own boat
When all were swimming down
I was fearing mother's frown.
Some days my sin, my faults haunt me still.
To have so much life, gives me a chill.
I fear the pain of having only one will make me fall
But mostly I drop into wanting to forget about it all.

The feeling in the first part of the WAE is consistent with her regret that she did not have children earlier. I sensed this had something to do with the chemistry between her and her partner being offset by a more potent relationship at work that made her feel worthy, possibly for the first time. Much of her melancholy for what could have been is also underpinned by a relationship with mother based on criticism and lack. Ms B was angry about this eight years ago when I first met her, but now has revealed the relationship with mother has mellowed as she now knows her grandson was made from egg donation. Ms B's relationship with mother has survived not only this revelation, but the years where her mother kept telling her she left everything too late, including how she potty-trained her son.

In the second half of the WAE (Figure 6.7), working with a median of 13, we find a considerable amount of words well over this benchmark, indicating a perseveration to get things absolutely correct to repeat an initial association. For this reason, I will be focusing my analysis of Part 2 in the WAE on those times recorded in fifths above the value 32, approximately three times the median, indicating Ms B may have begun to tire and stress over accessing the correct response. Of the 12 responses fitting this description, more than half of them contain correctly repeated associations. My process of analysing her most acute high numbers is to split them into two groups, one group of seven words correctly recalled and five that were not, to discover the meaning within the quarrel. Splitting, as a verb, is to divide, which I feel captures the problematic complex Ms B has been struggling with for most of her life.

In Figure 6.7, the stimulus word 'Child' commences a narrative sequence of feelings that bring to her consciousness a connection to the pressure she felt around her last attempt to become pregnant. The connection between stimulus word and associations provide a window in which she can separate from family and group, through a thin, narrow door before it is shut on her last chance to procreate. Her drive to be correct motivates her to work hard to get accuracy of recall, not realizing it took an increasing period of time to achieve the result, both in the WAE and in life. There was a slim chance of making a baby at 47, then suddenly the IVF took hold, and she was forced to close the door on a past identity she hadn't wanted to give up. As enthusiastic about her son as she now is, there was something she continued to avoid, namely, the future. Her son will grow up and he may want to go away to school, or live in a foreign country, and her daily life will not be as interesting as she was currently finding it. What would she be then? Motherhood began to appear as a valuable enriching identity.

| Word | Response | 2nd Word | Time | Fifths |
|---|---|---|---|---|
| Child | Baby | Baby | 6.37 | 32 |
| Glass | Window | Window | 8.39 | 42 |
| Part | Separate | Separate | 6.6 | 33 |
| Family | Group | Group | 9.7 | 48 |
| Narrow | Thin | Thin | 4.54 | 32 |
| Door | Shut | Shut | 14.62 | 73 |
| to Sleep | Snooze | Snooze | 10.2 | 51 |

**FIGURE 6.7** Correctly Recalled Words Above 32

| Word | Response | Second Word | Time | Fifths |
|---|---|---|---|---|
| to Pay Attention | Notice | Listen | 6.69 | 33 |
| to Paint | Artist | to Draw | 10.5 | 52 |
| Box | Chest | Case | 7.63 | 38 |
| Happiness | Good | Sad | 16.39 | 82 |
| to Abuse | to Hurt | to Hit | 1.89 | 9 |

FIGURE 6.8 Incorrectly Recalled Words Above 32

Examining Ms B's responses where the associated word (Response) is not correctly repeated (Second Word) the argument begins to reveal itself. The perspective of the omnipotent speaker shifts between articles of speech. The stimulus word 'to Pay Attention' was associated to the noun 'Notice' as in something to observe and later shifts to 'Listen', a verb with more personal connotation, as there is a 'doer'. The same pattern continues with the stimulus word 'to Paint' associated to the noun 'Artist' that later becomes 'to Draw' something she might wish to do.

The stimulus word 'Box' is a container that becomes a piece of furniture with 'Chest' and later transforms into 'Case' which may be read as spectacle case, jewellery case; a 'case' for a study, research, or medical record. The move from 'Chest' to 'Case' is therefore another attempt to imprint the impersonal with the personal. This perseveration of elevated responses peaks at 82 when Ms B responds to 'Happiness' as 'Good' but later brings her own personal feeling to the fore with the incorrect reply of 'Sad'. I wish to complete this part of the analysis on the stimulus word 'to Abuse' because although it was incorrectly repeated, as were the other four words in the Incorrectly Recalled set, it dropped well under the median suggesting that Ms B had easy access to the memory of being 'Hurt' and 'Hit' by mother when she was quite little, especially after a second baby came along. Ms B's acute sadness at not being able to make a second baby, like mother, her siblings and school gate friends, denies Ms B's access to the feeling she has a family, and not just one child. A second baby would be a second chance to repair, perhaps to find 'Happiness'.

After we had explored her experience of the WAE she said, 'It was all good, once I got over the right–wrong answer bit'. Perhaps her uptake could also be applied to the non-WAE aspects of life, to achieve the same feeling she regularly exuded, 'it's all good'.

## Ms D and Jung's Word Association Experiment

The WAE inspired three rescheduled appointments before Ms D could work up the courage to come back in to do this phase of the research. Her 'reasons' for cancelling were always masked behind a disorganized persona to do with scheduling that made her sound like a hyper-ventilating new mother rather than the highly managerial mother she had become. One cancellation came about two hours before we were due to meet. Each excuse felt like an important message of her ongoing affective communications, felt as: '*I am afraid to face something, afraid of how you might make me feel about myself*'. Each time I checked with her to see if she really wanted to do the WAE and each time her response was grateful that I would agree to re-schedule to another time.

Among the participants Ms D had the highest number of Complex Indicators, 155, as seen in the above table. The number is made up of a total of Stereotypes, False Reproduction of associated response words (errors), and Disconnection within associations and recalled responses to a stimulus word. The high/low numbers indicate an up and down pattern of how the perseveration of a complex continues over several words. The number of times a Repeated Word was used in the context of associations and responses is also recorded as part of a persevering pattern.

| *Time 1* | *Time 2* | *Stereotypes* | *False Repro.* | *Disconnect* | *Repeated* | *No. CI* |
|---|---|---|---|---|---|---|
| 33 | 25 | 22 | 41 | 0 | 8 | 155 |

**FIGURE 6.9** Ms D and Jung's Word Association Experiment

In the first half of the WAE, high response times, recorded in fifths, provide an at-a-glance picture of what is on her mind: money, stupidity (pride), cross (angry) parents, wallet (money) and money again (expensive), in parenthesis are the stimulus words. The highest numbers, or longest response times are to the words: 'Money', 'Stupid' and 'Pride', recorded at 36, 35 and 34 in descending order respectively.

Under these highest numbers there was another layer of high response values in fifths between 15 and 20. Starting high at 20 with the stimulus word 'to Die' Ms. D responds in opposition with 'to Live' but moves to the feeling of 'Sadness' incorrectly recalled, most likely as a felt response to the loss of her father just before her fourth successful IVF attempt. At lower response times, my eye had to become more discerning for the feeling of what had happened since I last saw her eight years prior while she was pregnant. 'Water', with a response of 18 to associate 'Drink' and 'Cup' was a blanked association. The problem with 'money' commences with the stimulus word 'to Pay' at a mere 8 but the complex kicked off with the previous word, 'Ship', begins to reveal the perseveration of a complex with the incorrectly recalled word 'Wreck'. Along this 'under feeling' there are associations to the word 'Angry' of 'Parents' and then incorrectly recalled as 'Cross'. This response comes soon after the second response of 'Stupid'. Near the end of Part 1, two words after 'Expensive' and matching responses of 'Money', Ms D associated 'to Fall' with 'Land' and later incorrectly recalls her earlier association as '"Hurt'.

In Figure 6.10 we see three affective layers of Ms D's process seeking to organize the depth of a shocking event felt as a trauma with the feelings that underpin it. I suspect this event has links to an earlier trauma, such as her difficulty to conceive, and both are connected to social standing. She hadn't realized she had to remember her first responses until later in the second round, but rather than lowering her number of false reproductions it increased them by three. Afterward, Ms D (who I realized had a daimon within, bursting to come forward) said she 'quite enjoyed' taking the WAE. A nervous type with a highly-strung disposition, Ms D's complexes performed a camouflage function under a veil of goodness and caring, secretly seething behind the structures of marriage, friends and family, as the most important things in her life. The only associations she was able to discuss were 'to Part' as in saying good-bye, 'Money' as it has been a big issue in her marriage, and 'Stupid' as to how she evaluated the marriage on their handling of money issues. 'Pride' brought her back to feeling stupid, another self-attack rather than a clean association. Ms D tended to blunt her thinking. Were we able to imagine Ms D as capable of making a relationship with her complexes at some point, perhaps later in her life, a *confessional narrative* could emerge, as I saw with other participants, that would have helped her to forge an empathic relationship with herself, allowing for agape, 'a combination of Eros, humane feeling and respect … cognizant of the shadow … as a function of the self' (Lambert, 1973, p. 20) that can arise when the

| Word | Response | Second Word | Time | Fifths |
|---|---|---|---|---|
| Ship | Water – Sea | Wreck | 2.33 | 12 |
| to Pay | Money | Money | 1.64 | 8 |
| Pride | Lion | Stupid | 6.73 | 34 |
| Angry | Parents | Cross | 3.04 | 15 |
| Rich | Poor | Poor | 1.29 | 16 |
| to Die | to Live | Sadness | 4 | 20 |
| Money | Coins | Wallet | 7.3 | 36 |
| Stupid | Spaniel | Dog | 6.93 | 35 |
| Expensive | Money | Money | 3.08 | 15 |
| to Fall | Land | Hurt | 2.42 | 12 |

**FIGURE 6.10** Trilateral Affects

other takes their life down a brave turn in the interest of individuation. Ms D's poetic naming of the problem might have then read like this:

> My mother did everything for me, to keep me in her mind.
> So it never occurred to me my mind was something I could find.
> I wanted to be a woman of substance,
> but it instead I am the life of the party.
> My husband's work almost went into the pan,
> And still I remained his number one fan.
> I never felt so humbled in my life.
> Except when I didn't want to be just a wife.
> I need to feel loved … it's true.
> Not by my daughter; she's makes me blue.
> But I am delighted by my son, he is such fun.
> I really do want to stay mother's pet and my husband's lover.
> I think the Oedipal thing is so over …

The word 'Pride' held one of her highest recorded response values. There was an outburst regarding discussion to her association with having 'pride', something she thinks she's been guilty of. This appeared to be her way of saying she could be stupid. I wondered if Ms D didn't like to think, as she seemed to blunt the need for the function, preferring to denigrate our process of exploration. Ms D took issue with any suggestion she avoided thinking, telling me she found it quite disturbing the last time she came to see me. It seemed what Ms D was blocking is not thinking but allowing herself to feel for herself.

> I really don't like spending too much time thinking about things. This is the way I've chosen to live my life … it just worried me about how dangerous it could become to over analyse things. If you have a busy enough and full enough life it could be dangerous.

Ms D thought having children changed a woman, especially by turning away from work toward family, but she maintained the need to find the right balance. She hasn't had to work for financial need and further felt lucky that she can do decorating work around the children.

Pride as a core complex pervaded the establishment of a 'couple' identity as a team she and her husband had worked through with great difficulties. Pride in how she has made a family unit work and that they are lucky, against very strong feelings that she is not good enough, smart enough, or anything like her mother, who she presents as the perfect nurturing 'Great Mother'. This is where pride hides. She wants to be as smart and good as her mother. The manufacture of good things in her life via marriage to a husband who had been able to create comforts, enabled her to overcome the inferiority of not being among the educated and cultural elite by putting emphasis on humanistic qualities. The affect these defences had on my interest in her 'delayed motherhood' since my first encounter with her in 2003, mirrored her own disappointment. Ms D correctly saw agape in my face during the Phase 1 interview but read my surprise regarding her *complexio oppositorum* paradigm shift incorrectly as criticism. In time however, I saw how she hid behind petulant sensitivity as the only way she knew how to get mother or husband to pay her attention. In between the lines, I could sense she could wear them down to a point of empathy to be in control. I felt shame was present for Ms D. She was used to mother letting her down easily and soothing her troubled brow. She did not have to feel more than defence. The veracity of her feelings, however, was shrouded in defiance and rebellion. She could not find the words for feelings she could only display in a highly-strung sort of way in order to dominate rather than join. I wondered how this difficulty with pairing/joining paralleled how she managed her mother, and vice versa, and how her daughter learned to mimic her demand for dominance. Hence in Figure 6.7, Trilateral Affects, the dimension of 'Angry' activated a parental role that often made her feel cross; she felt her daughter was controlling her, and it was mirrored in the way she tried to control me, as a repetition compulsion. Quite possibly her daughter's need of her was an attack on her narcissism. This may be one of the crucial developmental variants between women having children around 30 years of age and women having children after 40. Few women feel they've achieved much in the world before 30. Ms D was the youngest of the participants who believed she had delayed motherhood when she compared herself to contemporaries. However, the delay lurking in the shadows was Ms D's rage at finding she could not garner respect by mimicking mother's maternal preoccupation. Creating her own modern version of maternal subjectivity suited her better.

For all participating WAE women, the dream journal was a large part of their awakening to how they began to re-narrate their experiences. In Ms D's case, her dreams paralleled her conscious disappointment of unrequited love. By the end of the protracted dream work, two new thought feeling forms came into her awareness. 1. She got the life she wanted; 2. No longer did she want to be in control all the time. The WAE had stirred things up somewhat, but it was the creativity she found in her dreams after the WAE that brought her the possibility of more coherence.

## Further Implications

The common complex linking these women is the negative mother complex, which played Trickster games in their lives as a trauma most often seen through the death or absence of a father, literally or symbolically, to give rise to a male sibling with pride of place. What kept coming up as both privation and deprivation across affective behaviour and narratives within the life stories of the eight participants was the difference in the way girls and boys were raised as siblings, through parental expectations and in education, reflecting culture on gender. The memory of a male sibling enjoying primacy of place in the parental home over the daughter was acute and clear. The inability to feel valued by the masculine became encapsulated trauma seemingly against the feminine when they re-experienced fertility loss. While the archetype of the Trickster played with their emotions, reality and ability to believe in themselves, the galvanizing transformative dimension of their lives varied according to the way in which they sought recovery.

My sense with all the women who participated was the present absence of the male partner in relation to how internalized pressure around being late to motherhood affected their relationships. The women felt alone and isolated with their feelings of having to remedy their isolation, first by trying to make something of themselves in the world of work, or by making something close to meaning in the way they wanted to claim achievement as a mother. Many of the participants communicated as if they hadn't quite recovered from all the time they had lost, even when they achieved what they wanted, it wasn't expressed as if it was enough, there was always something more that was missing. I sensed the something more was that many of them had critical mothers and never felt fully received by them except for one participant who felt she was late to motherhood in her early 30s (Ms D), but was in fact in process of reconciling herself to not being perfect, like mother. Therefore, the loneliness they all felt in relationship to their mother was often a transference phenomenon in their partnership to the father of their children. In the next chapter, this will become more evident as we examine the super-ordinate themes across the representative three cases.

## References

Barone-Chapman, M. (2011). 'Pregnant Pause: Procreative Desire, Reproductive Technology and Narrative Shifts at Midlife'. In R. Jones (ed.), *Body, Mind and Healing After Jung: A Space of Questions*. London and New York: Routledge.

Beebe, J. (1981). 'The trickster in the arts', *The San Francisco Jung Institute Library Journal*, 2(2), pp. 21–54.

Freud, S. (1920b). 'Beyond the Pleasure Principle'. In J. Strachey et al. (eds), *The Complete Works of Sigmund Freud*, S.E. 21. London: The Hogarth Press and the Institute of Psychoanalysis, 1953–1974.

Huskinson, L. (2010). 'Analytical Psychology and Spirit Possession: Towards a Non-pathological Diagnosis of Spirit Possession'. In L.A. Huskinson and B.E. Schmidt, *Spirit Possession and Trance: New Interdisciplinary Perspectives*, London:Continuum, pp.71–96.

Jung, C.G. (1904–1906). 'The Association of Normal Subjects', C.G. Jung and F. Riklin. In *Collected Works, Vol. 2. Experimental Researches* (2nd edn). London: Routledge & Kegan Paul, 1992.

Jung, C.G. (1904–1909). 'Studies in Word Association'. In *Collected Works, Vol. 2. Experimental Researches* (2nd edn). London: Routledge & Kegan Paul, 1992.

Jung, C.G. (1918). *Studies in Word Association* (trans. M.D. Eder). London: Routledge & Kegan Paul, 1969.

Jung, C.G. (1930–31). 'The Stages of Life'. In *Collected Works, Vol. 8. The Structure and Dynamic of the Psyche* (2nd edn). London: Routledge & Kegan Paul, 1991.

Jung, C.G. (1931c). 'A Psychological Theory of Types. In *Collected Works, Vol. 6. Psychological Types* (2nd edn). London: Routledge & Kegan Paul, 1989.

Jung, C.G. (1934a). 'A Review of the Complex Theory'. In *Collected Works, Vol. 8. The Structure and Dynamics of the Psyche* (2nd edn). London: Routledge & Kegan Paul, 1991.

Jung, C.G. (1938). 'Dogma and Natural Symbols'. In *Collected Works, Vol. 11. Psychology and Religion*. London: Routledge & Kegan Paul, 1991.

Jung, C.G. (1940). 'The Psychology of the Child Archetype'. In *Collected Works, Vol. 9i. The Archetypes and the Collective Unconscious* (2nd edn). London: Routledge & Kegan Paul, 1990.

Kalsched, D. (1996). *The Inner World of Trauma: Archetypal Defenses of the Personal Spirit*. London & New York: Routledge.

Khan, M.M.R. (1963). 'The Concept of Cumulative Trauma' (2nd edn). In M.M.R. Khan *The Privacy of the Self*. New York: International Universities Press, pp. 42–58.

Kohut, H. (1977). *The Restoration of the Self*. New York: International Universities Press.

Lambert, K. (1973). 'Agape as a therapeutic factor in analysis', *Journal of Analytical Analysis*, 18(1), pp. 25–46.

Meier, C.A. (1984). *The Unconscious in its Empirical Manifestations Vol. 1: The Psychology of C. G. Jung with Special Reference to the Association Experiment of C.G. Jung*. Boston, MA: Sigo.

Petchkovsky, P., Petchkovsky, M., Morris, P., Dickson, P., Montgomery, D., Dwyer, J. and Burnett, P. (2013). 'fMRI responses to Jung's Word Association Test: Implications for theory, treatment and research', *Journal of Analytical Psychology*, 58(3), pp. 409–431.

Shin, Y-W., Lee, J-S., Han, O-S., Rhi, B-Y. (2005). 'The influence of complexes on implicit learning', *Journal of Analytical Psychology*, 50(2), pp. 175–190.

Silverstein, S.M. (2014). 'Jung's views on causes and treatments of schizophrenia in light of current trends in cognitive neuroscience and psychopathology research II: Psychological research and treatment'. *Journal of Analytical Psychology*, 59(2), pp. 263–283.

Vezzoli, C., Bressi, C., Tricarico, G. and Boato, P. (2007). 'Methodological evolution and clinical application of C.G. Jung's Word Association Experiment: a follow-up study'. *Journal of Analytical Psychology*, 52(1), pp. 89–108.

Winnicott, D.W. (1974). 'Fear of breakdown', *International Review of Psycho-analysis*, 1, pp. 103–107.

# 7
# TRAUMA AND TRANSFORMATION

A representational 'collective' of a woman's desire for procreative identity in midlife may be seen through the lens of personal and cultural complexes of the collective unconscious, functioning as conscious imperatives expressed through technology's ability to stand in for 'other' (Barone-Chapman, 2011). This 'other' is a substitute for an unmet known, most often recalled and referred to as 'my mother'. Technology is an unfamiliar other, arriving by expedient means, associated with increased age and declining fertility amidst sudden, mid-life imperatives to re-create and repair the mother-child union. Heretofore, I have reserved the place as *The Hunger to Fill an Empty Space* (Barone-Chapman, 2007) as there is a concentration of passion, energy, effort and plenty of animus around the achievement of delayed procreative identity.

Unravelling the 'complex indicators' within the Word Association Experiment (WAE) (Jung, 1904–1909, 1905) provided an in-depth view of the trauma around delayed motherhood, which led me to keep in mind the following questions: Has scientific medicine cut us off from experiencing the body through feelings and emotions? (Redfearn, 1985). What is our Western culture demonstrating through late motherhood that cannot be expressed any other way? At some point in each participant's development generative anxiety become activated (Raphael-Leff, 2007) through mother's ideas about her own reproductive circumstances which were used to instruct the daughter on how to organize her generativity when it was her time to make a choice. Longitudinal traumas between mothers and daughters are easily converted into these kinds of *creativity disturbances*. 'Creativity at the individual level is shaped by the societal context in which creative development and thought takes place' (Simonton, 2009).

Has the 'technological unconscious' (Rutsky, 1999) interfered with the 'nature' of all living things resulting in disenchantment with ordinary reproduction and mating? 'The cultural unconscious, in the way I use it, is an area of historical memory that lies between the collective unconscious and the manifest pattern of the culture' (Henderson, 1990, p. 103). Sam Kimbles (2014, p. 83–85) articulates this pattern as occupying three areas of experience at group level of family and in society: 1. intergenerational processes; 2. collective shadow processes; 3. cultural complexes playing a large role in producing social suffering. Identification of a cultural complex is useful because the messages of anxiety and fear contained within this type of complex is implicit, not explicit and therefore potentially more provocative as a *phantom narrative* (Kimbles, 2014, pp. 11, 21). Here, Kimbles also highlights how intergenerational processes, while providing structure and continuity, operate as places for unresolved grief and violence to re-enact historical context into the present. The WAE has shown how unravelling these assumptions can foster transmutation of suffering.

## The Wounding

Carrying forward the previous chapters to do with participant's testimony becomes a parallel process akin to inter-generational trauma, with this word oscillating toward situating the past of the woman when she was a child into the adult experience of the *pregnant pause*. This is a place where 'disintegration anxiety' (Kohut, 1977, p. 104), 'primitive agonies' (Winnicott, 1974) and 'cumulative traumas' (Khan, 1974, pp. 42–60) of unmet dependency needs find various justifications to delay motherhood as there has not been enough self to establish a 'protective shield against stimuli' (Freud, 1920b, p. 27). To these disturbances we may add the fear of being abandoned, unloved, or not kept in mind if the child does not perform to parental requirements to make the parent 'look good' to others. Super-ordinate themes revealed themselves as inter-woven schema across personal, cultural, and collective complexes of the unconscious.

## Theme 1: Becoming the Better Mother (Personal, Cultural and Collective Complexes)

This theme carried a lot weight in the minds of the women who desired procreative identity to redeem themselves from the idea that they had been a bad child who was unlovable. Indigenous cultural assumptions about the female body being ordained for motherhood aroused by an aspect of the feminine identified by Jung (1982, p. 115) as the woman who wants to be 'anything but like mother', is at base, resistant to changing her ideas about what is possible until she becomes accustomed to living through the persona of the good mother. A lack of being met by mother in a way that allowed her to develop autonomy and independence, led to prolonged adolescence, until the daughter did something to end the spell by making a baby. As Jung observed, there are stages when mother is associated to family, community, society, uterus – to oppose her can bring on disturbances in the menstrual cycle, failure to conceive, aversion to pregnancy, profuse vomiting, miscarriage, all the rejecting *material* to the female who struggles with *mater* who is head of the family. Jung went so far as to suggest the rejecting impulse could also be observed as making a woman clumsy with tools, in a world of influence where mother has no place. In other words, her sensate function was useless. Most of the participants were grateful for a good partner who provided object constancy, something they had not grown up expecting to find.

Delayed motherhood becomes a symptom of obstructions in early development including uncertainty with sexual identity and gender confusion, most often seen through disassociated relationship to the female body, as if the body was responding in collusion or rebellion, to messages learned earlier within the family and culture. My early hunch, that the female body was being neutered into performance of patriarchal values, appeared in the case studies as an abreaction, in conflict with the imperative to reproduce. Compounding this union of personal and collective influences was the emergence of a transcendent space between a woman's personal mother and the mother she thought she must be in order to qualify as *a good mother*. Most of the relationship with her mother set the stage of how Eros, the masculine god and carrier of the feminine, manifested. Yet an emotional cocktail of shame, regret and stigma presented a dark side for some of the women for whom, though the children had come through luck, IVF or ovum donation, there remained a residue of failure for having become the mother they never wanted to be, or even the mother they wished they had, but all too late in life.

## Theme 2: The Un-Mothered Child (Personal and Cultural Complexes)

What has emerged about technology and its relationship to delayed motherhood is not what I had predicted. I came to the subject expecting to discover that women had been cavalier about when to become mothers, if at all, because technology was being relied upon to solve the problem of ageing infertility. Here I was, demonstrating media's cultural influence on hearts and minds about women who delay motherhood. Instead, I found women with a profound inability to feel they had themselves been mothered and who were anxious about whether they would feel love towards the children they produced, no matter how they were created. The feeling of the un-mothered child had made them less available for a relationship where they were also loved in return, until midlife, as an act of rebellion against the primordial abandonment they had continued to experience from childhood. This goes some way in explaining how they learned that a relationship with an 'other' could be easily severed before they reached young adulthood.

Strangely, Ms D demonstrated this most acutely and perversely, having had too much of a doting mother, she initially believed her goals were to be the same. Engagement with her first-born, who happened to be a girl, went from hypertrophy of feminine interests to atrophy. Overnight it was as if her new-born daughter was asking too much of her. As a female child her first-born had unwittingly activated an attack on her narcissism, which kept Ms D in a position of wanting to run away from the infant, a pattern that continued. This enantiodromia (Jung, 1911–12, para. 581) led Ms D to want something different in motherhood by the time she had her second child, a son, that would be different from mother and her peer group. The difference was the move from maternal preoccupation to maternal subjectivity with autonomy and independence. I read Ms D's desire to become more interesting without procreative preoccupation, to be indicative of a negative mother complex, in the vein of, 'anything but like mother' (Jung, 1982, p. 115) than she was ready to face when we met for the last time. In effect, her idealization of mother, who responded to Ms D with acute sensitivity to every need, weighed heavily on her when thoughts of being different from mother, came into her mind.

## Theme 3: Maternal Gender Bias (Personal and Cultural Complexes)

All the participants had chosen 'non-uterine identity' (Samuels, 1989) through the world of work, where the absent, personal father could be found through the culture of the working world. This is an important theme that influences all the other themes. It came up as both privation and deprivation across affective behaviour and narrative shifts within the life stories of eight participants.

The existence of a male sibling, who had more privilege, encouragement, engagement and attention from mother than the daughter, was the present absence in the mother-child dyad. Patriarchal influence took the form of absent or wayward fathers, privileged brothers and betraying mothers. This theme emerged in every case where there was a brother, older or younger. 'That mask for the ambition to respectability which serves to make the status quo look more attractive – is what, in a culture dominated by the patriarchal animus, we eventually all suspect in the advice of our parents – in the advice of our most developed cultural forbears … when such integrity has grown rigid and inauthentic' (Beebe, 1992, p. 101–102). I came to realize these participants were demonstrating the very bones of delayed motherhood, distinguishing the making of a complex between personal experience, cultural and collective contexts. The affects before me at micro-level was emerging into a macro-view of how feminism emerged when the feminine could no longer quietly accept being thwarted to favour the masculine. Like the goddess Inanna (Brinton Perera, 1981; 1985), the participants had gone underground, hiding from engagement with men for fear they could not live up to the potency of their mothers, even if the potency had a negative impact on their lives. The story of their mother's relationship with them appeared as an attempt to canalize their personalities along softer values rather than any hint of also containing the masculine (Paris, 2007).

Within a *pregnant pause,* the needs of the body – warmth, nourishment and protection, what Ginette Paris regards as Psyche's needs – become concretized in 'an atmosphere where the heart finds its niche, its nest, its rest' but remains out of reach, outside of the cultural separation of 'winners' and 'losers' (Paris, 2007, p. 121). The 'having it all' narrative has been about having the entitlement of what was perceived to be masculine and feminine, polar validations of career and family previously only enjoyed by men, now a source of rising and acute anxiety in older women on the edge of their fecundity. From the perspective of post-Jungian psychology (Barone-Chapman, 2014b) 'having it all' is having access to both masculine and feminine energies, Logos and Eros, without biasing one because of biological gender and relegating the other as a lesser, inferior voice. Dominion over another may be part of an idealization of motherhood (Benjamin, 1988) occurring among anti-feminist and non-feminist women to redeem a sphere of influence through female de-sexualization and lack of agency, unwittingly preserving an older gender attitude toward sexuality that leaves women righteously clinging to de-eroticized caring (Benjamin, 1988, p. 92).

## Theme 4: A Life Lived in Two Parts (Personal, Cultural and Collective Complexes)

Finding maternal gender bias in favour of the masculine, in addition to the life pattern of 'first Adam then Eve' is crucial to all other findings. A re-creation of the original creation myth 'first-Adam-then-Eve' (Hillman, 1972) appeared as a life pattern within the earliest memories of participant's choices in their triangulation with parents and male siblings. As young women purposely choosing to use their minds to make non-uterine decisions tended to put them more in the world of men, the structure of their lives began to suggest an extended Apollonic phase. The favouring of the masculine over the feminine in their family cultures, and in the collective unconscious, associated with economic performance, ergo more value, was partly responsible for women's lives acquiring the appearance of a structure in two parts: first Adam then Eve. The reverse, First-Eve-then-Adam, became another kind of anomaly necessitating an enantiodromia ('an about face') before the participant reached the age of 40 (see Theme 1 – the better mother, Ms D, above).

Historically, from just a small glimpse into Freud's thinking of the feminine through one of his last writings in Vienna, it may be possible to see the necessity of feminist thought to salvage psychoanalysis from Freud's complaint 'psychology cannot solve the riddle of femininity' (Freud, 1933, p. 149).

> The difference in a mother's reaction to the birth of a son or daughter shows that the old factor of lack of a penis has even now not lost its strength. A mother is only brought unlimited satisfaction by her relation to a son; this is altogether the most perfect, the most free from ambivalence of all human relationships. A mother can transfer to her son the ambition which she has been obliged to suppress in herself, and she can expect from him the satisfaction of all that has been left over in her of her masculinity complex.
> 
> *(Freud, 1933, pp. 112–134)*

What is important about the finding of a favoured male sibling buried in all participants' stories of delayed motherhood are the deep wounds of early gendered grooming. The superior value placed on the masculine while the good things of the feminine in the daughter were difficult to see by parental caretakers. What could be seen in the present was how this biasing affected the women years later, realizing that for most of their adult lives they felt they might be less capable in life than a male. Yet all participants had enjoyed engagement in the world of work and career long past many of their peers, due to late onset of pregnancy around the fourth decade. The comparison goes some way toward suggesting how their choice in delaying motherhood resonates, at minimum, with having to prove something to themselves and others regarding the very definition of what embodying the feminine is about; normative, predictive generative identity via motherhood was not going to be enough. At least in the first half of life.

Out of this theme also comes the observation that 80 per cent of the participants had partnered with younger men, not older men who could potentially dominate them. In Jungian terms we could view the younger age of their partner as being the 'age' of their animus, less developed in some respects. Partnering with a younger man when the desire to procreate became a form of 'midlife awakening' represents an attempt to turn back time and tide, to recapture something lost over time, such as a more youthful appearance (Friese, Becker and Nachtigall, 2008; Goffman, 1963).

## Theme 5: Too Much Mother (Personal and Cultural Complexes)

Seligman forecasted that the rise of divorce in Britain would amount to over one million children losing their fathers in the six years that followed 'as if he had died, and perhaps, psychologically, in a more dangerous way'. Such a number drew her to raise the question of the symbolically missing father, defined as unavailable by both mother and child. She asked the same kind of questions I find myself asking now of my cases, 'Why is he allowing himself to be, effectively, obliterated? Is he being excluded or is he excluding himself?' (Seligman, 1985, pp. 71, 79). Evidence from her case material suggested unconscious collusion between mother and child to satisfy each other's needs aims to forestall a phase of sharing and conflict.

The term Seligman uses to describe the children of such a dyad, 'the half-alive ones', is powerfully constricting. She connotes a kind of vampirism when she describes:

> a large number of ego-damaging mothers' as withdrawn, self-absorbed, efficient but affectionless … rigidly controlling, domineering and intrusive, or else seductive and castrating, puritanical and guilt-breeding or as tyrannizing their children by illness, more often feigned than real … others that cannot release a child, exploit or scapegoat him. There are also jealous mothers who vacillate between hostility and remorse.
>
> *(Seligman, 1985, p. 73)*

The totality of this kind of mother, the 'All-Too-Present Mother' was identified by Seligman from work by Newton and Redfearn (1977) drawn from Mahler, Pine and Bergman (1975) which in effect echoes Jung's (1921, para. 307) earlier warning of the psychic effects of the parent's unlived life upon the child. An obsession to fix the parents' failings, rather than find their own destiny, all too often forsakes other callings of their own desire and design until much later in life. Jung's attention on the psychic effect of the parent's unlived life, such that s/he identifies with them (Kay,

1981, p. 203–219) may include a daughter trying to become the husband that mother couldn't keep, the wife to the father mother could not be, and a better mother than her own, should children happen.

At root, affects are learnt through the perverse proportions motherhood can take (Welldon, 1992), as a result of a breakdown of interior mental structures, 'whereby the mother feels not only emotionally crippled in dealing with the psychological and physical demands from her baby, but also impotency and the inability to obtain gratifications from other sources' (Welldon, 1992, p. 83). The over-riding felt experience coming from all participants was their memory of being a child who did not find acceptability of her desires in the face of the mother (Raphael-Leff, 2010, p. 543).

## Theme 6: The Negative Mother Complex – Transforming or Terrible?

On a cultural and collective level in terms of identifying complexes, all eight participants expressed an experience of early trauma with a critical negative mother, competition with a male sibling who had pride of place in the home, and the subsequent struggle to make a self that they could not otherwise find (Zinkin, 2008) through uterine activity. This unconscious 'choice' played into a modern revision of Hillman's (1972, pp. 217–225) archetypal pattern within the collective unconscious identified through the creation myth, 'First Adam then Eve', says something about how archetypal patterns may evolve over time. Much of the negative mother complex encountered in research with women in a phase of a pregnant pause, adheres to a family myth where, as children and into adulthood, they were required to be in service to archetypal features of the parental role (Kradin, 2009). If a daughter is kept in an adolescent phase of development permission to procreate is implicitly withheld, as the mother archetype will not have been 'humanized' or installed (Mathers, 2001), into her own being. This eternal daughter, a Puella, unconsciously waits for the father to return in the form of a male other. Unable to find the man within, the animus who would serve her in a heroine's quest to 'fight the dragons' of childhood, puberty and mid-life (Neumann, 1954) she struggles to bring her body back to mind. Such an intrapsychic disunion between masculine and feminine takes time to unfold, and time waits for no woman without the help of bio-technology. Yet it appeared the women had learned something about naming and claiming what had been elusive in the early part of their lives, necessitating a whole body and soul experience.

> In a disenchanted world the body is the last receptacle of the holy ... of an enriched and deepened psychological life ... they suggest that the interiorization of psychological life into the subject conceived as a bodily location is not an ontological necessity but the effect of a cultural shift ... These conclusions were also reached by Zinkin (1985). He points out that the shift from Freud to Jung is a shift from the body to the self as the psychologist's central field of reference.
> *(Brooke, 1991, pp. 171–172)*

With acknowledgment of archetypal realms, Jung bridged millennia of images to feeling tones, also referred to as affect, which 'precisely speaking, [is] neither "in" the body nor "in" the image but in the "between" [of] both body and image' (Brooke, 1991, p. 219). Thus, without attunement with early caregivers the installation of good and evil becomes embattled between 'openness' and 'closedness', brightening and darkening effects (Brooke, 1991; Boss, 1977, pp. 109–14) at the root of all affect.

This research, developed through the use of the personal language of mythopoetics is an attempt to best describe the wisdom of the unconscious (Grotstein, 2000, p. 5; Kalsched, 2014, pp. 204–205), to bridge developmental affect through the language of archetypes, because 'psyche spontaneously *personifies* its affects (both good and bad) around forms giving 'structures' that are universal ... inner 'persons' of the psyche [which] may be constellated by personal experience in the real world, but are not reducible to outer persons alone' (ibid., p. 190).

In the process of unpacking delayed motherhood I have discovered the pervasive nature of the Negative Mother Complex in operation until the approach to midlife and the second return to mother. Often it imbues a rise to spirituality, concomitant to the reliance on biotechnology. The cultural unconscious, a second layer of influence, extending the boundary of the personal into a larger familial group from peers to social and other media, displays a nature and mode of expression. Here I found the favouring of a male sibling to be a dominant factor in arousing envy in a daughter, largely due to a patriarchal mother. While a complex can be negative, positive or both, in the case of most of these participants it could be said to have been bordering on pathological affect at earlier points in their development, in a panoply of complexes across personal, cultural and collective touch points. By 'touch point' I am referring to the point at which a complex is activated. What I found in dreams and narratives was the pattern of repetition – disruption – repetition – emerging transformation. The pattern most often related to a conflicted position, for or against collaborating with an 'other'. This further revealed deep-seated feelings about patriarchy and misogyny as unconscious problems with gender. As Tricksters' agents in aid of developing womanhood, with the aim of making an individuated self, all ideas of being second-class to a more privileged male sibling may turn to folly at midlife.

Over time, self-awareness had catalysed participant's complexes such that all the women came away feeling they had undergone a deep change. I put much of this transformation down to the experience of undergoing the WAE and an ability to mentalize the process. The more intrigued each woman was in fully engaging with her unconscious use of her body as symptomatic of the time necessary to process whatever cumulative trauma had been splintered off from consciousness, the more meaning the process held for her. For experience to have meaning, feeling must be able to enter body, mind and/or spirit. 'If body, mind and spirit don't map together in a person there is a semantic failure between Self and ego, which can't grow through sharing body-meaning' (Mathers, 2001, p. 80). This makes for difficulty in forming relationships with others, as a developmental retrospective.

## Theme 7. Redemption and Reparation (A Global Idea)

Women who find themselves in the pregnant pause are asking for the re-balancing of Logos and Eros, to regain 'Medusa's head' before Athena's projections turned against her. Wirtz (2014, p. 236) finds the archetype of sacrifice to cast a 'light on the dialectic between victim and sacrifice … why we suffer loss … [a] psychic necessity, to which we are compelled by fate.'

Complexes exist in the psyche where observed phenomena functions like the character of Trickster, going to great lengths to obscure observation of phenomena, attention to inter-subjectivity, repetitive patterns, highly charged affects, including time collapsing and lengthening. Trauma as we have seen in the case studies has many faces and forms. One archetypal form is the shape shifter known as Trickster, who carries a dual nature, part animal, part divinity, capable of complex torture and rescuing, bears noteworthy resemblance to the transformative axis of Sophia and Lilith (Neumann, 1955, pp. 82–83), wise women who are not just good or bad, but transformative in the service of the transmutations of pain and suffering. Trickster has also been described as a 'soul in hell'; known for 'transformation of the meaningless into the meaningful' reflects 'Trickster's compensatory relation to the 'saint' (Jung, 1972, p. 457). Trickster is therefore the necessary but often destructive ingredient for metabolizing 'death of time, death of language and death of narrative' (Connolly, 2011, p. 611) transforming trauma originating in maternal deprivation. As a messenger of the underworld, Trickster's methods include sacrificing naïveté, ego, even victimhood itself, if required, and is uniquely placed to hold the negative and positive until the meaning and purpose of each woman's creation myth becomes installed as a psychic reality. The new myths of creation are plural, such that installation of their reality is outside of time, in perpetual motion.

Thanks to biotechnology midlife is now a very long moment. Medical reproductive biotechnology is apt to be perceived, during a pregnant pause (see Definitions; Barone-Chapman, 2011) in a prior life narrative, as a benign form of patriarchal authority, a returning, mothering-oriented, prodigal father coming home to give his middle-aged daughter permission to alter time. In the course of a woman's life such a sudden transformation raises the possibility that an early relational disturbance, with an inhibiting or prohibiting affect, has been preventing 'the trauma [to] be "forgotten", and "remembered" instead of being always present' (Cavalli, 2012, p. 598).

## Discussion

The term 'trauma-culture' (Luckhurst, 2003), may have its genesis in cultural expression but its roots form a backward glance to early childhood experience as a female abject and a dissociated view to it, as reflected in both Neumann's (1955) *Fear of the Feminine*, and the Myth of Lilith, (expanded on in the next chapter). The mother archetype includes maternal solace, sympathy, female authority, wisdom transcending reason, and helpful instincts (Jung, 1972, p. 15), but these seemingly positive attributes exist in transitory ambivalent spaces as well the negative pole, sometimes in parallel through archetypal expression such as the goddess of fate, Kali, the loving but terrible mother, and Lilith, the devouring mother. Taken at face value the mother archetype arouses great hope for love and fear of rejection, ripe for disappointments and failures at the personal level accounting for the 'veil' of perception through which a *participation mystique*, also known in psychoanalytical terms as projective identification, take place. This is the relevant junction to seeing into the role trauma holds in the case studies as a 'veil' in the perception bridge between the archetype as symbol and the meaning of human behaviour in the physical world.

In trauma, feeling is dead, a 'match' to the dead mother, a pattern described by psychoanalyst Andre Green (1993) as a way of seeing into patients who cut themselves off in various ways, under-achieve and repeatedly demolish intimate relationships at the point of reaching great intimacy. Green's extensive experience led him to understand the patient's internal world as dominated by a cruel, life-altering imago (archetype) from early childhood when the mother went through a depressed episode. The child experiences a fall from grace when mother was no longer a source of vitality, becoming self-absorbed, distant and cold. In tracking the death of the emotional bond between mother and child, Green defined the result as leaving a 'psychoses blanche', or blank psyche (Green (1993). Meredith-Owen (2011, p. 675), also finds it 'as a potential *coniunctio oppositorum*' with an open question 'into the roots of narcissistic disorder, and in particular, dissociation'.

The link between trauma and dissociation has been well established (Carrion and Steiner, 2000; Van Der Hart, et al., 2004; Dorahy and Van Der Hart, 2007), but not their link to delayed motherhood. Jung's description of the mother-daughter connection through the achievement of motherhood, has to do with forward and backward movement through '… the bridge of the momentary individual, [that] passes down into the generations of the future … gives the individual a place and a meaning in the life …' (Jung, 1941, para. 316). With this perspective and attending tensions in mind, it is highly relevant to this research on complexes to do with late motherhood to consider Jung's (1972, pp. 21–25) view of how the negative mother complex manifests in the daughter as identification or resistance to her. The 'feminine side' can become confounded and thwarted, depending on whether the Self becomes exalted or perverted on subjects such as motherhood, fatherhood and the demands these relationships can make.

The transformative potential of libido as 'creative, procreative, but possess[ing] an intuitive faculty … a force of nature, good and bad at once, or morally neutral' (Jung, 1911–12/1952d, para. 182) is born from the tension of opposites from which all energy proceeds (Jung, 1928c, paras 34, 78). It is creative, destructive and life changing, with the capacity to have brought about the professional split between Jung and Freud on the use and function of a symbol. Following that event,

> The "creative illness" of 1913-19 signified Jung's personal willingness to return to the Mother as the basis of his psychology, and it left traces of the matriarchal in many places in his work – in the excessively positive value he places

upon the unconscious, in his interest in health and growth, an in his unqualified acceptance of synchronicity. This matriarchal thinking, however appealingly argued, can seem to a hard-nosed patriarchal science to be inspirational at best, and at worst loosely mystical and credulously magical.

*(Beebe, 1992, p. 84)*

For teleological reasons, I will continue with Jung's basis to view a symbol, such as a negative mother complex, as capable of transcendence by mediating between opposites and effecting transitions leading to transformations of psychic states (Bovensiepen, 2002). Jung's work on archetypes, complexes and symbols is relevant to the female psyche in midlife and the essence of a pregnant pause, which carries with it the tension of the opposites, also known as ambivalence, with high toned feeling, riding on the back of the mother archetype and the goal of transformation through a 'night sea journey' (Jung, 1911–12/1952e, para. 308; Jung, 1911–12/1952c, paras 484, 541, 555, 577). This journey, in every case, whether it is based on Egyptian, American Indian, or Greek myths transpires over the 'waters of the unconscious', (water and night symbolizing the unconscious journey from the 'terrible' mother to a rebirth). This transformation has been the crucial evidence in the findings from the WAE. Even when mother is too good, the daughter continues to induce mother to serve her self-interests, perhaps due to envy. 'For Jung, the space of the third begins as a gap of opposition and misunderstanding and grows into a space of conversation where new things happen' (Belford Ulanov, 2007, p. 589). It is beyond what is female or male, conscious or unconscious, it is neither/nor/both /and; it is the new perspective.

## References

Barone-Chapman, M. (2007). 'The hunger to fill an empty space: an investigation of primordial affects and meaning-making in the drive to conceive through repeated use of ART', *Journal of Analytical Psychology*, 52(4), pp. 389–541.

Barone-Chapman, M. (2011). 'Pregnant Pause: Procreative Desire, Reproductive Technology and Narrative Shifts at Midlife', in R. Jones (ed.) *Mind, Body and Healing after Jung*. London: Routledge.

Barone-Chapman, M. (2014b). 'Sulphur Rises Through the Blackened Body'. In D. Mathers, (ed.), *Alchemy and Psychotherapy: Post-Jungian Perspectives*. London and New York: Routledge.

Belford Ulanov, A. (2007). 'The third in the shadow of the fourth', *Journal of Analytical Psychology*, 52, pp. 585–605.

Beebe, J. (1992). *Integrity in Depth*. College Station, TX: A&M University Press.

Benjamin, J. (1988). *The Bonds of Love: Psychoanalysis, Feminism, and the Problem of Domination*. New York: Pantheon.

Boss, P. (1975). *Existential Foundations of Medicine and Psychology*. Trans. S. Conway and A. Cleaves. London and New York: Jason Aronson, 1979.

Bovensiepen, G. (2002). 'Symbolic attitude and reverie: problems of symbolization in children and adolescents', *Journal of Analytical Psychology*, 47(2), pp. 241–257.

Brinton Perera, S. (1981). *Descent to the Goddess: A Way of Initiation for Women* (Studies in Jungian Psychology by Jungian Analysts No. 6). Toronto: Inner City Books.

Brinton Perera, S. (1985). 'The Descent of Inanna: Myth and Therapy'. In E. Lauter and C. Schreier Rupprecht (eds), *Feminist Archetypal Theory: Interdisciplinary Re-visions of Jungian Thought*. Knoxville, TN: University of Tennessee Press, pp. 137–186.

Brooke, R. (1991). *Jung and Phenomenology*. Pittsburg, PA: Trivium Publications.

Carrion, V.G. and Steiner, H. (2000). 'Trauma and dissociation in delinquent adolescents', *Journal of the American Academy of Child & Adolescent Psychiatry*, 39(3), pp. 353–359.

Cavalli, A. (2012). 'Transgenerational transmission of indigestible facts: from trauma, deadly ghosts and mental voids to meaning-making interpretations', *Journal of Analytical Psychology*, 57(5), pp. 597–614.

Connolly, A. (2011). 'Healing the wounds of our fathers: intergenerational trauma, memory, symbolization and narrative', *Journal of Analytical Psychology*, 56(5), pp. 607–626.

Dorahy, M.J. and Van der Hart, O. (2007). 'Relationship between trauma and dissociation: A historical analysis'. In E. Vermetten, M.J. Dorahy and D. Spiegel (eds), *Traumatic Dissociation: Neurobiology and Treatment*. Washington, DC: American Psychiatric Pub., pp. 3–30.

Freud, S. (1920b). 'Beyond the Pleasure Principle', *Standard Edition of the Complete Psychological Works of Sigmund Freud, Vol. 18*. London: Hogarth Press.

Freud, S. (1933). 'Lecture XXXIII: Femininity', *New Introductory Lectures on Psychoanalysis, SE, Vol. 22*, London: Hogarth Press, pp. 112–134.

Friese, C., Becker, G. and Nachtigall, R.D. (2008). 'Older motherhood and the changing life course in the era of assisted reproductive technologies', *Journal of Aging Studies*, 22(1), pp. 65–73.

Goffman, E. (1963). *Stigma: Notes on the Management of Spoiled Identity*. New York: Simon & Schuster.

Green, A. (1993). 'The dead mother', *Psyche*, 47(4), pp. 205–240.

Grotstein, J. (2000). *Who is the Dreamer Who Dreams the Dream? A Study of Psychic Presences*. Hillsdale, NJ: The Analytic Press.

Henderson, J. (1990). 'The Cultural Unconscious'. In *Shadow and Self: Selected Papers I Analytical Psychology*. Wilmette, IL: Chiron Press.

Hillman, J. (1972) *The Myth of Analysis: Three Essays in Archetypal Psychology*. Evanston, IL: Northwestern University Press.

Jung, C.G. (1904–1909). 'Studies in Word Association'. In *Collected Works, Vol. 2. Experimental Researches* (2nd edn). London: Routledge & Kegan Paul, 1992.

Jung, C.G. (1905). 'The Reaction Time Ratio in the Association Experiment'. In *Collected Works, Vol. 2. Experimental Researches* (2nd edn). London: Routledge & Kegan Paul, 1992.

Jung, C.G. ([1911–12]1952c). 'The Dual Mother'. In *Collected Works, Vol. 5. Symbols of Transformation* (2nd edn). London: Routledge & Kegan Paul, 1995.

Jung, C.G. ([1911–12]1952d). 'Introduction to Part 2: The Concept of the Libido'. In *Collected Works, Vol. 5. Symbols of Transformation* (2nd edn). London: Routledge & Kegan Paul, 1995.

Jung, C.G. ([1911–12]1952e). Symbols of the Mother and Rebirth'. In *Collected Works, Vol. 5. Symbols of Transformation* (2nd edn). London: Routledge & Kegan Paul, 1995.

Jung, C.G. (1921). 'The Type Problem in Poetry'. In *Collected Works, Vol. 6. Psychological Types* (2nd edn). London: Routledge & Kegan Paul, 1989.

Jung, C.G. (1928c). 'On Psychic Energy'. In *Collected Works, Vol. 8. The Structure and Dynamic of the Psyche* (2nd edn). London: Routledge & Kegan Paul, 1991.

Jung, C.G. (1941). 'The Psychological Aspects of the Kore'. In *Collected Works, Vol. 9i. The Archetypes and the Collective Unconscious* (2nd edn). London: Routledge & Kegan Paul, 1990.

Jung, C.G. (1972). *Four Archetypes: Mother, Rebirth, Spirit, Trickster*. London: Routledge.

Jung, C.G. (1982). *Aspects of The Feminine*. London and New York: Ark Paperbacks.

Kalsched, D. (2014). *Trauma and the Soul: A Psycho-Spiritual Approach to Human Development and its Interpretation*. New York and Hove, East Sussex: Routledge.

Kay, D. L. (1981). 'Paternal Psychopathology and the Emerging Ego', *Journal of Analytical Psychology*, 26(3), pp. 203–219.
Khan, M.M.R. (1974). *The Privacy of the Self*. New York: International Universities Press, Inc.
Kimbles, S. (2014). *Phantom Narratives: The Unseen Contribution of Culture to Psyche*. New York and London: Rowman & Littlefield.
Kohut, H. (1977). *The Restoration of the Self*. New York: International Universities Press.
Kradin, R., (2009). 'The family myth: its deconstruction and replacement with a balanced humanized narrative', *Journal of Analytical Psychology*, 54(2), pp. 217–232.
Luckhurst, R. (2003). 'Trauma culture', *New Formations*, 50(1), pp. 28–47.
Mahler, M.S., Pine, F. and Bergman, A. (1975). *The Psychological Birth of the Human Infant: Symbiosis and Individuation*. New York: Basic Books.
Mathers, D. (2001). *An Introduction to Meaning and Purpose in Analytical Psychology*. Hove: Routledge.
Meredith-Owen, W. (2011). 'Jung's shadow: negation and narcissism of the self', *Journal of Analytical Psychology*, 56(5), pp. 674–691.
Newton, K. and Redfearn, J. (1977). 'The Real Mother: Ego–Self Relations and Personal Identity', *Journal of Analytical Psychology*, 22(4), pp. 295–315.
Neumann, E. (1994). *The Fear of the Feminine and Other Essays On Feminine Psychology*. Bollingen Series LXE 4. Princeton, NJ: Princeton University Press.
Neumann, E. (1955). *The Great Mother: An Analysis of the Archetype*. New York: Pantheon Books.
Paris, G. (2007). *Wisdom of the Psyche: Depth Psychology After Neuroscience*. East Hove, Sussex and New York: Routledge.
Raphael-Leff, J. (2007) 'Femininity and its unconscious "shadows": Gender and generative identity in the age of biotechnology', *British Journal of Psychotherapy*, 23(4), pp. 497–515.
Raphael-Leff, J. (2010). '"Generative Identity" and Diversity of Desire', *Group Analysis*, 43(4), pp. 539–558.
Redfearn, J. (1985). *My Self, My Many Selves*. London: Karnac.
Rutsky, R.L. (1999). *High Technē: Art and Technology from the Machine Aesthetic to the Post Human*. Minneapolis, MN: University of Minnesota Press.
Samuels, A. (ed.) (1985). *The Father: Contemporary Jungian Perspectives*. London: Free Association Books.
Samuels, A. (1989). *The Plural Psyche*. London: Routledge.
Seligman, E. (1985). 'The Half-Alive Ones'. In A. Samuels (ed.), *The Father: Contemporary Jungian Perspectives*. London: Free Association Books.
Simonton, D.K. (2009). 'Political Pathology and Societal Creativity', *Creativity Research Journal*, 3(2), pp. 85–99.
Van Der Hart, O., Nijenhuis, E., Steele, K. and Brown, D. (2004). 'Trauma-related dissociation: conceptual clarity lost and found', *Australian and New Zealand Journal of Psychiatry*, 38(11–12), pp. 906–914.
Welldon, E.V. (1992). *Mother, Madonna, Whore: The Idealization and Denigration of Motherhood*. London: Karnac.
Winnicott, D.W. (1974). 'Fear of breakdown', *International Review of Psychoanalysis*, 1, pp. 103–107.
Wirtz, U. (2014) *Trauma and Beyond: The Mystery of Transformation*. New Orleans, LA: Spring Journal Inc.
Zinkin, L. (1985). 'Paradoxes of the self', *Journal of Analytical Psychology*, 30(1), pp. 1–17.
Zinkin, L. (2008). 'Your self: did you find it or did you make it?', *Journal of Analytical Psychology*, 53(3), pp. 389–406.

# 8
# CREATION AND DESTRUCTION

Through the writings of Jung's first consort, Sabina Spielrein, whom he treated, analysed and trained, only later to be analysed by Freud, we can see from one of the first female psychoanalysts, how early confusion around pain and pleasure from her father's corporeal punishment resulted in uncertainties around creation and destruction (Covington, 2006).

Sabina Spielrein's interest and involvement in sexual problems began early, leading to her becoming Jung's patient at the Burghölzli Psychiatric Hospital at the University of Zurich, a case well documented by her biographer (Carotenuto, 1982), as well as her achievement in becoming one of the first psychoanalysts to address the basic question of psychoanalysis: the reason for sexual repression (Kerr, 1986; McCormick, 1994). In her way of thinking, along with repression comes the ego's fear response of becoming lost in the other (ibid, p. 188) which led her to amplify and link the sexual act as 'the reproductive instinct' to the idea of destruction (Spielrein, 1994). Her further postulation in regard to the avoidance of intimacy with men is not based on the potential of social ruin expected in the early twentieth century in which she lived. The basis is learned avoidance of too much closeness with mother, else it arouses her prolonged possessiveness. Despite Spielrein's many contributions, both Jung and Freud diminished the value and significance of her work (McCormick, 1994, p.188), yet both men publicly acknowledged her contributions to their ideas (Covington, 2006).

> In every love, one must distinguish between two conceptual orientations: the first – how one loves; the second – how one is loved. In the first, one is the subject and loves the externally projected object: in the second, one becomes the beloved and loves the self as the object ... In the beloved, object-images gain intensity through incorporation, leading the love, directed against the self, to self-destructive acts; self-criticism, martyrdom, and even complete

extinction of one's sexuality (castration). These are merely different forms and degrees of self-destruction.

*(Spielrein, 1994, p. 169–170)*

It may be said that Spielrein's desire for dissolution made her too open to the narcissistic aims of parental figures in Jung and Freud, which made her unable to re-integrate (close) for self-preservation. The self-destruction process Spielrein identifies through feeling of being in love, may be likened to one identified by Michael Fordham (1976, pp. 18–32) in observing how infants when opening to external stimulation, is referred to as 'de-integration' and closing as re-integration to cope with and learn to absorb experience in a dose they find comfortable, a process Fordham linked to the installation of 'ego' (Mathers, 2001, p. 164) when development is going well. For a woman caught in a pregnant pause, opening and closing to 'other' may become stuck in opening too quickly, unable to close, or unable to open without feeling acute anxiety, as the archetype of Self cannot locate the feeling involved to communicate them (Mathers, 2001, p. 164). Failures in opening and closing constitute the feeling of 'dis-integration' as in a relationship failing, because an archetype was not properly installed by mother to show what mothering looked like, nor father with fathering (Mathers, 2001). 'Developmentally, complexes are essential, non-pathological structures – unless an archetype installs prematurely. For example, ego is a complex with a vital reality testing function' (Mathers, 2001, p. 164). Fear of opening and closing sequences can then become too heightened, if there hasn't been enough relationship between Self and ego installed to reality test against anxious preoccupation. Expanding from family to larger systems of culture and national identity, it's easy to see 'when gender performance is culturally demanded … any differentiation between what is and what ought to be' (Hume [1740/1888]2003), becomes lost in a blackened body of shame (Barone-Chapman, 2014b). My way through this psychosocial project on delayed motherhood has been to question Jungian gender theory 'in the spirit of another Jung; the Jung of the symbolic, the mythic, and the subtle body' (McKenzie, 2006, p. 401; Barone-Chapman, 2014b, pp. 218–219).

Re-discovering the founding analytical fathers' relationship to the feminine launched the investigation of a social problem to do with misogyny continuing into the present (Barone-Chapman, 2014a). Generations of Jungians have accepted Jung's ideas from the first half of the twentieth century, privileging the male to develop a relationship with the archetype of the feminine, anima, while at the same time criticizing the female who was developing a relationship to her inner masculine, the animus. 'It is a fundamental tenet of analytical psychology that imbalances in conscious attitude tend to produce a compensatory unconscious movement' (Samuels, 1985, p. 3).

The Lilith myth, as told in the Hebrew creation myth in the Alphabet of Ben Sira (Vogelsang, 1985) lends itself to this inquiry. The story of this first woman, sometimes called 'the first Eve' to Adam, the first man, is relevant to this exploration, as the crux of the myth was meant to discourage the female who would be the male's equal. The myth of Lilith has survived for several thousand years. Destruction (blackening) plays a crucial part between Adam and Lilith, who were both created out of the same earth, and therefore created equal in value. As the myth has been told over millennia, trouble occurred between them when Lilith refused to lay beneath Adam, as she wanted to be on top. In the archetypal image of Lilith, Vogelsang finds the feminist challenge to society's patriarchal values on the collective level as a new paradigm on the personal level for women to face inner conflict between worth and desire (Vogelsang, 1985, p. 149). Adam and Lilith could be having a love relationship 'entered into for its own sake, not for an advantage of any kind', but instead their psychic energy is in service to the ego's goals. The myth is not about Lilith attempting to dominate Adam, but to claim her birthright of equality. 'If we realize that the anger and aggressiveness women feel toward patriarchy is a reaction to the contempt and scorn society has, over the centuries, heaped on the woman … We will be able to understand the destructive fury this scorn has unleashed in women and perhaps deal with both cause and effect' (Vogelsang, 1985, p. 153).

Barbara Koltuv (1986) finds in Lilith and her successor Eve, two sides of the feminine, one instinctual and the other destructive, but both necessary for spiritual and psychological integrity. She explains how the myth presents the lack of a child as the handiwork of Lilith, as if she has won. 'It is said that the daughters of Eve suffer Lilith's pain at each diminishment of the moon … like Hecate, her powers are greatest at the instinctual crossroads of a woman's life: at puberty, at each menstruation, at the beginning and end of pregnancy, motherhood and menopause' (Koltuv, 1986, p. 81). The legend of Lilith suggests woe to woman who will not obey the laws of a patriarchal God who commands her to be 'underneath' Adam, for if she disobeys, she would follow Lilith into an eternal barren state and become unseen in the world. Some versions of the story say that Lilith eats her young and is jealous of Eve who knows she was made from Adam and therefore cannot be his equal. The patriarchal message is clearly embedded within this creation myth: a woman who wishes to conceive children must cleave to man and nurture him and his children (Koltuv, 1986, p. 85, cited from the Zohar I 20a; Scholem, 1977), 'for a woman enjoys no honor save in conjunction with her husband'. But this is only half the myth. Lilith and Eve are two halves of a whole woman on an intra-psychic level (Koltuv, 1986, p. 87), working through ambivalence between birthing/nurturing desires and producing ideas/nourishing works. Without integrating both, mediating both, a woman is either cast out from herself, or from society. In her seminal work, *The Book of Lilith*, Koltuv recovers for women a connection to the instinct and sexuality of the body, inner knowledge and experience over logic and law (Koltuv, 1986, p. 122)

Sigmund Hurwitz (2009, p. 31–32), finds the Lilith figure also appearing outside of Jewish mythology in the lore of Babylonians, Assyrians, Arabs, Sumerians and Hittites, though it has been in existence in Jewish mythology for the longest at 2,500 years occupying an important place within the realm of demonic images. Hurwitz tells us that Lilith's first appearance was that of the Terrible Witch Mother, an archetype documented across millennia in many cultures, unchanging until the Talmudic-Rabbinic and Greco-Byzantine traditions when her demonic persona split into a dual nature. To a woman she will arouse feelings of being faced with 'the terrible, devouring mother' trying to 'harm pregnant women and to steal their new-born children ... always poised to kill the child ... [as] conveyed in early texts as "the strangler"' (Hurwitz, 2009). The evolution of the feminine in consciousness according to Hurwitz, proceeds from the Great Mother as 'a bipolar, archetypal figure, in that she contains the aspect both of the nurturing, caring mother and of the terrible devouring mother' (Hurwitz, 2009). In parallel, Lilith as a demonic figure earns her dualistic persona through the seduction of men as a 'divine whore' who is a seducer of all men for all time until the Day of Judgement (Hurwitz, 2009, p. 31). In this context Lilith is the eternal homewrecker who will not allow men to be faithful and women to bear and raise their children. Lilith as an archetype is therefore integral to unpacking the basis of a *pregnant pause*, when the daughter believes it is not safe for her to feel fecund. Paralyzed under Lilith's influence, projections onto men make them appear unsuitable as partners and fathers. Thus, we get both a fear and a fascination with the archetype of a powerful feminine force in the unconscious with Lilith, only to yield a great ambivalence.

Lilith's flight to the Red Sea to escape Adam and the intentions of the Father-God, produce loss on both sides: Adam no longer had contact with the first human feminine and must do with the feminine function in Eve, while Lilith no longer has a place in conscious life, and must live in the feminine unconscious (Vogelsang, 1985). Hurwitz asks if Lilith's exit was akin to modern fairy tales in terms of a 'magic flight' acknowledging the contribution of Marie Louise Von Franz (Von Franz, 1970, p. 132) on the theme of a lengthy period of loneliness as a prerequisite to escaping evil (Hurwitz, 2009, p. 184). Drawing from various Hebrew texts Hurwitz does not find an actual 'flying' nor a 'fleeing' as Adam was not found in the texts to be in pursuit. Therefore the 'flight' is a retreat in psychological terms taking place at the same geographic point, the Red Sea, where the children of Israel were delivered from their Egyptian overlords. Hurwitz (2009, p. 182) reminds us that the story of Lilith in the Hebrew text of Ben Sira was written by a man for men, and therefore finds the problem largely with the male psyche and the fear of the feminine and has little to do with the woman. 'The dominating attitude of patriarchal man is ... at bottom, nothing more nor less than an expression of his deep-seated fears and his uncertainty of womankind ... behind these fears must also lie a certain fascination' (Hurwitz, 2009, p. 184). Hurwitz cites Karen Horney's (1932) work on 'the problem of a man's fear of women' (Horney, 2009, p. 195) finding it less an issue of castration (Freud) and more a threat to self-esteem, but all too narrow when compared to the impact of the totality of what the mother archetype symbolizes for the child in all its positive and negative aspects (Jung, 1943). Following Jung's thought, Hurwitz cites the fear of the transformative nature of the anima to be a root cause due to 'a disturbed original relationship between the child and his [her] mother, who at the same time represents the embodiment of the mother archetype' from which the anima must be freed (as if from the womb of the unconscious, an ever present danger of swallowing consciousness) if it is to make 'the transition from the matriarchal to the patriarchal phase' (Hurwitz, 2009, p. 196).

We might ask if fear of the feminine lies entirely at a man's doorstep as we move into the next section of this chapter to consider the disruptions and developmental failures leading to the activation of unconscious fears that Lilith will be at the helm. As already stated, many of the women involved in giving testimony on late motherhood, had been groomed to feel inferior to the masculine, by being less considered, desired and entitled than a male sibling, resulting in a view they might be less capable in life than a male. That most of the participants enjoyed engagement in the world of work long past many of their peers until onset of pregnancy around the fourth decade, goes some way to suggesting how late motherhood resonates, at minimum, with having to prove something to themselves and others about their value in a male dominated world. Normative, predictive generative identity via motherhood was not possible for many of the participants until their masculine worth had been established. Uncannily, birth control, biotechnology and a woman's right to choose when to reproduce has overturned Freud's (1933, p.149), basis of femininity as 'biologically given and thus "bedrock" to the psychical field' (Hillman, 1972, p. 292). Yet, dichotomously this same Freudian tenet has contributed to the new developmental twist on the creation myth, 'first-Adam-then-Eve' (Barone-Chapman, 2014a, p. 47). 'We are cured when we are no longer only masculine in psyche, no matter whether we are male or female in biology' (Barone-Chapman, 2014a) When the feminine in either gender is denigrated, we find a link to the alchemical subtle body becoming physically and psychically blackened, precipitating a sulfuric decay to rise so that the problem as it is felt can dissolve (Barone-Chapman, 2014b).

> Female masochism, penis envy, and women's weak superego must be understood as results of the imposition of patriarchal law upon women. Freud's theory is revolutionary in content because it reveals more deeply and completely than any other psychological theory the misery women will suffer as long as they live under the "law of the father".
> 
> *(Flax, 1990, p. 158, citing Mitchell, 1974, p. 15–23)*

and,

> The family is the source of women's oppression because under patriarchal domination it is the agency in and through which women and men are engendered-replicating men who dominate, women who submit.
> 
> *(Flax, 1990, p. 145)*

This is where gender certainty narrows the opportunity to become whole, in an alchemical sense of the syzygy.

In all of Neumann's (1955, p. 226) 'Great Round' perceptions of how the feminine develops and transforms there is 'the phenomenon of reversal' (ibid., pp. 75–83) within the feminine along the axis of fertility and death occupied by the archetypes of Good Mother and Terrible Mother respectively, both these polarities are part of the ordinary mother. This includes the mother of maternal preoccupation, subjectivity and ambivalence. Transformation is described as compensation along an axis holding positive and negative poles conceptualized as the opposites, Sophia and Lilith. Both are also necessary to depict the intersubjective space between mother and daughter in 'doer and done to' relationships (Benjamin, 1998), which lead to the feeling of either/or choices of submission or resistance to the other's demand (Ogden, 1994).

The processes Neumann (1955, pp. 75–83) describes as necessary to unravel the uroboric condition of being 'not yet born' has been mythologized through the image of a snake wrapping around itself into a circle to devour its own tale. Differentiation of ego from life-giving and life-threatening processes, in order for true autonomy to occur requires the Great Mother to descend from her lofty dominance in the unconscious through archetypally inspired developmental rituals imagined as: 1. Separation from parental figures in order for masculinity and femininity (the opposites) to emerge from uroboric unity. 2. Engagement with the heroic journey whereby the ego aligns itself to heroic masculinity to win its freedom from matriarchal dominance. While much of Neumann's thinking here is an expansion of Jung's regarding the effect of the feminine principle upon the man (see also Neumann, 1954, *The Fear of the Feminine*) we have seen in modernity the application of both rituals in the lives of women; a life lived in two parts.

For far too long such trans-generational transmissions of authoritative patriarchal patterns have had a profound impact on daughters and sons under pressure to collude with the parental need for the child to act as a receptacle for the parent's unendurable high-toned feeling states such that, eventually, the child knows no other way but to enact the part that has been assigned (Knox, 2003, p. 221). From these 'traumas' come dissociation with the body as being part of the self, in favour of a 'false self' (Winnicott, 1965), which operates from a split off ego, to separate mind from the body, the site of traumatic experience (Winnicott, 1965).

Understanding Lilith as an archetypal power is relevant to a daughter who comes under a separation spell after years of fusion, if she can have a relationship with the father, or a 'father figure' with mitigating influence based on the valence of his own attitudes toward the feminine. If he 'values the feminine and in his attitude reflects this regard, his attitude will counteract the influence of the collective…[but if father] does not participate in her life, she will be forced to deal with the collective unconscious … before she can realize her shadow qualities'.(Vogelsang, 1985, p. 156).

Women who delay motherhood have shown up feeling they have betrayed themselves in some way, as if ruined by Lilith, 'the character of enchantment leading to doom' (Neumann, 1955, p. 81). In such an archetypal image we find a woman's inner conflict between worth and desire part of a feminist challenge to society's patriarchal values (Vogelsang, 1985, p. 149). Reconstruction movement now suggests that we need to make clear inquiries into the construction of double-bind curtailment of female authority (Young-Eisendrath, 2013 p. 187).

## Lost and Found

The biological imperative to reproduce (Rich, 1976; Chodorow, 1978) appears at midlife as a way to make familial bonds for the repair of old maternal and relational wounds. Though,

> it is typically patriarchal to set the tone and agenda to what will most profit at various times in life, rather than let biology, the wishes and choices of others, set the bar for outcomes, the former abandoned father's daughter follows on from making a career of her own to also make time for maternity with the adroitness of Trickster. She comes to it with logos and determination the "time is now" for rebirth and renewal. There will be time to regress to the Eros of motherhood later.
>
> *(Barone-Chapman, 2017, p. 202)*

A mid-life baby for a growing percentage of women is a means of redemption from her trauma with the patriarchal 'mother monster' (a way of referring to mother's animus) which led to a transmutation of feeling and regard, constructive empathy for the young woman they knew as a child. Trickster's methods sever ties to earlier defences of the self, such as naïveté and victimhood. The many faces of trauma and transformation serve to track the multiple shifts in personhood necessary to achieve parity in a patriarchal society, and how motherhood continues to be a conduit to acceptable female parity. Patriarchy is not limited solely to men, though as James Hillman (1985) insisted, 'it was a birth right of both sexes …' though [it is] something 'patriarchy has tried to deny' (Beebe, 1992, p. 102). Patriarchy can take up form within any number of archetypes and genders. It is important to see it as a system, rather than a gender. By delaying motherhood, a woman buys time to forge her mettle in a patriarchal society to prepare to form a matriarchal community with other women. Women who delay motherhood have spent more time in work and career, especially where competition for advancement is keen, which can leave them with the sense that what women do to other women (Chesler, 2009) in social settings and at the school gates, may be more daunting.

Cosgrove's (2003, p. 95) citation of two quotes from Kristeva are worth noting as we think about our relational selves through the spectre of being consigned as other, the moment we start to be thought of, and to think of ourselves as 'mother'. The loving mother, different from the caring and clinging mother, is someone who has an object of desire (Kristeva, 1986, p. 251). To accord proper theoretical ground to this perspective, Kristeva adds, 'Nobody knows what a "good enough" mother is. I wouldn't try to explain what that is, but I would try to suggest that maybe the good enough mother is the mother who has something else to love besides her child, such as her work, her husband, her lovers, etc.' (Kristeva, 1984, p. 23). Whether she is understood as a symbol, a subject, an archetype or ordinary human, becoming a mother to be other is akin to the function of a wounded healer. Courage is required to tackle such a dual nature. This is how training analysands work through the mother complex, and how my participants found renewal: Once they became a mother, their own mother was no longer a monster. Implicitly delayed until midlife, a turn to motherhood has become a psychosocial destination that opens the door to an eclipse of maternal pre-occupation, ambivalence and subjectivity, requiring only the attribution of value to the child as *other*.

## References

Barone-Chapman, M. (2014a). 'Gender Legacies of Jung and Freud as Epistemology in Emergent Feminist Research on Late Motherhood'. In L. Huskinson (ed.), *The Behavioural Sciences in Dialogue with the Theory and Practice of Analytical Psychology*. Basel and Beijing: MDPI.

Barone-Chapman, M. (2014b). 'Sulphur Rises Through The Blackened Body'. In D. Mathers (ed.) *Alchemy and Psychotherapy: Post Jungian Perspectives*. London and New York: Routledge.

Barone-Chapman, M. (2017). '*Trickster, Trauma and Transformation: The Vicissitudes of Late Motherhood*'. In E. Brodersen and M. Glock (eds), *Jungian Perspectives on Rebirth and Renewal: Phoenix Rising*. London and New York: Routledge.

Beebe, J. (1992). *Integrity in Depth*. College Station, TX: Texas A&M University Press.

Benjamin, J. ([1998]2004). 'Beyond Doer and Done To: An Intersubjective View of Thirdness', *The Psychoanalytic Quarterly*, 73(1) pp. 5–46.

Carotenuto, A. (1982). *A Secret Symmetry: Sabina Spielrein Between Jung and Freud*. New York: Random House.

Chesler, P. (2009). *Woman's Inhumanity to Woman*. Chicago, IL: Chicago Review Press.

Chodorow, N. (1978). *The Reproduction of Mothering: Psychoanalysis and the Sociology of Gender*. Berkeley, CA: University of California Press.

Cosgrove, L. (2003). 'Feminism, postmodernism and psychological research', *Hypatia*, 18(3), pp. 85–112.

Covington, C. (2006). 'Sabina Spielrein: out from the shadow of Jung and Freud', *Journal of Analytical Psychology*, 51(4), pp. 527–552.

Flax, J. (1990). *Thinking Fragments: Psychoanalysis, Feminism, and Postmodernism in the Contemporary West*. Berkeley and Los Angeles, CA: University of California Press.

Fordham, M. (1976). *The Self and Autism*. Library of Analytical Psychology, Vol. 3. London: Heinemann.

Freud, S. (1933). 'Lecture XXXIII: Femininity', *S.E.*, 22, London: Hogarth Press, pp. 112–135.

Hillman, J. (1972). *The Myth of Analysis: Three Essays in Archetypal Psychology*. Evanston, IL: Northwestern University Press.

Hillman, J. (1985). *Anima: An Anatomy of a Personified Notion*. Dallas, TX: Spring Publications.

Horney, K. (1932). 'Die Angst vor der Frau' [The problem of a man's fear of women], in *Internationale Zeitschrift für Psychoanalyse*, Vienna, Vol. XVIII, p. 5.

Hume, D. (1740/1888/2003). *A Treatise of Human Nature*. Mineola, New York: Dover Philosophical Classics.

Hurwitz, S. (2009). *Lilith – The First Eve: Historical and Psychological Aspects of the Dark Feminine*. Einsiedeln, Switzerland: Daimon Verlag.

Jung, C.G. (1943). 'Psychological Aspects of the Mother Archetype.' In *Collected Works, Vol. 9i. The Archetypes and the Collective Unconscious* (2nd edn). London: Routledge and Kegan Paul, 1990.

Kerr, J. (1986). 'Beyond the Pleasure Principle and Back Again: Freud, Jung and Sabina Spielrein'. In P.E. Stepansky (ed.) *Freud Appraisals and Reappraisals: Contributions to Freud Studies, Vol. 3*. Hillsdale, NJ: Analytic Press.

Knox, J. (2003). *Archetype, Attachment, Analysis*. Hove & New York: Routledge.
Koltuv Black, B. (1986). *The Book of Lilith*. York Beach, ME: Nicolas Hays, Inc.
Kristeva, J. (1986). *The Kristeva Reader*, ed. T. Moi. New York: Columbia University Press.
Mathers, D. (2001). *An Introduction to Meaning and Purpose in Analytical Psychology*. Hove: Routledge.
McCormick, K. (1994). 'Sabina Spielrein: Biographical note and postscript.' *Journal of Analytical Psychology*, 39(2), pp. 187–190.
McKenzie, S. (2006). 'Queering gender: anima/animus and the paradigm of emergence', *Journal of Analytical Psychology*, 51(2), pp. 401–422.
Mitchell, J. (1974) *Psychoanalysis and Feminism*. New York: Pantheon.
Neumann, E. (1954). *The Fear of the Feminine and Other Essays on Feminine Psychology*. Princeton, NJ: Princeton University Press.
Neumann, E. (1955/1996). *The Great Mother. An Analysis of the Archetype*. Trans. R. Mannheim. London: Routledge.
Ogden, T.H. (1994). 'The analytic third: working with intersubjective clinical facts', *International Journal of Psycho-Analysis*, 75, pp. 3–19.
Rich, A. (1976). *Of Woman Born: Motherhood as Experience and Institution*. New York and London: W.W. Norton & Co.
Samuels, A. (ed.) (1985). *The Father: Contemporary Jungian Perspectives*. London: Free Association Books.
Scholem, G. (ed.) (1977). *Zohar: The Book of Splendor: Basic Readings from the Kabbalah*. New York: Schocken Books.
Spielrein, S. (1994). 'Destruction as the cause of coming into being.' *Journal of Analytical Psychology*, 39(3), pp. 155–186.
Vogelsang, E.W. (1985). 'The confrontation between Lilith and Adam: the fifth round', *Journal of Analytical Psychology*, 30(2), pp. 149–163.
Von Franz, M.L. (1970). *An Introduction to the Psychology of Fairy Tales*. Zurich and New York: Spring Publications.
Winnicott, D.W. (1965). 'Ego Distortion in Terms of the True and False Self'. In D.W. Winnicott (ed.), *The Maturational Processes and the Facilitating Environment*. London: Maresfield Library Press.
Young-Eisendrath, P. (2013). 'The female person and how we talk about her'. In E.L.K. Toronto, G. Ainslie, M. Donovan, M. Kelly, C.C. Kieffer and N. McWilliams (eds), *Psychoanalytic Reflections on a Gender-free Case: Into the Void*. Hove and New York: Psychology Press.

## Further Reading

Appignanesi, L. (1984). 'Julia Kristeva in Conversation with Rosalind Coward', *Desire*. London: Institute of Contemporary Arts, pp. 22–27.
Chodorow, N. (2014). *Femininities, Masculinities, Sexualities: Freud and Beyond*. Louisville, KY: University Press of Kentucky.
Jung, C.G. (1940). 'The Psychology of the Child Archetype'. In *Collected Works, Vol. 9i. The Archetypes and the Collective Unconscious* (2nd edn). London: Routledge and Kegan Paul, 1990.
Weir, A. (1986). *Sacrificial Logics: Feminist Theory and the Critique of Identity*. New York: Routledge, p. 182.

# 9
# THROUGH A MOTHER MONSTER

> The heroic consciousness of the ego has an upward path … [and so] places a negative sign upon digressions and descents. For example, submersion under the sea in the heroic view is a "night sea journey" through a mother-monster, out of which one emerges having gained an insight or integration, or a virtue. The immersion is to be endured for the sake of later advantages on the path …
>
> *(Hillman, 1972, p. 284)*

Late motherhood is emerging as a symbol of early unrequited love with parental objects that 'remains unconscious [such that] repetition occurs without understanding, [and] a pattern is established for an endless cycle of repetitive non-generative activity' (Conforti, 2003, p. 94). Delayed motherhood has emerged in a biotechnological age as another form of power, control and resistance (Showalter, 1992; Gilligan, 2003; 2013; Swartz, 2013).

My objective, in addition to identifying thematic complexes and a method of researching the unconscious, has been to critique, raise questions and wonder about the effects of technology on the state of play between the feminine and masculine since the 1950s. In one sense, I have infused into emerging social constructs a form of animism by linking the gestation period of this research to Jung's (1958, para. 589) interpretation of UFO sightings in 1947. In effect this phenomenon foreshadowed a new age, replete with a rise in animism, reliance on technology, the logos of science and its shadow aspect that magical thinking means anything can and should be possible through science. How paradoxical it is that Max Weber's (1947) phrase, 'disenchantment with the world' in its depiction of modernity's demystification of objects in the world as having life continues to apply to conditions in favour of scientific ways of preserving and making new life in many forms. Consider how stem cell research, robotics, and cloning, will make reproductive technology look archaic in the near future.

This book has considered delayed motherhood as if we were analysing a dream. It began with a critical literature review on social problems with the feminine re-emerging and found new ground on the back of the early gender thoughts of Freud and Jung. Alongside this phenomenological observation, there were others. Women were unconsciously, yet purposely making non-gendered choices, so that the structure of their lives began to suggest they needed to prove something about holding the masculine before the feminine could reveal herself. The creation myth, 'First Adam, then Eve' (Hillman, 1972) applies to a life lived in two parts. Their need to tell the story of their journey toward motherhood took on a confessional quality, where 'the body experiences of [childhood], childbirth and becoming a mother [become] fundamental, catalytic crises of selfhood' (Quiney, 2007). While a child remains puerile when it must retain an inflated view of a parent, such schemata appears when new ways of being with the other are found, so she no longer has to carry the constricting, critical possessive mother archetype. Part of this work has allowed a kind of joy in observing women discover they do not have to carry the 'empty space' for the absent father's return. The absent father has lost his protected and idealized position.

Freud and Jung's views became evidence of patriarchy as background while feminist inspired psychoanalytical thinking and Queer theories allowed me to find new meanings of the embodied feminine through a recapitulation of a union of opposites into a union of epistemology and ethos (Barone-Chapman, 2014a). The essence of Jung's (1933, para. 291) frame of modernity has been to associate physical disorders to a psychic origin, un-altered by modernity or female advancement, outside of essentialist gender performance. Jung left remnants of the mother scattered across his work – from the unquestionable value he places upon the unconscious... 'to a hard-nosed patriarchal science to be inspirational at best, and at worst loosely mystical and credulously magical' (Beebe, 1992). But such a construction left his work open to accusations of being 'inspirational' or merely 'mystical and magical' (Beebe, 1992, p. 84). Both are plausible and yet neither are totally accurate.

The significance of delayed motherhood against lowered fertility rates in geographies with the longest history of industrialization (Nelson, 2004), in terms of gender, culture and archetypal patterns has involved a closer look at psyche's discontents and how they can undergo a transformation into a new consciousness. Through the lens of delayed motherhood and the language of alchemical transformation (Mathers, 2014) a subtle field is emerging in the spheres of politics, biotechnology, activism, economics and law. The pendulum swings toward the right and the left. This makes achieving and nurturing, penetrating and receiving, between genders, and within gender, vital for finding integrity in simple acts such as growing a child's mind, body and soul.

## Summary of Complex Findings

Complexes are a normal part of the psyche and have three qualities – a root system indicating something in the past; a nature in how that affect is displayed; and a mode of expression, dependent upon circumstances, that are 'negative' (shadow), 'positive' (hero) or 'bipolar' (a combination of both). The following parts of a complex have been revealed in this study:

1. PERSONAL COMPLEX – A traumatic history with primary caregivers, in particular the personal mother, while father was protected through absence and other distance defences in the triangle with a male sibling, which carried an additional benefit of imbuing delayed motherhood as a protection against androcentric interruption.

2. CULTURAL COMPLEX – An upsurge in take up of biotechnology methods also imbue delayed motherhood with affects in the form of a rebellion against cultural hetero-normative expectations. Women who are also mothers are more easily managed in a patriarchal society, which produces a fractured view of 'Us' vs. 'Them' (Singer, 2009), dynamics where women are categorized as those who mother and those who do not as a way of determining an ability to caretake.

3. COMPLEXES OF THE COLLECTIVE UNCONSCIOUS – Repetition of the Creation Myth – 'First Adam, Then Eve', has acculturated women to devalue feminine activities and to place superior value on male activities until mid-life when a search for re-integration of splintered aspects of psyche takes place in modern society. Discovering evidence of three qualities of a complex, with links between personal, cultural and the collective unconscious, along gender lines, led me to conclude that a trauma complex about mother is at the core of delayed motherhood as a condition of gender rebellion against matriarchal order.

'Under these circumstances, when the traumatic complex is triggered, the core of the psyche is laid bare and there is a psychological imperative, experienced by both the individual and, in identification, [with intimate other] that this vulnerable core must be regulated and protected at all costs' (West, 2013, p. 85). Consequently, a woman is at once distracted and preoccupied, unable to relate to others (a process of mentalization) as a result of a wound to the core self (ibid, p. 85). This research demonstrates the importance of allowing a daughter to psychologically separate from the mother who has been disappointed in her relationship with the father, which has led her to take over the daughter's instincts and impulses as an entitled castrating mother. Daughters put under pressure to comply in such an atmosphere reported finding intimacy intimidating because their primordial relationships were entrained in a fear response. Further evidence revealed how the unconscious desire to remain safe from pregnancy fuelled by the avoidance of intimate relating created a double bind of longing for something the daughter felt unworthy of having. The superior, competing mother had thwarted both uterine and non-uterine, agentic endeavours, which contributed to arousing increased desire for a baby when time appeared to be running out. Most of the women had experienced the loss and grief of several miscarriages, a form of archetypal grief inspiring both depression and anger (Brewster, 2018) sufficient to persevere in attaining a maternal self.

Latent desire for a return to 'normalcy' through the creation of a family was in turn a spontaneous need to undo years of being complicit in destruction of a relational self. But it also emerged as a *massa confusa* originating as a projective identification (Schwartz-Salant, 1988) of gender identity with hetero-normative parents where mother was more dominant and influential in the home than father. Most of the mothers represented among the participants who delayed motherhood, had been critical, disparaging their daughters as not competent enough to manage life, let alone motherhood. Yet few of the mothers had ever also worked or enjoyed a career outside of homemaking.

Therefore, the revolt against the biological imperative to reproduce was not so much an overt rebellion but a quest for authentic, reparative relating which took time to create with a significant partner, following the uncertain hyper relationship mother displayed toward patriarchy (father) through her animus. The frequency of the archetypal critical 'witch' mother creating inequality among her children by biasing the son over the daughter, while ignoring the father/partner into a place of present absence was a phenomenon of the research in itself, consistent with insecure attachment findings elsewhere (Gerhardt, 2004, pp. 25–31).

In conclusion, late motherhood is connected to a personal area of difficulty that can also be found in cultural and collective complexes. The biological imperative to reproduce at midlife is a way to repair old attachment wounds by making new familial bonds.

As a means of redemption from the patriarchal 'mother monster' women are seeking a solution through Eve, not Adam. Mothers of such women can also undertake reparative measures to humanize the inequality they demanded in their mother-daughter relationship. Trickster's methods sever ties to earlier defences of the self, such as naïveté, victimhood and arrogance. The many shifts in personhood necessary to achieve matriarchy in a patriarchal society continues to be a conduit to acceptable female parity. Patriarchy is not limited solely to men. Patriarchy can take up form within any number of archetypes and both genders. It shows up most openly through 'false-father values ... [associated] with the negative mother's animus – haste, double-dealing, emphasis upon a collective persona, and expediency' (Beebe, 1992, p. 101), often leaving a daughter in a wasteland of inauthentic rigidity. Passion, even rage, breaks the bonds of this patriarchal animus to reach for a higher level of integrity, opening to anima in support of moral initiative (ibid, p. 102). 'Persona integrity – that mask for the ambition to respectability which serves to make the status quo look more attractive – is what, in a culture dominated by the patriarchal animus, we eventually all suspect in the advice of our parents' (op cit.). By delaying motherhood, a woman buys time to forge her mettle in a culture seemingly complicit with patriarchal values, to prepare to form community with other women, where the competition will be keener (Chesler, 2009). Longitudinal misogyny of women may be a patriarchal mirror projection to keep women busy competing with other women, as born out in the myth of Lilith, who became a frightening memory to pregnant women and Eve, the first woman to lay beneath Adam. However, delaying the initiatory ritual of motherhood is also a project replete with the goal to cross fertilize opposites, to find a transcendent function throughout the phases of a *pregnant pause*. Only later will it be understood as if it were a dream, accompanied by the 'wish for transcendence' (Beebe, 1993, p. 81). This is the way through the desire for motherhood at midlife. Staying with the tension of opposites to find a union of spiritual reality with the 'empirical reality of life … [that] together forms a whole' (Jaffe, 1970, p. 21). In order to create something new, often called 'the third' to function as a liberator in service to a work of art, idea, or a baby, the new king of consciousness is asking to be born. Anima and Animus must wrestle with choices and limitations. In every case where it concerns a baby, new definitions for rebirth, renewal and sovereignty must be found, to return later as someone who can report in to Self on all that has been learned. Cultural Complexes have shown that our objects of desire (or repulsion) are not solely of our own making. They need need discerning integrity.

## References

Barone-Chapman, M. (2014a). 'Gender Legacies of Jung and Freud as Epistemology in Emergent Feminist Research on Late Motherhood'. In L. Huskinson (ed.), *The Behavioural Sciences in Dialogue with the Theory and Practice of Analytical Psychology*. Basel and Beijing: MDPI.
Beebe, J. (1992). *Integrity in Depth*. College Station, TX: Texas A&M University Press.
Beebe, J. (1993). 'Jung's Approach to Working with Dreams'. In G. Delaney (ed.), *New Directions in Dream Interpretation*. Albany, NY: SUNY Press, pp. 77–101.
Brewster, F. (2018). *Archetypal Grief: Slavery's Legacy of Intergenerational Child Loss*. London: Routledge.
Chesler, P. (2009) *Woman's Inhumanity to Woman*. Chicago, IL: Lawrence Hill Books.
Conforti, M. (2003). *Field, Form, and Fate: Patterns in Mind, Nature and Psyche*. New Orleans, LA: Spring Journal Books.
Delaney, G. (1993). *New Directions in Dream Interpretation*. Albany, NY: SUNY Press.
Gerhardt, S. (2004). *Why Love matters How Affection Shapes a Baby's Brain*. London and New York: Routledge.
Gilligan, C. (2003). 'Letter to readers, 1993.' In *In A Different Voice: Psychological Theory and Women's Development*. Cambridge, MA: Harvard University Press.
Gilligan, C. (2013). *Joining the Resistance*. John Wiley & Sons.
Hillman, J. (1972). *The Myth of Analysis: Three Essays in Archetypal Psychology*. Evanston, IL: Northwestern University Press.
Jaffe, A. and Jung, C.G. (1970). *Memories, Dreams, Reflections*. Trans. R. Winston and C. Winston. New York: Random House Books.
Jung, C.G. (1933). 'The Meaning of Psychology for Modern Man'. In *Collected Works, Vol. 10. Civilization in Transition* (2nd edn). London: Routledge & Kegan Paul, 1991.
Jung, C.G. (1958). 'Introductory to Flying Saucers: A Modern Myth'. In *Collected Works, Vol. 10. Civilization in Transition* (2nd edn). London: Routledge & Kegan Paul, 1991.
Mathers, D. (ed.) (2014). *Alchemy and Psychotherapy: Post Jungian Perspectives*. London and New York: Routledge.
Nelson, A.M. (2004). 'A qualitative study of older first-time mothering in the first year', *Journal of Pediatric Health Care*, 18(6), pp. 284–291.
Quiney, R. (2007). 'Confessions of the New Capitalist Mother: Twenty-first Century Writing on Motherhood as Trauma', *Women: A Cultural Review*, 18(1), pp. 19–40.

Schwartz-Salant, N. (1988). 'Archetypal Foundations of Projective Identification', *Journal of Analytical Psychology*, 33(1), pp. 39–64.
Showalter, E. (1992). *Sexual Anarchy: Gender and Culture at the Fin de Siècle*. London: Virago Press.
Singer, T. (2009). 'A Jungian approach to understanding "us vs. them" dynamics', *Psychoanalysis, Culture & Society*, 14(1), pp. 32–40.
Swartz, S. (2013). 'Feminism and psychiatric diagnosis: reflections of a feminist practitioner', *Feminism & Psychology*, 23(1), pp. 41–48.
Weber, M. (1947). *Theory of Social and Economic Organization*, Trans., A.M. Henderson and Talcott Parsons. New York: Oxford University Press.
West, M. (2013). 'Trauma and the transference – countertransference: working with the bad object and the wounded self', *Journal of Analytica Psychology*, Vol. 58, pp. 73–98.

## Further Reading

Toronto, E.L.K., Ainslie, G., Donovan, M., Kelly, M., Kieffer, C.C., and McWilliams, N. (eds), (2013). *Psychoanalytic Reflections on a Gender-free Case*. Hove and New York: Psychology Press.
Young-Eisendrath, P. (2013). 'The female person and how we talk about her'. In E.L.K. Toronto, G. Ainslie, M. Donovan, M. Kelly, C.C. Kieffer and N. McWilliams (eds), *Psychoanalytic Reflections on a Gender-free Case*. Hove and New York: Psychology Press.

# EPILOGUE

> Historically, cross-culturally, a woman's status as child bearer has been the test of her womanhood. Through motherhood, every woman has been defined from outside herself: mother, matriarch, matron, spinster, barren, old maid – listen to the history of emotional timbre that hangs about each of these words. Even by default motherhood has been an enforced identity for women, while the phrases "childless man" and "nonfather" sound absurd and irrelevant to us.
>
> *(Rich, 2015, p. 261)*

In the shadow of a *pregnant pause* is the role 'toxic masculinity' (read socially conditioned masculinity; Salam, 2019) has played in the trajectories of female children who did not know whether mother would ever champion them on to greater things in life. Early learning that boys have more value has followed generations of women into the workplace, divisively implying they forego motherhood. I am suggesting through this work on the psychosocial currents of late motherhood, that men need to stop and review the effects toxic masculinity has had on their own lives and the people they love, in favour of more modern ideas of what it is to be and live as a man they could respect. What this means is owning distress and disappointment as a valuable emotion. Learning hardness is the Achilles heel of weakness, and violence is a call for help. These conditions are put in place early, at home and in schools, by mothers and other males, and though it crosses colour lines, all too often it is men of colour who are at the punishing end of a racially biased patriarchy. Not unlike the gender biases of ultra-conservatives attempting to control women's bodies by fabricating biased laws. Since August 2018 we now have ten guidelines from the American Psychological Association (APA) confirming that males can be affected, mentally and physically by falling in line with traditional male ideology. The first of these guidelines reads, 'Psychologists strive to recognize that masculine identities are constructed based on social, cultural and contextual norms.' What it doesn't say, is that the same holds true for women.

We are undergoing a rapid evolution of spirit and soul in the body, where biotechnology increasingly plays a larger part. 'It may be that the new epoch we are entering will see the birth of a very different image of God or Spirit, a new understanding of the instinctive intelligence with the processes and patterns of nature, and how the unseen or inner dimension of reality influences and interacts with this physical dimension' (Baring, 2013, p. 223).

A woman without a child is often asked questions about her fecundity and procreative identity not required of women who became mothers at an earlier age. Such interrogations reflect the pressure within culture to 'complex' the childless woman. After a certain age, as her peers procreate, the woman who does not/cannot for reasons she may be unaware of, faces the arduous task of separating the basis of her womanhood and possible 'femininity' (or lack of) from the potential instinctual and socially conditioned expectation that a woman can only be a mother. It seems for change to occur a seemingly un-reasonable woman at midlife must ask, 'why not' of her insurers, the National Health Service (UK), her friends and family.

Initially I did not enter into this investigation fully convinced the topic of a mid-life *pregnant pause* (Barone-Chapman, 2011) was a feminist issue. Rather, my initial thoughts led me to see if personal and cultural complexes were getting in the way of a female adhering to a predictable archetypal pattern I saw disrupting relations between the genders. Through my clinical practice, I came to see women as struggling with 'indigenous' cultural assumptions about their bodies being ordained for motherhood, extending a long period of adolescence while striving for accomplishment in the world of work, coming to motherhood later than was considered the norm in personal, social, health and cultural contexts. I came to wonder if there might be a reparative process at work, the closer they came to embrace the 'older woman' archetype of Witch/Crone, the archetype who comes to disturb innocence. It is common in midlife, if there has been an extended adolescence, for this particular archetype to invite herself into a woman's life. For some it can feel like a pause out of time, part complex, part possession, part naïveté, and part patriarchal medicine.

The rise of late desire for motherhood began to appear as an Anima Mundi problem requesting revisioning. The goddess Inanna, known as the 'Evening Star, Queen of the Land and its fertility, Goddess of War, Goddess of Sexual Love, the Healer, Life Giver, and Composer of songs' (Shaindel Senensky, 2003, p. 163), came into my mind as a means for a woman to seek a connection to the dark feminine when she cannot easily comply with the patriarchal animus of the mother archetype. Inanna undertakes a descent to reclaim the 'dark feminine'. The meaning of this 'semi-death' in the underworld for older women undergoing fertility treatment inspires them to rise up with equalizing wisdom and ruthlessness, withstanding patriarchal influence, themes grounded in mutuality, respect, and conscious communion. Therefore, an ethical position to mutable and evolving expression and repression of the feminine necessitates an in-depth understanding of these ingredients as liberating, alchemical, individuating interactive by-products. The social burden of the technological unconscious is both personal and cultural in the form of policy making that needs to raise the ceiling on assisted reproductive technology (ART) in the National Health Service to reflect the longer period of developmental maturation required in a culture that places value on masculine performance. Not long ago (29 October 2018) on BBC radio came the news that some women in the UK were being refused IVF treatment over the age of 34, when the nationally publicized ceiling is 39 in line with NICE (National Institute for Health and Clinical Excellence) guidelines. The ceiling remains too low to accommodate the seismic shifts of mid-life, which does not necessarily coincide with menopause or turning 40. I propose the ceiling is lifted to include woman up to the age of 45 years.

Women who have delayed motherhood in the biotechnological age report feeling the shift to procreative identity as both subtle and seismic, conscious and unconscious. Unlike current movements, #MeToo and the Men's Movement, feminist anthropologists Coontz and Henderson (1986a, pp. 36–42) found no evidence of strife or struggle in the move from matrilineal to patrilineal inheritance laws (Brodersen, 2016, p. 45). Over time, 'patrilocal lineages exerted increasing control and reproductive power over in-marrying wives from other clans. Such wives lost their natal, lineage claims and became outsiders, subordinated producers within kin corporate groups where they were no longer owners and had less say over the allocation of consumption' (Coontz and Henderson, 1986a, p. 131). We can also track through to modern medicine's ability to alleviate pain to discover how sex differences account for women's higher pain sensitivity than men, likely underpinned by biopsychosocial responses that cause them to be under-treated for pain, and more likely to be dismissed on psychosomatic grounds (Fillingim, King, et al., 2009). Early evidence of gender bias has shown up on pain treatment which may be impacted by the way gender sterotypes effect the way judgements are formed – women are expected to tolerate higher levels of pain than men (Hoffman and Tarzian, 2001; Norman, 2019; Earp, Monrad, LaFrance, et al., 2019). We can extend this bias to all matters concerning a woman's body, to imagine the meaning and purpose delayed motherhood conveys as if it was a conscious act of resistance. However, behind the public and media objections there is a long evolutionary trajectory which brings us to this very fraught gender non-relational moment in time. A non-pathos ethical position regarding non-participation in essentialist notions of feminine performance mirrors an internalized delayed response, often associated with some kind of dissociation through trauma. Women's trauma has both accessible history and non-accessible residue of memories that belong to the turn away from a matriarchal order. Whether the subject is women's reproductive rights, un-welcomed sexual advances, women in office, the cabinet or any position they find meaningful, gender bias continues to leave women feeling men operate more in opposition than as contributing partners.

What would equality look like? '… both partners [could become conscious of the] need to develop their capacities for truth-telling, mindfulness, and vulnerability, and their ability to dialogue when they are in conflict' (Young-Eisendrath, 2019, p. 118). Within this kind of mutuality, delayed motherhood becomes a means to re-balance long-standing inequality born out of the 'First Adam, then Eve' path through obliquity until bumping into a procreative solution to that obliquity. This is the point at which the transmutation of early suffering begins.

The new myths of creation born of biotechnology, are outside of developmental psychology, but never free from its lessons. Motivated to redeem and repair, older women are transforming kinship ties for the transformation of earlier and longstanding trauma. Re-embodying the feminine through late motherhood emerges as a new union of epistemology and ethos, requiring both deconstruction and reconstruction. In its wake there is an opportunity for more variation in mothering, on which rests the future of a more varied relationship to self, daughter, son, and significant others. When the feminine is equal in value to the masculine the children know the soul of the world will be fertile for them. When this order is out of order the creative and fecund world turns upside down and backward until the search for what is sacred in the Anima Mundi can be reclaimed: matriarchy and patriarchy in parity.

## References

American Psychological Association (2018) 'APA Guidelines for Psychological Practice with Boys and Men', https://www.apa.org/about/policy/boys-men-practice-guidelines.pdf, accessed 3 September 2019.

Baring, A. (2013). *The Dream of the Cosmos A Quest for the Soul.* Wimborne: Archive Publishing.

Barone-Chapman, M. (2011). 'Pregnant Pause: Procreative Desire, Reproductive Technology and Narrative Shifts at Midlife'. In R. Jones (ed.), *Body, Mind and Healing After Jung: A Space of Questions.* London: Routledge.

Brodersen, L. (2016). *Laws of Inheritance. A Post-Jungian Study of Twins and the Relationship between the First and Other(s).* London and New York: Routledge.

Chesler, P. (2009). *Woman's Inhumanity to Woman.* Chicago, IL: Lawrence Hill Books.

Coontz, S. and Henderson, P. (1986a). 'Introduction: "Explanations" of Male Dominance'. In S. Coontz and P. Henderson (eds), *Women's Work, Men's Property: The Origins of Class and Gender.* London: Verso, pp. 1–42.

Earp, B.D., Monrad, J.T., LaFrance, M., Bargh, J.A., Cohen, L.L. and Richeson, J.A. (2019). 'Gender bias in pediatric pain assessment', *Journal of Pediatric Psychology*, 44(4), pp. 403–414.

Fillingim, R.B., King, C.D., Ribeiro-Dasilva, M.C., Rahim-Williams, B. and Riley, J.L. (2009). 'Sex, gender, and pain: a review of recent clinical and experimental findings', *Journal of Pain*, 10(5), pp. 447–485.

Hoffman, D.E. and Tarzian, A.J. (2001). 'The girl who cried pain: a bias against women in the treatment of pain', *Journal of Law, Medicine & Ethics*, 29, pp. 13–27.

NHS (2013). 'New NICE Guidelines for NHS Fertility Treatment', https://www.nhs.uk/news/pregnancy-and-child/new-nice-guidelines-for-nhs-fertility-treatment/', 3 September 2019.

Norman, A. (2019). *Ask Me About My Uterus: A Quest to Make Doctors Believe in Women's Pain.* New York: Hachette Book Group, Inc.

Rich, A. (2015). *On Lies, Secrets and Silence: Selected Prose, 1966–78.* New York and London: W.W. Norton & Co.

Salam, M. (2019). 'In Her Words: What is Toxic Masculinity?', *The New York Times*, 22 January 2019. Accessed 22 January 2019.

Schwartz-Salant, N. (1988). 'Archetypal foundations of projective identification', *Journal of Analytical Psychology*, 33(1), pp. 39–64.

Shaindel Senensky, S.S. (2003). *Healing and Empowering the Feminine. A Labyrinth Journey.* Wilmette, IL: Chiron.

Young-Eisendrath, P., (2019). *Love Between Equals: Relationship as a Spiritual Path.* Boulder, CO: Shambhala.

# DEFINITIONS

**Affect:** 'By the term affect I mean a state of feeling characterized by marked physical innervation on the one hand and a peculiar disturbance of the ideational process on the other. I used emotion as synonymous with affect. I distinguish – in contrast to Bleuler (v. *Affectivity*) – *feeling* (q.v.) from affect, in spite of the fact that the dividing line is fluid, since every feeling, after attaining a certain strength, releases physical innervations, thus becoming an affect'.

- *Collected Works Vol. 6* 'Psychological Types', 'Definition', § 681.

**Archetype:** 'Archetypes are not simply intellectual concepts but are imbued with feeling, which gives them their power to affect us in a most visceral fashion. You know when you are gripped by an archetype, such as falling in love. Or when you are possessed by the "witch"; or the "hero". They have characteristics with which we may be familiar and encountering them in their archetypal form increases their impact significantly because archetypes are numinous (which means they are possessed of a spiritual quality/energy which increases their force and may be felt as overwhelming)'.

- Williams, R. (2019). *C.G. Jung: The Basics*. London and New York: Routledge, p. 39.

**Axiom of Maria:** 'A precept in alchemy: "One becomes two, two becomes three, and out of the third comes the one as the fourth". Jung used the axiom of Maria as a metaphor for the whole process of individuation. *One* is the original state of unconscious wholeness; *two* signifies the conflict between opposites; *three* points to a potential resolution; *the third* is the transcendent function; and *the one as the fourth* is a transformed stated of consciousness, relatively whole and at peace'.

- Sharp, D. (1991) *C.G. Jung Lexicon: A Primer of Terms and Concepts*, Toronto: Inner City Books, p. 33.

**Collective (Unconscious):** 'There are a number of ways in which unconscious forces play their part. The collective unconscious is a real fact in human affairs. It would need volumes to explain its various ramifications. We all participate in it. In one sense it is the accumulated human wisdom which we unconsciously inherit; in other senses it implies the common human emotions which we all share'.

- 'Jung Diagnoses the Dictators' (1939), In W. McGuire and R.F.C. Hull (eds), C.G. *Jung Speaking, Interviews and Encounters*, Princeton: Princeton University Press, 1973 and 1976, p. 139.

**Complex:** 'Complexes are in truth the living units of the unconscious psyche, and it is only through them that we are able to deduce its existence and constitution ... The *via regia* to the unconscious, however, is not the dream, as [Freud] thought, but the complex, which is the architect of dreams and of symptoms'.

- *Collected Works Vol. 8*, 'A Review of the Complex Theory', § 210.

***Complexio Oppositorum:*** The following is in reply to a letter from the Revd David Cox on the subject of Religious Belief (*Collected Works, Vol. 18*, The Symbolic Life 'Jung and Religious Beliefs', p. 730) 'If my identification of Christ with the archetype of the Self is valid, he is, or ought to be, a *complexio oppositorum*. Historically this is not so. Therefore, I was profoundly surprised by your statement, that Christ contains the opposites. Between my contention and historical Christianity there stretches that deep abyss of Christian dualism – Christ and the Devil, good and evil, God and Creation. Beyond "good and evil" simply means we pass no moral judgment. But in fact, nothing is changed. The same is true when we state that whatever God is or does is good. Since God does everything (even man created by him is his instrument) everything is good, and the term "good" has lost its meaning. "Good" is a relative term. There is no good without bad. I am afraid that even revealed truth has to evolve. Everything living changes. We should not be satisfied with unchangeable traditions'.

- C.G. Jung *Letters*. Selected and edited by G. Adler in collaboration with A. Jaffe. Translated by R.F.C. Hull. Two vols, Vol. 1, 1906–1950, Vol. 2, 1951–1961. Princeton: Princeton University Press, 1973 and 1976, § 1650–1652.

**Consciousness:** 'By consciousness I understand the relation of psychic contents to the *ego* (q.v.), in so far as this relation is perceived as such by the ego. Relations to the ego that are not perceived as such are *unconscious* (q.v.). Consciousness is the function or activity which maintains the relation of psychic contents to the ego. Consciousness is not identical with the psyche (v. *Soul*), because the psyche represents the totality of all psychic contents, and these are not necessarily all directly connected with the ego, i.e., related to the it in such a way that they take on the quality of consciousness. A great many psychic complexes exist which area not all necessarily connected with the ego'.

- *Collected Works, Vol. 6* Psychological Types, 'Definitions', § 700.

**Counter-Transference: 1)** '... the analyst's countertransference becomes a fertile planting ground for the numerous and intense projections the patient tries to disown. In this process, the analyst can become coloured by the projective counter-identification and begin to bend to the passive or not so passive pressures to act out certain roles, functions, or affects that the patient places within him [her]. These are all clinical dynamics that seem very much in line with Jung's description of *participation mystique*. It is also what Betty Joseph (1985) speaks to regarding how the patient comes to use the analyst and pull the analyst into various unconscious and interpersonal states of mind. The patient, in an emotional and interpersonal manner, manages to herd the analyst into certain ways of being that complement the roles, functions and affects the patient is struggling with', p. 108.

- Waska, R. (2014). 'Modern Kleinian Therapy, Jung's *Participation Mystique* and the Projective Identification Process'. In M. Winborn (ed.) *Shared Realities: Participation Mystique and Beyond*. Skiatook, OK: Fisher King Press.

**2)** 'The premise is that countertransference is, of its nature, an imaginal enterprise and, viewed as active imagination, it may offer a very particular way of amplifying the analysand's experience'.

- Schaverien, J. (2007). 'Countertransference as active imagination: imaginative experiences of the analyst', *Journal of Analytical Psychology*, 52(4), pp. 413–431.

**3)** 'I would suggest that resonance occurs when the analyst's tuning fork vibrates with the patient's psychic material through the unconscious. When this experience is in the body, the feelings are not clear or thought through, and the analyst has to be able to sustain the state of not knowing and confusion more than usual'.

- Stone, M. (2006). 'The analyst's body as tuning fork: embodied resonance in countertransference', *Journal of Analytical Psychology*, 51(1), pp. 109–124.

**Cultural Complex:** 'The term "cultural complex" arises from two different aspects of Jung's psychology. Let us start with the term "complex" because this was the first area of research for Jung. Through the word association test Jung noted that there occurred a delayed reaction time to certain words which as experimentally repeatable. Jung observed that the delay was caused by the arousal of particularly strong emotions in connection with specific trigger words. He coined the term "complex" to account for this phenomenon ... When we speak about a cultural complex, we are moving from an individual psychology to the psychology of the group – which can dwell both within the "collective" psyche of the group and the group level of the psyche embedded within the individual. In 1962, Joseph Henderson presented a paper at the Second International Congress for Analytical Psychology entitled "The Archetype of Culture" where he defined this layer of the psyche which he postulated as existing between the personal and the archetypal (Henderson, 1964) ... In the last few years Tom Singer (2002) and Sam Kimbles

(2000) have coined the term "cultural complexes" to elaborate on this level of psychological experience'.

- Kirsch, T.B. (2004). 'Cultural Complexes in the History of Jung, Freud and Their Followers'. In T. Singer and S.L. Kimble (eds), *The Cultural Complex: Contemporary Jungian Perspectives on Psyche and Society*. New York and London: Routledge, p. 185.

**Enantiodromia:** 'This characteristic phenomenon practically always occurs when an extreme, one-sided tendency dominates conscious life and in time an equally powerful counter position is built up, which initially inhibits the conscious performance but subsequently breaks through conscious control.'

- *Collected Works, Vol. 6*, 'Definitions', § 709

'Every psychological extreme secretly contains its own opposite ... There is no hallowed custom that cannot on occasion turn into its opposite, and the more extreme a position is, the more easily may we expect an enantiodromia, a conversion of something into its opposite'.

- *Collected Works, Vol. 5*, 'The Dual Mother,' § 581

'... a reverse of the personality into its opposite character type. He embraces the shadow and indeed for a time becomes identified with its energies and qualities'.

- Stein, M. (2010). *Jung's Map of the Soul: An Introduction*, Chicago and La Salle, IL: Open Court, p. 208.

**Interpretive Phenomenological Analysis (IPA):** 'Phenomenology through the research methodology of interpretative phenomenological analysis is concerned with exploring the lived experience of the participant or with understanding how participants make sense of their personal and social world. On the other hand, discourse analysis and conversation analysis are concerned with describing the linguistic resources participants draw on during conversations, the patterns those conversations take, and the social interactional work being performed during them'.

- Smith, J.A. (2008). *Qualitative Psychology: A Practical Guide to Research Methods, 2nd Edition*. London: Sage Publications, p. 3.

IPA also emphasizes that the research exercise is a dynamic process with an active role for the researcher in that process. One is trying to get close to the participant's personal world, to take an 'insider's perspective', but one cannot do this directly or completely. Access depends on, and is complicated by, the researcher's own conceptions; indeed, these are required in order to make sense of that other personal world through interpretative activity. Thus, a two-stage interpretation process, or double hermeneutic, is involved. The participants are trying to make sense of their world; the researcher is trying to make sense of the participants trying to make sense of their world. IPA is therefore intellectually connected to hermeneutics and theories of interpretation (Packer and Addison, 1989; Palmer, 1969; Smith, 2007). Note from the author: The possibility of both empathic and questioning hermeneutics dynamics emerged as a parallel research method with the term 'clinically informed' IPA, referring to transference and countertransference dynamics originating in the consulting room.

**Objective Psyche:** 'Jung uses the phrase ... to discuss the view that the unconscious is a realm of "objects" (complexes and archetypal images) as much as the surrounding world is a realm of persons and things ... The deeper one goes into the objective psyche, moreover, the more objective it becomes because it is less and less related to the ego's subjectivity'.

- Stein, M. (2010). *Jung's Map of the Soul: An Introduction*. Chicago and La Salle, IL: Open Court, p. 208.

**Pregnant Pause**: 'A pregnant pause comes on as passionately as first love, with all the expectation of satisfying the need of a deep, meaningful relationship with another that cannot be broken by a change of fortune or heart' (Barone-Chapman, 2011, p. 181). The pregnant pause brings into awareness unconscious processes asking for a narrative shift in midlife as part of a reparative motif (Barone-Chapman, 2011). Note from the author: During the course of writing this book I came to realize the 'Pregnant Pause' is a trilogy in which becoming pregnant is the centre stage to repair what had traumatized a woman earlier in her life, causing her to arrive late to procreative desire. The Pregnant Pause becomes both crucible and bridge between a life lived in two parts, first as Adam who is the hunter gather, and later as Eve who tends home and hearth. Thanks to the advancement of biotechnology, it is now, more than at any other time in human history, possible to forecast the conditions in which a woman will ground herself at mid-life in order to conceive, and to re-ascend if necessary or if desired, afterward. A 'baby' comes in many forms. Within a life lived in two parts, a teleological view holds the possibility of finding meaning and purpose for every notion of reparative creativity.

- Barone-Chapman, M. (2011). 'Pregnant Pause: Procreative Desire, Reproductive Technology and Narrative Shifts at Midlife', in R. Jones (ed.) *Body, Mind and Healing After Jung: A Space of Questions*. London: Routledge.

**Projection:** 'Means the expulsion of a subjective content into an object; it is the opposite of *introjection* (q.v.). Accordingly, it is a process of *dissimilation* (v. *Assimilation*), by which a subjective content becomes alienated from the subject, and is, so to speak, embodied in the object. The subjects gets rid of painful, incompatible contents by projecting them, as also of positive values which, for one reason or another – self-depreciation, for instance – are inaccessible to him [her]'.

- *Collected Works, Vol. 6, Psychological Types*, 'Definitions'm § 783

**Shadow:** 'The personal unconscious is personified by the shadow'.

- *Collected Works, Vol. 14, Mysterium Coniunctionis,* § 128

'The shadow is a living part of the personality and therefore wants to live with it in some form. It cannot be argued out of existence or rationalized into harmlessness'.

- *Collected Works, Vol. 9i,* 'Archetypes of the Collective Unconscious', § 44.

**Transference**: 'This bond is often of such intensity that we could almost speak of a 'combination.' When two chemical substances combine, both are altered. This is precisely what happens in the transference. Freud rightly recognized that this bond is of greatest therapeutic importance in that it gives rise to a *mixtum compositum* [composite mixture] of the doctor's own mental health and the patient's maladjustment'.

- *Collected Works, Vol. 16,* 'The Psychology of the Transference', § 358.

# INDEX

Adam and Eve: life pattern of 'first Adam then Eve' 2, 12, 28, 91, 93, 101, 104, 110, 111, 117, 123; Lilith and 101–103, 112
affect: defined 119; vs. feeling xviii, 119. *See also* Trilateral Affects
affective symptoms 43t, 45t
agape 82–84
Alexander Stewart, J. 30
*Alphabet of Ben Sira* 101, 103
ambivalence 95–97. *See also* maternal ambivalence
anima 24, 25, 28, 112; animus and 1, 24, 25, 28, 29, 101, 112, 116; fear of the transformative nature of the 103–104; Jung and 24, 25, 28, 101, 103; Marion Woodman on 2–3; motherhood and 1, 103, 112 (*see also* Anima Mundi); patriarchy and 2–3; Sigmund Hurwitz on 103–104
Anima Mundi 116, 118
animism xvi, 13, 109
animus 3, 29, 63, 92, 93, 101; anima and 1, 24, 25, 28, 29, 101, 112, 116; Jung on 24, 25, 28; motherhood and 30, 63, 87, 106, 112; patriarchal 29, 90, 112, 116 (*see also* mother monster archetype). *See also* masculinity: in women
anxiety: disintegration 67, 88. *See also* fear(s)
Apollonic archetype 28
archetypes 49; nature of 119. *See also specific archetypes*

assisted reproductive technology (ART) 14, 15, 18, 26, 56, 117. *See also* in vitro fertilization; reproductive technology
Axiom of Maria 119

'bad mother.' *See* mother monster archetype; negative mother complex
Baraitser, L. 4
Baring, A. 116
Becker, G. 3, 19, 20, 28
Beebe, J. 90, 96–97; on delayed motherhood 113; on Jung 96–97, 110; on patriarchy 90, 97, 106, 110, 112
Belford Ulanov, A. 97
Ben Sira. *See Alphabet of Ben Sira*
Benedek, T. 6
Benjamin, J.: on femininity 2, 28–29, 32, 105; on identification 25, 32, 40; on mother-child relationship 1–2, 4, 32, 105
"biological clock," 3, 19
'bipolar' archetypal figures 103, 111. *See also* opposites
bipolar aspects of mother complex 63
bisexuality: Freud and 24–25; gender and 24–25, 28, 33
Brooke, R. 24, 93–94
Butler, J. 32, 33

Campbell, P. 14–15
cases. *See* Ms A; Ms B; Ms D
Cavalli, A. 20, 95
child archetype 39, 67
Chodorow, N.J. 2, 3

Christ 120
Chronos 26
collective complexes 71, 88–92, 112
collective psyche 13, 68, 121; transformation of xvi, 13, 19
collective representations 67
collective unconscious xiii, 28, 33, 42, 49, 55, 87, 93, 105; complexes of the xvii, xviii, 34, 41, 49, 111; cultural unconscious and xv, 87; formation 67; nature of 67, 120; personal unconscious and 26, 71
complex indicators (CI) in Word Association Experiment 69, 70, 72, 73, 81, 87. *See also* Word Association Experiment: complexes and
complexes 14, 68; of the collective unconscious xvii, xviii, 34, 41, 49, 111; nature of xv, 14, 120; parts of 111; Word Association Experiment (WAE) and 68–75, 79, 81–84. *See also specific topics*
*complexio oppositorum* 6, 46, 84; can happen to anyone 59–60; definition and nature of 120
confession 48, 55, 60, 110
confessional narrative 82
Conforti, M. 6, 109
consciousness: borderlands of 1, 32; bringing unconscious contents to 40; definition and nature of 120; ego and xvii, 26, 71, 109, 120; 'new king of consciousness' 20, 68
Coontz, S. 117
Cosgrove, L. 4–5, 106
countertransference (CT) 39–40, 43t, 45t
creation and destruction 6, 26, 96, 100–102. *See also* good and terrible mother; Lilith
creation myths 12, 28, 29, 55, 95, 101, 102, 118; James Hillman on 91, 93, 110. *See also* Adam and Eve; Lilith
creativity disturbances 87
crone archetype 116
cultural complex 14, 87, 89–93, 116; definition and nature of 14, 111, 121; identification of a 88; of the term 121–122
cultural unconscious xv, 87–88

'dark feminine' 116
de Beauvoir, S. 3
de-gender equality xiii, xiv, 32
Demeter 63, 64
Demeter-Kore myth 63
demonic figures 102–103
despair, narrative of 78f
destruction 6, 26, 51, 95, 96, 100–102. *See also* good and terrible mother; Lilith

devouring mother 3, 96, 103
diagnosis, psychiatric 28
'disenchantment with the world' 13, 109
disintegration anxiety 67, 88
'domestication of women' 6
double binds 64, 68, 105, 111
doubt: as ethical benchmark xiii, 34. *See also* self-doubt
Douglas, C. 29, 30

ego xvii, 26, 34, 100–102, 105, 123; complexes and 68, 71, 101; consciousness and xvii, 26, 71, 109, 120; Dale Mathers on 94, 101; duality of 2, 40; Murray Stein on the xv, 26, 123; Self and 26, 28, 94, 101; and the Trickster 68, 95; and the unconscious xv, 33, 34, 68, 105, 120
Electra complex 62
emotion 119. *See also* affect
emptiness. *See* 'Hunger to Fill an Empty Space'
enantiodromia 6, 56, 89–91, 122; as ageless 60–62; definition and nature of 122
Erikson, E.H. 13
Eros 89; a complex view of mother and 62–65; Logos and 29, 90, 95, 106; over-development of 62, 63, 96
ethical benchmark, doubt as an xiii, 34
ethical methodological juncture 31
ethical positions 34, 116, 117
ethical questions 32, 33
ethics, feminine 30
Eurich-Rascoe, B.L. 50

false self 105
fear(s) 56, 67, 69, 73, 74f, 75f, 88, 103–104; of becoming a mother 50; double helix of 46, 69; of the feminine 30, 95, 103, 105; gender-related 30, 54; patriarchy and 30, 50, 103
feelings 119. *See also* affect
female body as symbol 1–2
feminine hero. *See* hero, feminine
feminine inferiority 27, 104
feminine revolution 15
feminine/feminist psychosocial dilemmas 25
femininity/the feminine: acceptance of 27; fear of the 30, 95, 103, 105; Freud on the 'riddle' of 28, 91; Jessica Benjamin on 2, 28–29, 32, 105; repudiation of 27 (*see also* misogyny). *See also* anima
feminism 25, 28, 29, 31, 32; patriarchy and 1, 15, 27, 29, 31, 102, 105
'feminist,' connotations of the term 31
'feminist' anger against patriarchy 15

feminist research 1, 29, 31
feminist terminology 27
feminist writings xvii, 25, 33
fertility 11, 16, 19, 42. *See also* infertility
fertility crisis 55, 60
fertility treatment 34, 53, 55–56, 116. *See also* reproductive technology
Flax, J. 6, 104
Fordham, M. 101
Freud, S. 40, 91, 93, 96; gender and 24–25, 27–29, 33, 34, 51, 91, 104, 110; vs. Jung xviii, 29, 49, 93, 96; on repetition compulsion 33, 40; Sabina Spielrein and 100, 101; on sexuality xv, xviii, 25, 33, 91; symbols and 96; on transference 124; on trauma 67, 88; and the unconscious xviii, 33, 68, 120; Word Association Experiment (WAE) and xv, 68
Friese, C. 3, 19, 20, 28

Garden of Eden. *See* Adam and Eve
gender 27–28; nature of 25. *See also specific topics*
gender certainty, assumption of 29
gender equality. *See* de-gender equality
gender identity 16, 32, 50, 112. *See also* queering patriarchy and the feminine
gender rebellion 50, 53–54, 111. *See also* rebellion
goddesses 90, 96, 116. *See also* Lilith
good and terrible mother 5–6, 16, 96, 97, 102–105. *See also* negative mother complex
'good enough' mother xvi, 4, 106. *See also* 'too good' mother
'good mother' 55, 88, 89
Green, A. 96

Hades 42, 63
'having it all' narrative 90
Henderson, J.L.: on cultural unconscious xv, 87–88; 'The Archetype of Culture' 121
Henderson, P. 117
Henwood, K.L. 15–16, 27
hermeneutics and Interpretive Phenomenological Analysis (IPA) 40–41, 122–123
hero, feminine 6; to denounce destruction as the 50–51; in search of the 30–32. *See also* Young-Eisendrath, P.
heroic journey of the feminine, new 30
heroines 55, 63, 93; vs. feminine heroes 30. *See also* Young-Eisendrath, P.
heroism 2, 48, 105
heterosexuality 29, 32, 33

Hillman, J. 46, 93, 104, 109; archetypes and 46, 93; on creation myth 91, 93, 110; on ego 28, 109; gender and 27–28, 91, 104; individuation and 5; on patriarchy 106; on Self 28; on termination 27
Hollway, W. 3
homosexuality and heterosexuality as oppressive system of classification 32, 33
hooks, bell xi–xiii
Horney, K. 103
Hume, D. 101
hunger for a child i, 2, 45
'Hunger to Fill an Empty Space, The' (Barone-Chapman) 55, 87
Hurwitz, S. 102–104

identification, Jessica Benjamin on 25, 32, 40
identity: crisis of 55; social identity vs. self-definition 19. *See also* Self
identity influencers 14–18
in vitro fertilization (IVF) xvi–xvii, 11, 20, 43, 45, 58–61. *See also* assisted reproductive technology
Inanna 90, 116
individuation 3, 19, 20, 31, 32, 61, 64, 67, 82–83; axiom of Maria as metaphor for 119; night sea journey and 5; union of opposites and 4, 31. *See also* 'night sea journey'
infanticidal fantasies 52, 54, 55, 72, 74, 103
infertility 6, 42, 64; ageing 89; age-related 19, 89. *See also* fertility; fertility treatment
Interpretive Phenomenological Analysis (IPA) xv–xvi, 34, 40–42, 75, 77, 122–123; hermeneutics and 40–41, 122–123
intersubjective field xvii, 29, 31, 41, 46, 62
intersubjective space 40, 41, 46, 54, 105
intersubjectivity xvii, 2, 31, 32. *See also* maternal subjectivity

Jaffe, A. 113
Jagose, A. 32, 33
Jesus Christ. *See* Christ
Johnson, S. 17–18
Joseph, B. 121
Jung, C.G.: on masculinity 25, 28, 33, 63, 68; on patriarchy 29, 33, 110. *See also specific topics*

Kaa, D.J. van de 11, 12
Kairos 26
Kalsched, D. 20, 67
Kast, V. 28
Khan, M.M.R., on trauma 14, 64, 67, 88

Kimbles, S.L. 88, 121–122
kinship libido 15
Koltuv, B.B. 102
Kore 42, 63
Kraemer, S. 4
Kristeva, J. 4, 30, 106

Lambert, K. 48, 82
Leusinger-Bohleber, M. 6
libido xv, 15, 20; transformative potential of 96
Lilith 5, 54, 55, 95, 102, 103; Adam and Eve and 101–103, 112; as archetypal power 96, 102–103, 105; and competition between women 112; flight to the Red Sea 103; mother-daughter relationship and 105; motherhood and 105; myth of 95, 101–103, 112; pregnant pause and 103; pregnant women and 112
living meaning, subjective and affective spaces of the body containing 2, 31
logos: of science 13, 109 (*see also* science). *See also* Eros: Logos and
love. *See* agape; Eros
Lowinsky, N. xiii

Maria, Axiom of 119
masculinity 91, 105; bisexuality and 25, 33; favouring xiv, 2, 90, 91; ignoring the masculine through denigration 43, 53; Jung and 25, 28, 33, 63, 68; Marion Woodman on 30; patriarchy and 2, 5, 30, 31 (*see also* patriarchy); Queer and 32–34; toxic 115; in women 28, 33, 53–55, 68, 104 (*see also* animus)
maternal ambivalence xi, 5, 11, 17, 102; case material 59, 61, 62; increasing 6; vs. maternal preoccupation and subjectivity xvi, 3, 64, 105, 107; 'permission' to acknowledge 4
maternal individuation 61. *See also* individuation
maternal object as symbol 1–2
maternal preoccupation 3, 46, 57, 62, 90, 105
maternal self 49–55
maternal subjectivity xvi, 3, 45, 46, 62, 84, 90, 105, 107. *See also* intersubjectivity
Mathers, D. 94, 101
McAdams, D.P. 48
Meredith-Owen, W. 96
Merleau-Ponty, M.M. 2, 31
midlife xvi, 5; biotechnology and 95; Jung's theories of 29; *In Midlife: A Jungian Perspective* (Stein) 26–27; re-making of individuation in 32 (*see also* individuation). *See also* pregnant pause; *specific topics*
'midlife awakening' 92
midlife complexities xviii, 12–14
'miracle mom' 19, 20
misogyny 34, 94, 101, 112; 'bedrock' of 27–28
mother archetype 63, 93, 95–97, 103. *See also* mother monster archetype
mother complex 4, 63, 107. *See also* negative mother complex
mother monster archetype 5, 61, 106, 109, 112
Ms A, case of: requests special meeting to make special request 43–44; to denounce destruction as feminine hero 50–51; gender bias 52; the maternal self 51–55; Word Association Experiment (WAE) and 71–76, 72t; spoiling mother 75
Ms B, case of 44, 59; to demonstrate repair and recovery is possible 56–57; unconscious rebellion 57–59; Word Association Experiment (WAE) and 76–80, 77t
Ms D, case of 45–46, 85, 89–91; to demonstrate *complexio oppositorum* can happen to anyone 59–60; enantiodromia is ageless 60–62; Word Association Experiment (WAE) and 80–84
mythology 26, 28, 42, 49, 63, 90, 93, 95. *See also* creation myths; goddesses; Lilith

Nachtigall, R.D. 3, 19, 20, 28
narcissistic injury 43, 64
narrative interpretations 75–78
narrative shifts xii, 11, 12, 90; in midlife 123
narratives 15, 17–20; confessional 82
negative mother complex xii–xiii, 84, 90, 96, 97; activation of a complex 94; meaning failure 94; problems with collaboration 94; as transforming vs. terrible 93–94
Neumann, E. 95, 104, 105
'night sea journey' 55–56, 97, 109
Noack, A. 4
normative framework 15, 27

objective psyche 123
Oedipal phase 2
Oedipus complex 32, 83
opposites: union of 4, 29, 31, 32, 110. *See also* 'bipolar' archetypal figures
'other' 50, 64, 87, 89, 94, 101
otherhood of mothering 1
otherness 2, 3, 40

Paris, G. 15, 90
Parker, R. 4
patriarchal animus 29, 90, 112, 116. *See also* mother monster archetype
patriarchal medicine 95, 116
patriarchal science 97, 110
patriarchal values 50, 89, 102, 105
patriarchal views of the feminine 5, 28–31, 105. *See also* queering patriarchy and the feminine
patriarchy 27, 28, 45t, 90, 94, 102, 104–106, 115, 118; Adam and Eve and 12, 102, 112; anima and 2–3; and competition between women 112; and the family 6, 104; fears and 30, 50, 103; and the female body xvii, 49–50, 89; feminism and 1, 15, 25, 27–29, 31, 102, 105, 110; Freud and 28–29, 33, 104, 110; humanising patriarchy's masculine archetypes 5; John Beebe on 90, 97, 106, 110, 112; Jung and 29, 33, 110; Lilith and 102, 112; Marion Woodman on 2–3, 5, 30; motherhood and 3–5, 13, 16, 25, 30, 48, 90, 94, 102, 105, 106, 111, 112 (*see also* mother monster archetype); nature of 106, 112; psychiatry, diagnosis, and 28–29; transition from matriarchal to patriarchal phase 104; use of the term 27. *See also* queering patriarchy and the feminine
Persephone 42, 63
perseveration 70, 71, 72f, 73, 75, 79–81
phantom narrative 88
Pines, D. 63, 64
Powell, S. 2
pregnant pause 88, 123; definition and nature of 123
'Pregnant Pause: Procreative Desire, Reproductive Technology and Narrative Shifts at Midlife' (Barone-Chapman) xii, 123
procreation: desire for 2, 62 (*see also* hunger for a child); reasons for delaying xvii, 34. *See also* specific topics
projection 121, 123; definition and nature of 123. *See also* specific topics
projective identification 63, 96, 112
psychiatric diagnosis 28
'Psychological Aspects of the Mother Archetype' (Jung) 63
psychosocial identity, development of 13
psychosocial phenomena xv–xviii, 11, 12

queer theories 29, 110
queering patriarchy and the feminine 32–34
Quiney, R. 110

Raphael-Leff, J. 24–25
'real mum' 18–20
rebellion xi, 45t, 89, 111, 112; against domination of the biological imperative xiii, 32, 33; unconscious 57–59. *See also* gender rebellion
redemption 54, 55; reparation and 95, 118 (*see also* reparation)
redemptive motif, delayed motherhood as a 55
redemptive (unifying) symbol(s): child as a 12; Trickster as bearer of 68
reflexivity 31
reparation 56–57, 116; of old wounds 106, 112; redemption and 95, 118 (*see also* redemption)
reparative creativity 123
reparative motif xii, 12, 123
repetition compulsion 33, 40–41, 84
reproductive technology x, 95. *See also* assisted reproductive technology; fertility treatment; in vitro fertilization; 'Pregnant Pause'
'Return of the Repressed' (Stein) 26
return to mother 20, 63, 96. *See also* second return to mother
'return to the mothers' 20, 96
Rich, A. 115
Rowland, S. 28
Rubin, G. 6

sacrifice 95
Samuels, A. 64, 101
science 13–15, 19, 54, 109, 110; logos of 13, 109; patriarchal 97, 110; religion, mythology, and 49
scientific medicine 50, 54, 87
Second Demographic Transition (SDT) 11
second return to mother 2–3, 94
Sedgwick, D. 40
Sedgwick, E.K. 33
Self xiii, 26, 30–31, 96; archetype of the 101, 120; ego and 26, 28, 94, 101; feminine 64; wound to the core self 111. *See also* identity; maternal self
self-blame 20
self-definition vs. social identity 19
self-destruction 100–101
self-doubt 5, 53, 73
self-esteem 2, 3, 103. *See also* narcissistic injury
selfishness 4, 14, 15, 61, 62
Seligman, E. 2, 31, 92
sexual orientation 29, 32, 33
sexuality 100; Freud on xv, xviii, 25, 33, 91. *See also* Eros; libido

shadow 82, 111, 115, 122; collective unconscious and 105; definition and nature of 124; Eros and 62, 82
shame 4, 5, 44, 46
Shelton, N. 17–18
*Silence of the Lambs* (film) 30
Simonsen, K. 2, 31
Simonton, D.K. 87
'sin' 48, 78, 78f
Singer, T. 88, 121–122
Smith, J.A. 41, 122
'social clock' 6, 13
social construction 16, 25, 50. *See also* animism
social identity vs. self-definition 19
sovereignty xiii, 2, 16, 48
Spielrein, S. 100–101
Stein, M. 20, 122; on complexes 71; on the ego xv, 26, 123; on midlife 5, 26; on 'objective psyche' 123; 'Return of the Repressed' 26
Stephenson, C.E. xvi
stigma 19
subjectivity: maternal xvi, 3, 45, 46, 62, 84, 90, 105, 107. *See also* intersubjectivity
Swartz, S. 28
symbolic equation 6, 60, 75

technological unconscious 50, 87, 116–117
teleological purpose 20, 49
teleology 12, 49
terrible mother. *See* good and terrible mother
Thanatos narrative interpretation 77–78
Tillich, P. 26
time 26; dimensions of 26
time riddle, Jung's 63
'too good' mother 56, 97
touch points 94
transference 40, 43t, 45t, 124; definition and nature of 124; erotic 15
transformation: of collective psyche xvi, 13, 19; trauma and (*see* trauma and transformation). *See also under* negative mother complex
transformative nature of the anima, fear of the 103–104
transformative potential of libido 96
trauma 61, 93, 96; acculturated through distant relationships 14; affect and 81; and creativity disturbances 87; cumulative 14, 64, 67, 88, 94; definitions and uses of the term 20, 67; and delayed motherhood xiii, 20, 61, 64, 68, 87, 111, 123; and dissociation 96, 105, 117; forgetting and remembering 20, 95; forms of 95; gender and 74, 84–85, 111; Masud Khan on 14, 64, 67, 88; mother monster archetype and 106, 112; negative mother complex and xii, 93, 94; redemption from 95, 106, 112; and the self 67, 105; Trickster archetype, Trickster games, and xii, 68, 84–85, 95, 112; women's xvi, 61, 94, 106, 112, 117, 118
trauma and transformation 20, 41, 95, 118; many faces of 95, 106, 112
trauma complex 111
trauma culture 15, 95
Trickster archetype 39, 68, 76, 85, 95
Trickster games xii, 84
Trickster's method 95, 106, 112
Trilateral Affects 82f, 84

unconscious 34; ego and the xv, 33, 34, 68, 105, 120; Freud and the xviii, 33, 68, 120; Jung and the xvii–xviii. *See also* collective unconscious
underworld 42, 63, 95, 116

vampirism 92
Vande Kemp, H. 50
Vogelsang, E.W. 102, 105

Weber, M. xvi, 13, 109
Weiner, Y. 26
Welldon, E.V. 93
West, M. 111
Wiesner-Hanks, M. 27
Winnicott, D.W. 4, 67
Wirtz, U. 95
witch archetype 102–103, 112, 116, 119
'Women and Later Life' (Henwood) 15–16
Woodman, M. 30; on anima 2–3; on patriarchy 2–3, 5, 30
Word Association Experiment (WAE) xvi, 25–26, 41, 68–70, 87, 121; administration 42, 69–70; analysis of WAE results 70–84; archetypes and 49; complexes and 68–75, 79, 81–84; Freud and xv, 68; Ms A and 55, 71–72, 72t; Ms B and 76–77, 77t; Ms D and 80–84; overview 69; sexuality and xv; transformation and 88, 94, 97
Word Association Test (WAT). *See* Word Association Experiment
wounded healer xiii, 39, 106

Young-Eisendrath, P. xiv, 2, 16, 33, 117